Scéal

by Gary Hope

"Scéal," by Gary Hope. ISBN 978-1-62137-592-0.

Library of Congress Control Number: 2014915422

Published 2014 by Virtualbookworm.com Publishing Inc., P.O. Box 9949, College Station, TX 77842, US. ©2014, Gary Hope. All rights reserved. No part of this publication may be reproduced, stored in a retrieval system, or transmitted in any form or by any means, electronic, mechanical, recording or otherwise, without the prior written permission of Gary Hope.

Manufactured in the United States of America.

1

I was born in October of 1950, the best month and year to be born, in my opinion. I was told that my mother was in downtown Red Springs that fateful day, enjoying the Fall Festival parade, which included some tractors, a new Ford, an almost new Chevrolet and some horseback riders…pretty fancy stuff for our little town. Then, as a Palomino horse and rider passed by, I decided it was time; they rushed my mother over to Womack Army Hospital in Fort Bragg and shortly thereafter I made my appearance in the world. I don't remember it. I was born at Fort Bragg because my father was in the Army at the time, his name was Andy Hope—that's all, just Andy Hope, no middle name. The Army insisted he have a middle initial for their records, so he chose the letter J. So, officially in the Army he was Andy J. Hope. My mom's name was Doris Townsend, one of six children, all of whom had middle names except my mom…I don't know why that was. Nearly everyone I've ever known had middle names, except Andy Hope and Doris Townsend…maybe it was fate they had met; but, maybe not. A few years later, after my dad's Army career, he promptly joined the Navy; why, I don't know. I think he just liked being gone and not being tied down, which he proved when he disappeared from our lives 5 years later and we never heard from him again, until a phone call one night 15 years later telling us he had died (more on this story later).

My little sister, Anne, was born three years after me and we were nurtured and raised by our Mom, of course, but also by our grandparents, Grover Cleveland Townsend and Ida Elizabeth Townsend, with whom we lived until we left for college. There were also many aunts and uncles and cousins around all the time, it was a grand, joyful and charmed boyhood I lived—my sister may look at it a bit differently; there were times when my playfulness may have extended the boundaries a little—but I think she's forgiven me for most of the tricks I played on her…I hope she has. Anne? Please?

The year my dad left us, my sister and I visited him in Athens, Tennessee; I was 5 and she was 2…it would be the last time we ever saw him. He picked us up in Red Springs and drove us over the mountains to Tennessee; incredibly enough, my sister and I both remember that trip. We stayed with our Granny Hope, while our dad was at work at the radio station where he had a country radio show. We both remember chasing lizards up the walls on the outside of the house, a strange memory, and I remember being in the car with my dad when we stopped at a softball game and they wanted him to play, but he had me, so all he did was bat once and hit a home run—I was very proud of him.

Each night at the radio station, we would listen to him, and he would end his show saying, alright Gary and Anne, time for you to go to bed. We thought that was the coolest thing EVER! What a great dad we had. This was in 1955 and a very young Elvis Presley was making the rounds of the radio stations trying to publicize his songs and himself, when one magical night my dad interviewed him on his radio show. The only thing I remember was my dad asking Elvis to close the show by telling Gary and Anne it was time to go to bed, which Elvis did…how awesome was that? Elvis talking to me and Anne (more on Elvis later, by the way).

That is the extent of my fatherly memories…good ones, as memories go, but too few, way too few. However, I don't hate him, or blame him, or even miss him really; there were times I missed the concept of having a father. But I can't say I really missed him at all…my life was charmed in so many other ways, it probably wouldn't have been fair for me to have had a great father as well. I was as happy as a boy could possibly be. Surrounded by love, spoiled rotten and blessed with the best circumstances imaginable—at least I thought so.

When my dad left us, we were living in Norfolk, Va., because that's where he was stationed in the Navy; so there we were, my mom with two little kids to take care of and no child support and no family in Virginia to help. How she got through that is amazing to me…I couldn't have. But, she did somehow; she got a job, kept house and raised two children in an era where mothers didn't work—they stayed home in the 1950's and the husbands worked. Soon, however, the demands of working and caring for two kids by herself became overwhelming. My Aunt Mary, living in Red Springs, volunteered to keep me when I started first grade. My mom just couldn't afford the day care for us both; plus, I loved Red Springs and my Aunt Mary. One of the few memories I have of living in Norfolk then was pleading with my mom to change my middle name to Red Springs—which was way better than Raymond, in my opinion.

So, off to Aunt Mary's house I went for the first grade…And except for her giving me an enema one night, I had an absolute blast. About once a month or so, Aunt Mary would put me on the bus (6 years old) and I'd ride up to Norfolk to stay with my mom and Anne for a few days. It was quite the adventure back then; certainly no hint of danger, the bus driver took care of me and gave me sandwiches. But, my Mom wanted me back and was able to get a better paying job where she could afford daycare, so I moved back to Norfolk for three years—2cd, 3rd and 4th grades. Unfortunately, I don't remember much about it, except for the great Christmas' my mom always planned. Then, the best news of all happened…my mom got a job at Fort Bragg and we all were moving back to Red Springs with my grandparents…oh happy days! That's the selfish look I suppose, certainly from my Mom's perspective, moving back in with your parents, with two small children couldn't have been the ideal life for a young, attractive 30 year old woman.

But for me it was PARADISE! First of all, my grandparent's house was perfect…PERFECT! My grandfather was a first rate gardener and planter, and his goal was to feed us from his garden. In the back yard we had several peach trees, an apple tree, a fig tree, a pecan tree, two grape vines (one with blue grapes which was so big you could climb inside the grapevine and hide in it and another vine with white grapes). Still in the back yard, further out, he planted watermelons (one of my three favorite foods), plus cantaloupes and strawberries.

On one side of the house he had planted about 10 plum trees and another pecan tree and on the other side of the house was the main garden, normally potatoes, green beans, cabbage, corn, field peas, lettuce, tomatoes, radishes, turnips, etc., etc., etc…and my favorite—a pomegranate bush! Across the street from us were blackberry bushes with the most luscious tasting berries you could find. No wonder today and all my life really, I've been a fruit-a-holic; what a garden of Eden we enjoyed. I can still smell the aromas of my grandmother canning jellies and jams and canning all the vegetables for us to eat in the winter. And the memories of all of us sitting on the back porch shucking corn, shelling peas and swatting flies…glory days. We stored potatoes in the barn out back; a huge stack of spuds maybe 4-5 tall in a 10' circle—enough to last all winter and spring until the next crop came in.

And, 95% of this gardening work was done by my grandfather, who was paralyzed on his right side and only had the use of his left hand and leg—pretty amazing stuff! He had a man come in with a mule and plow each spring to turn the ground over; other than that he did it all with his hoe and various other tools, one handed and one legged. Except for helping dig some potatoes, and picking beans and corn, I mostly just threw dirt clods at my cousins and sister and played tricks on all those around me whenever I could. My grandmother (Granny) was my favorite subject for tricks, after lunch she would lay down for a short nap; when I was sure she was asleep, I'd take her glasses off her face and replace them with sunglasses. When she woke up, she would go around the house turning lights on, opening up shades, wondering out loud why it was so dark in the house. She also loved watching a few soap operas in the afternoon; she would sit in her rocking chair and get so engrossed in those shows, she never knew I was sneaking up behind her, untying her apron and tying it around the slats in her rocker—effectively tying her to the chair. There was a "little" danger in it for me, my grandfather DID NOT PLAY ! I could do all these things (and more) as long as he was out in the garden. You did not want to get him mad, his walking cane could leave quite a welt across your back or legs.

My grandfather had an old tackle box hidden in the bottom of his closet, but he had to know I could find it—he HAD to know that—knowing me. Anyway, it had things in it that blew my mind back then—things I'd never seen before and didn't think I'd ever see again. He had a chunk of petrified wood that amazed me—I wanted to hold it and feel it; and, he had some old coins from the late 1800's in there. Truly, amazing things for a nosy, little kid to see. He was also somewhat of a hoarder and saver, which I must have inherited from him…I'm sort of the same way. He would save the rubber bands the daily paper came tied in; he saved snuff boxes, jars, bottles, nails, screws…he wouldn't throw anything away. I don't blame him, I'd love to have some of those snuff boxes today. In later years, after my grandmother died and I had a driver's license, he would have me drive him over to the next county to the ABC store and he'd buy a ½ pint of something—I never knew what it was, or where he kept it—and I looked, to no avail. That was one secret he could keep from me.

I loved him with all my heart, I was always a little scared of him, but I loved him—he understood me and would even giggle at some of the tricks I played on poor, little Anne. A year before he died, he asked my mother to take him to see the ocean and the mountains one more time…we did that; I wish we'd done more for this great man.

My grandparents' house, my house as well, had a tin roof—you don't see those anymore, but it was awesome during rainstorms. The sound of rain on that roof could put me to sleep any time of day or night. Of course, there was no air conditioning in those days, but you didn't miss things you never had. I'm sure it was warm in the summer, I remember always turning my pillow over to the "cool" side trying to sleep; but with the windows open and screen doors, I never remember being uncomfortable. We had a gas heater in the front of the house and a coal stove at the rear of the house—the middle was just cold in the winter. But that was okay, we didn't mind. We had one bathroom, with a bathtub (no shower) for the five of us, which seemed normal to me—why would we need more than that?

Our house had this big wide front porch that wrapped around to the side as well. I could (and did) ride my bicycle back and forth on that porch when it rained. It also had a swing that seated 2-3 adults or 4-5 kids as well as several chairs…all great vantage points to watch the rain, or to watch people walk by, to sit and eat grapes, or to do nothing at all but enjoy being a boy. The swing had this big thick, shaggy, blue rug in it…we were told my father made that rug. I never knew if that was true or not, why would anyone make that up? But since I didn't have anything else of my father's, that rug was always special to me. I wish I'd kept it when the house was sold and torn down…but I didn't, now it resides in my mind only—but that's good enough. When I go back to visit in Red Springs now, I always visit the lot where our house was located. It's nothing more than a paved lot next to the Piggly Wiggly now. A paved lot full of the best memories a person could ever have; full of more love and fun and adventure than I deserve. A paved lot…A paved lot.

There was also a Chinaberry tree in the front yard, (a tree that was easy to climb and that had these little, red "chinaberries" growing in it). One of my favorite pastimes was to climb up high in the tree, hide as best I could and drop chinaberries on passing cars. Hard to explain why, but it was so much fun that one day I brought my dog up in the tree with me for him see how much fun it was…he didn't think so. He squirmed so bad that I lost control of him, he fell out of the tree and broke his leg. Not one of my better decisions.

Back in those days, we were never asked what we wanted to eat; my grandmother and Hazel cooked, and we ate what they cooked…if you didn't like it, you had the choice of not eating it, simple as that. But I don't ever remember that happening. I do remember fried chicken and white rice on Sundays after church; and I remember field peas and corn and Irish potatoes (the best kind) and pinto beans. My grandfather liked to use his fork and mash up his pinto beans into a mush; I thought this looked cool so I started doing it as well. They didn't taste any different, it just looked cool. Anne and I were also permitted to have one Pepsi per day (10 oz. bottles back then). I would save mine for nights when some of my favorite shows came on:

Gunsmoke, Have Gun, Will Travel, Perry Mason, Andy Griffith, the Dick Van Dyke Show…good programs that didn't need nudity and sex and filthy language to be good and entertaining. I would always put my Pepsi in the freezer for about 20 minutes before I wanted to drink it, this way, it would have some icy chunks in it that would be heavenly to drink. The only snacks I remember us having were fruit from the yard, or the always available peanut butter sandwich—peanut butter being the second of my three favorite foods, along with watermelon and bacon…I have simple tastes. Every once in a great while, mama would get some popsicles and put them in the freezer for us—oh, what a treat that was. They came on two sticks, so you could break them in half and eat just one at a time—made it last so much longer—oh me, I wish I had a grape popsicle right now! These memories only confirm that which I already knew…I had it made! I knew it then and I know it now…I have always been blessed; I don't know why, I certainly don't deserve it; but somehow the Lord has chosen to bless me throughout my life—and I certainly do appreciate it. More on this later.

2

"Whether you think you can or can't, you're right."

I would be extremely remiss if I didn't spend some time describing a lovely, lovely woman in my childhood who was not a blood relative, but who was definitely a part of our family...Hazel Mae Ray, one of the best human beings I've ever known. Hazel was, in the vernacular of the times and her own definition, a Negro. Later, she would become Black, however, in her own words, she never became African-American. As she told me at my mother's funeral, I've never been to Africa, my parents weren't from Africa, my grandparents weren't from Africa and their grandparents weren't from Africa...I'm a Black American woman. I agree with you 100%, Hazel.

Hazel worked for our family, heck, she took care of our family; we relied on her and depended on her for nearly everything. My grandmother was frail and had a bad heart and my mom worked and was gone 10-12 hours a day, so Hazel became our surrogate everything. We loved her...and she loved us. She would cook us breakfast before school, she knew how to cook the eggs just right, cooked enough so the white didn't run, but not enough to keep the yellow part from running—oh yes, I liked the yolk runny. Two of those eggs and bacon on some toast with homemade grape jelly—oh my Gosh!!! I think I'm going to cry. She also made my sister pancakes that weren't completely cooked either; for some weird reason, Anne liked the inside of her pancakes runny. Now as odd as these two breakfast menus seem, it takes great care and experience to achieve this runniness consistently. How Hazel was able to do this, day after day, in retrospect, seems very admirable—if not downright amazing.

She helped Granny cook all the meals as well, can the fruit, shuck the corn, shell the peas, peel the potatoes, wash and iron the clothes—any and all duties around the house...which included taking care of me and Anne. Which was half easy, and half very hard, that is all I'm going to say. My favorite times with Hazel were during the summers when we were out of school and I had time to just hang around and talk to her...she had so much common sense it made the world seem easy to understand. She explained things to me in a way that made perfect sense—hard things, things that I couldn't ask other people for the fear of offending them. But I knew that no matter what I asked Hazel, she wouldn't be offended; she knew I was curious and I knew she would still love me. As an 11 year old, I wanted to know things, like, why the palms of Hazel's hands were very light colored while the rest of her was black. As she explained, it was because the Lord made us so that we worked with our palms, so they ended up scrubbing and scouring which wore the skin and color off them quicker. To prove this point, she showed me the bottom of her feet, which were also a lighter color because she walked on them all day. As she explained it, we are all the same, just a little different color and when the skin wore off, we are all just alike underneath that skin. Made perfect sense to me.

Hazel was special to me…to all of us; we depended on her for so many things. She had a son named Johnny who was about 6 years older than me; he was already over 6 feet tall when I was barely 5 feet tall. And, he was a good athlete, how good I don't know, because in those days the schools were segregated and we didn't get to see each other play. But I do know that Hazel somehow coerced Johnny and a few of his friends to play some pick-up baseball games with me and some of my scrawny friends. We thought we were good, and I guess we were for 11-12 year skinny punks; but we were WAY overmatched by Johnny and his friends. They hit balls farther than I thought was possible by a human being. We were awed. Amazingly, and I don't understand why, but Johnny and his friends enjoyed playing with us, and we all had a great time. I know somehow Hazel was behind those games and making us friends…that's the kind of things she would do.

Years later after we were all grown up and had moved on and away from Red Springs, I met Hazel for the last time at my mother's funeral. She was just as beautiful as she was 25 years earlier; her hug was just as comforting and her smile just as warming. A year or two after that sad day, I learned Hazel had died. That too was a sad day…I didn't get to tell her goodbye, or how much I loved her and appreciated all she had done for me. That's my fault for not making that minimal effort; shame on me, but you know what Hazel would've said about it? "No need to worry honey, I know how you loved me, just as I loved you."

My beautiful little sister loved Hazel as well and she needed Hazel's comfort more than me, because of all the tricks I subjected her to. I know she thought it was meanness on my part, but I never looked at it that way…I just thought my pranks were funny. But poor Anne didn't see the "fun" in it at all…in fact, she would get so mad at me steam would be coming out of her ears. For example, in our little town, for some unknown reason, you could dial the last three digits of your telephone number, hang up the receiver and the phone would ring—I don't why it would do that, but it did. So, me being me, I'd make the phone ring when Anne was in the next room, then I'd answer it and say "no…Anne's not here—bye." Well, let me tell you, she would get so mad at me, but I just thought it was funny; and the madder she got, the funnier I thought it was.

Other times, as I sat around doing nothing in particular, I'd see her go outside for something and I'd lock the screen door, locking her out…then I'd hide. Temper, temper, temper…she had one and I must say, I did all I could to exploit it…I guess that was meanness, but to me it was just fun and tricks—heck, I did that stuff to everyone, she was just more accessible. And, I knew I could get away with all that stuff because my mom loved me so much…I was her pet—Anne knows it, and accepts it. I know our mother loved us both with all her heart, but I could seldom do wrong, whereas Anne was a loaded pistol at times and could be hard to handle. I know there were times when she wanted to join in and hang around with me, but I was three years older and just didn't want my sister tagging along. Completely different now…I'm still three years older, but I wish she was with me all the time. Who wouldn't…she's smart, gorgeous, talented, successful, funny and most important of all…she loves her big brother—even after all that, she still loves her big brother. She's a good old girl.

More on Anne later…now, back to my childhood in beautiful, bucolic Red Springs, garden spot of southeastern North Carolina. Home of Trouble, June Bug, Pony, Lizard, Tunk, Moonface, Hollywood, Jub and many other assorted nicknames, in-laws and out-laws. I loved living in Red Springs, I'd probably live there now if my wife had Alzheimer's and didn't know where we were. (Just kidding Susan). Simple days and simple pleasures in the mid 1950's to the early 1960's. Throwing dirt clods at each other, playing hide and seek, hitting rocks with an old baseball bat, riding our bikes all over town and all the pickup games of baseball, football and basketball we played…treasured memories, treasured times.

Our good friend Phillip Bragg, who lived halfway between me and my friend Dickie, had a basketball goal (as we all did), but his was in his driveway, which was a crushed coal surface. Since he lived in the middle, we played there at lot; after an hour or two of bouncing that ball on coal and wiping sweat from your face with your coal blackened hands, we were about as dirty as dirty could get. But we didn't care…we were playing ball—that was all that mattered. Same way we played baseball in Ed Leigh's backyard, where the train tracks ran through the outfield. It was always fun when the train came by, I'd save an old penny and put it on the tracks and let the train crush it into an ultra-thin piece of metal…I thought that was so cool. I always wanted to do that with a nickel…but couldn't afford it. A nickel meant something then…you could buy 5 baseball cards, 5 pieces of candy or even get a cherry coke at the drug store…no way I could afford to flatten a nickel…no way!

We all collected baseball cards back then (some of us still do), our goal was to get all the players from each team, a full set—or, just get ONE Mickey Mantle card. One Mantle equaled everything else. He was the man, he was our hero, he was what we all wanted to be—good looking, powerful, popular and the best baseball player on the best team in the world. (my apologies Willie). First thing I'd do in the morning was to check the box scores to see how Mickey did the day before; one hit –great, two or three hits, I was walking on air; but an 0 for 4 day would break my heart. Just saying the name could make you happy…Mickey Mantle, Mickey Mantle…it rolled off your tongue and sounded so incredulous—how could he not be great. Later in life I wondered if he'd been named Irvin Jones, would he have been as good as he was, or as popular as he was. I don't know, but I sure am glad he was named Mickey Mantle.

Obviously, I was a Yankees fan growing up, but also a Green Bay Packer fan as well. Mama worked with a guy who was in love with her (she was never in love with him), but he was a nice guy named Maury Perrinboom. Maury was from Green Bay and truly loved the Packers and he got me hooked on them. He would have a friend of his from Green Bay send me the Monday morning papers from Green Bay after each football game…I thought that was great and saved those papers for years. This was in the glory days of the Packers when Vince Lombardi was coaching, Bart Starr was the quarterback, they had Jim Taylor, Paul Hornung, Willie Davis, Ray Nitschke, their whole lineup was NFL all-stars and future Hall of Famers. I loved the Packers…still do. Paul Hornung was the golden boy on those teams, halfback and field goal kicker; blonde haired and handsome, he won the Heisman Trophy while at Notre Dame and was the playboy of the league—before Joe Namath came along.

Hornung wrote a book at that time called "Football and the Single Man," Maury got a copy of it and somehow got Hornung to sign it "to Gary, best wishes, Paul Hornung." Thrilled could not describe how I felt about that gift…I still have the book and will always treasure it—for the memories. Maury also sent me a book by Vince Lombardi called "Run To Daylight," I still have that one as well. Yes, old Maury was a good guy, but he could never convince my mom to marry him—she just didn't love him that way, he was more of a friend to us all. Too bad for Maury (more on him later).

From time to time in the summers, we would camp out in our backyard—a great adventure. Dripping candle wax on your fingers and hand, listening to the AM station from Chicago after dark, chasing fireflies, and telling the most outrageous lies we could think of. Sometimes, late at night we would roam the streets, walking through town, past the grocery store, which sometimes had some fruit delivered out front for in the morning. I remember stealing a banana once and running like wildfire with my ill-gotten gains…I still feel guilty about that and hope to reimburse Piggly Wiggly at my earliest convenience. In fact, maybe I won't, now that I think about it. My first so-called job outside of home was at Piggly Wiggly; I was 15 or 16 (no minimum age laws back then). I went to work there one Saturday morning at 9:00 and worked till 6:00 that evening; I was so glad to see 6:00 come only to have my bubble burst when the manager said, "okay, everyone mop the floors." You cannot be serious! Work all day, and then mop floors? But, I mopped floors with the others, dreaming of what I was going to do with my first paycheck. I went back the following Wednesday to collect my check, in anticipation of that glorious day. $5.67…How could that be? 10 hours of working and mopping for $5.67??? There had to be a mistake, what are all these minuses from my check? Taxes? What?? Minus for this, minus for that; thoroughly heartbroken I had learned a valuable lesson—never work at Piggly Wiggly again—EVER! So there you go, I figure my work that day makes up for my ill-gotten banana…Piggly Wiggly, we're even.

3

"Experience is not what happens to you. It is what you do with what happens to you."

Another job I had during summers was picking watermelons. We were paid 1 penny per watermelon and for me and my friends, we thought this was a pretty good deal. You get to hang around with your buddies and make some money and eat the hearts out of all watermelons you wanted. They would bring us lunch out to the fields; we would break open a melon and wash our hands in it. A tractor and flatbed trailer would be on one end of the field and 8-10 of us would line up and relay the melons toward the trailer. Someone would count them, then we'd load them on a trailer and each person would be paid 1 penny for each melon we loaded. Plus, you could take home a couple of melons each day—since this was one of my three favorite foods; it was a win-win situation for me. The money wasn't good, I'll admit, but at least they didn't take out taxes, and the side benefits were extraordinary.

There were only two things I didn't like about that summer job…the first was the occasional snake—don't like 'em, don't care what kind they are, I don't like 'em. The second thing was the ride out to the farm. My friend Michael Davis (more on him later) would pick me up and drive me and a couple of others to the fields—he being the only one with a car. The problem was that he would drive 100 mph! It scared the pure fire out of me…but what can you say in front of your friends? You can't whimper or cry, so you just hold your breath and hope he doesn't kill us all…he didn't. But a few years later, he did wreck his new Corvette and almost killed himself; fortunately he only lost his spleen and broke some bones. At least none of us was in the car with him that day…he was indeed a crazy guy.

Those lazy summers were so much fun and I was very blessed to have so many great friends and such a large family to share time with. Seemingly, every week or two we would have guests, ranging from regulars like Aunt Myrtle, who called my Granny Ida—I'd never heard anyone call her anything except Granny before—it was very strange thinking she actually had a name other than Granny. They would sit and gossip for a couple of hours each week and catch up on all the floozies and drunks in town. My aunts and uncles also made fairly regular visits to see their mom and dad. Uncle Earl only lived across the field from us, so we saw him and Aunt Annie Lou regularly, and I even let Scott and Branson share a peanut butter sandwich with me occasionally. Uncle Paul and Aunt Dot would visit from Charlotte about once a month (more about this in a previous book) and Uncle G.C. and Aunt Ginny would visit with their 6 kids every month or two. However, Uncle Donald, Aunt Pat and their three kids would only visit from Florida about once a year…this was very special. Uncle Donald was just a big kid in my opinion…he was one of us. He liked to play and cut up and just have fun—he was up for anything. He married his wife Pat when she was just 14 years old…they had their first baby when she was 16, then another a couple years later, then another—all beautiful babies and children. I had a special place in my heart for the youngest of his three kids Brenda—more on Brenda later, a lot more.

Uncle Gurney and Aunt Margaret would visit from St. Paul's every so often and Uncle Gurney would pull quarters out of your ears! And, he'd let you keep the quarters! I always figured they were rich. And I guess they were, but being rich didn't spare them the tragedy of losing their only son in a swimming accident when he was only around 19 or 20 years old…they were never the same. A tragedy like that changes people…parents shouldn't outlive their children. My Aunt Mary, who I lived with for two years, had moved to Orlando, Florida. It was always special when she visited because I KNEW I was her favorite…I'm special that way. But it was even better when I got to visit her in Florida!

I would ride the train down there (again, in the late 1950's and early 1960's it was safe for a kid like me to travel by himself). I only had one problem, on one trip…the trains would stop at most towns and the conductors would walk through the cars and announce the name of the town where we were stopped. I had been dozing when I thought I heard the conductor yelling out "Orlando, Orlando, Orlando"…I jumped up, grabbed my bag and got off the train just in time; it was a close call. However, I didn't see Aunt Mary anywhere on the platform…to be sure she wouldn't be hiding from me—that's something I would do, not her. I looked all around, and no Aunt Mary, then I looked up at the sign in the train station and it say "Deland." When the guy was yelling out "Deland," I heard it as "Orlando." Oh boy!

Fortunately, the people in the train station took pity on me—cause I'm special—and called the Orlando terminal and got the message to Aunt Mary, they put me on the next train south, where she met me in ORLANDO. What a magical time I had with her—this was all pre- Disneyworld. But there was Gatorland…big gators, little gators, dangerous gators; you could walk over a little wooden bridge and throw them pieces of bread—very exciting. Aunt Mary knew how to entertain. She would take me swimming, we went to Silver Springs and rode in the glass bottom boats and she even took me on a tour of the new Tupperwear plant! Well, she could've skipped that one, but they gave out free samples at the end of the tour, so…

My favorite memory with Aunt Mary in Orlando was the night she took me to a drive- in (me in my pajamas) to see "A Hard Day's Night," the Beatles first movie. I was completely smitten and spellbound—in fact, the spell is still working overtime in my simple, little brain! The bug had been planted that one fateful night in early 1964 when we all saw the Beatles on the Ed Sullivan Show—that show changed the world as we knew it. Musically, culturally and sociologically…things would never be the same again.

Another memorable boyhood trip was with our Little League up to Baltimore and Washington to see some major league baseball games. Our first stop was in Baltimore, at the old Memorial Stadium. Guess who they were playing? The New York Yankees! Mantle, Maris, Whitey Ford, Elston Howard, Tom Tresh, Bobby Richardson, Clete Boyer…I could go on and on about their lineup, but the only one that really mattered was of course Mickey Mantle —the "Mick," the Man, my hero. We got to the ballpark early on a drizzly, rainy night, not even sure if they would get to play the game or not—we were praying. First thing we did was all run down the steps to the Yankees dugout and wait for the players to come out…well, actually waiting for THE PLAYER to come out. Finally, here he comes, the Mick, standing right in front of me, ten feet away…it was as if one of the Greek god's had descended upon earth and landed right in front of me. Blonde hair underneath that iconic NY hat, massive forearms and shoulders that looked as if they would burst from the uniform. I was so star struck I completely froze; did not ask for an autograph and did not speak…at least I didn't pee on myself. Fortunately, I finally had the presence of mind of take his picture before he trotted out to the field—a picture I treasured for many, many years.

Well, the Mick played left field that night…we all yelled to him and he waved back to us; he went 0-2 and the game was called after 6 innings because of the rain. Disappointing? Yes, but my friends…I saw the man in person, in all his glory and greatness, and I will never, ever forget that. The rest of our trip was quite uneventful…we went over to Washington, visited the White House and the monuments, etc. We even went to see the woeful Washington Senators play the Cleveland Indians…Washington had Frank Howard, who was huge, and Cleveland had a guy with one of the great names in baseball—Rocky Colavito. But, I remember nothing of the game, other than Rex Bullock caught a foul ball…after seeing the Mick, all else was achingly dull and even mundane. But what could you expect, after you'd been to the mountain top, seen the glory, and experienced your life, long dream.

I remember our first trip to Hardee's, in Lumberton, we had no fast food restaurants in Red Springs; in fact, we had no restaurants in Red Springs—unless you consider the Bus Station a restaurant. So, the trip to Lumberton, to the first Hardee's anywhere near us, was very exciting. This would have been in the early 1960's…there was no indoor seating, you went up to the window and ordered and they gave it back to you outside—very chic at the time. Hamburgers were.15, cheeseburgers were.20, fries.10, milk was.12 (which seemed expensive to me, you could buy a carton of milk at school in the lunchroom for.03), Pepsi or coke was.10 and.15 (small and large) and milkshakes were.20.

And it was all good! Very good in fact, we all looked forward to the 18 mile drive over to Lumberton to feast on this incredible menu…A hamburger for.15…truly amazing. I was in the car once with my friend Michael Davis, we were going to over to Lumberton to eat at Hardee's; he and his brother Stanley and I were all in the back seat and his parents, Holmes and Sara (who were excellent people), were in the front seat. We were very excited and hungry. Michael was sitting in the back seat directly behind Holmes, who was driving, and it was summertime and all the windows were down. Michael, being Michael, had been drinking a Pepsi in a glass bottle, he decided he was going to throw it out the window and try to hit a sign with it (sounds strange now, but really it was not that uncommon in those days to do that, or to simply throw your trash out the window as well). So Michael rears back to backhand the bottle out the window and when he does, he whacks Holmes in the back of the head, knocking him out! Holmes slumps over, blood is gushing out of the back of his head, Sara is screaming at Holmes while reaching over to grab the steering wheel. She keeps us in the road, while screaming at Holmes to wake up, which he eventually does and we somehow get pulled off the side of the road with no further damage, except to Holmes' head and the blood on the car seat. Was Michael punished? No, I guess the whole ordeal scared us all so bad that no punishment was needed. The really bad end to this story (except for the gash in Holmes' head) was that we turned around and went back home…no hamburgers, no fries, no milkshakes—poor, poor, pitiful us.

My mother worked then at Fort Bragg as a civilian employee at the JFK Special Warfare Center. She was very smart and eventually became the civilian controller there, responsible for a budget at that time of over $187 million dollars. I was very proud of her, she was smart, talented and very attractive as well –my sister has all those genes passed onto her; I got the bad genes. Fort Bragg was about 26-27 miles from Red Springs and several people carpooled together to save on gas, one of those being my cousin Jack Smith –maybe the most intense competitor I've ever played with or against. However, one day my mother knew she had to work late so she drove to work by herself that day. After work, driving home in the dark, in her old, large Buick (a tank of a car), she had an accident…a bizarre accident indeed. I was in the 8th grade at the time, so it must have been around 1963.

The facts, as I know them from my mom and several other witnesses are as follows: she was just coming into the Red Springs area, not far from my friend Allen Simpson's house, when suddenly she saw a man lying in the road directly in front of her. As she started to swerve into the other lane to avoid running over the man, she noticed an oncoming car in the other lane coming right at her, so she aborted the swerve into the other lane and had no choice but to run directly over the guy in the road. Keep in mind, this whole scenario took just a second or two to unfold—no time to think, no time for anything except what reactions and reflexes occur. So, unfortunately, she hit the guy lying in the road and felt the sickening thump of the wheel as it ran over his body. She was so concentrated on the man in the road that she never saw the oncoming vehicle in front of her The man in the other car, we're guessing, thought my mother was going to swerve into his lane, so he swerved over into her lane. When she actually stayed in her lane, the unavoidable happened…a head-on collision of two cars going 50-60 mph.

The poor man in the other car died on impact, my mother sustained untold major injuries and broken bones. I remember seeing her in the hospital where she had tubes in her mouth and nose and bandages all over her and they didn't know if she'd survive or not. She was in the hospital at Duke for several months…not weeks—months. Miraculously, the man in the road that my mother ran over did not die. When the ambulances all got there and took my mother away and the dead man away, they then lifted the man in the road—whom no one knew, he didn't have a wallet on him—put him on a gurney, strapped him down and lifted him into the ambulance for the trip to the hospital. Before the first aid person could get into the ambulance and start the engine, they heard the back door open and a shut. They thought maybe someone else was checking on the man strapped down, so the ambulance driver got out, went around to the back of the ambulance, opened the door and saw an empty gurney. The straps had been broken and the man was gone. No trace whatsoever...the police and all emergency personnel searched everywhere...they never found that man and never heard anything from him ever again.

I was in shock and scared to death for my mom; I don't why or how this happened, but Sara and Holmes Davis took me into their home (with Michael and Stanley) to live with them until my mom got out of the hospital several months later. Remember me telling you earlier they were excellent people? They were. It was in their house that I heard the first album of the Beatles (Meet the Beatles). They treated me as though I was their third son; it seemed natural and loving during my months there. Why I went there, instead of staying with my grandparents, I don't know. I just felt supremely blessed to be cared for by these two gracious, loving, wonderful people.

4

"Many people die at 35, but aren't buried till they're 75."

Growing up like I did, playing ball nearly every day, riding my bike all over town, skateboarding (yes, I skateboarded back then), climbing trees, doing all the things boys do —and things they shouldn't do; I never really got hurt, I think the Lord was watching over me, preventing me having any serious injuries. I never had any broken bones (till I broke my finger at football practice in high school), only had stitches once when Furman Humphrey (more on him later) kneed me in the lip on the opening kickoff of a backyard football game. I still have my appendix, my tonsils and I guess all my other parts except some hair that refuses to grow on the top my head. My most painful injury, in more ways than one, was when I was kicking a football in the back yard—practicing field goals. I kept teeing it up higher and higher to get more distance I presume; finally, I had it teed up so high that on my follow through my knee hit the bottom of my jaw, while my tongue was hanging out and I nearly bit my tongue off. I found out pretty quickly that tongues BLEED…they bleed a lot! I ran into the house, found mom and she was scared out of her wits. Luckily for us, Dr. Johnson's office was just across the block from us, through the First Baptist Church parking lot. She grabbed me and we ran over there and Dr. Johnson took me immediately into his office. After cleaning up all the blood and diagnosing my badly bitten tongue, he told my mom that he was going to stitch it up. Huh? Stitch it up? You mean sewing my tongue? I don't think so…I got off that table and started running and didn't stop till I got to my room and locked the door. Unfortunately for me, my mom did not agree with my actions. Once she forced me to open the door and finished scolding me and threatening me (told me she better NEVER hear me complain about my tongue hurting), she made me go outside, cut some switches, bring them to her, whereupon she thrashed me good. Not only was my tongue killing me, now my backside was on fire—it was not a good day for me.

Another inglorious day in my childhood happened behind the school, where we had all gathered to play a pickup game of baseball. We never had a problem getting people to play. First, we loved it, second, there was nothing else to do in Red Springs except play ball—well, that's my opinion anyway. We were all there, you know the names, it wasn't far for all of us to walk or ride our bikes. One of our friends, Dee Singleton, had money; not sure how he had money, but he did. His dad was a known card shark and I think Dee had some of those genes as well; all I know, is that Dee had money and always had a nice car…he was 2-3 years older than me.

As we were all gathered trying to choose up fair teams, Dee drove up and parked behind the small bleachers near the third base line, out of the way so his car wouldn't be hit by a foul ball…smart thing. I quickly grew bored with the choosing of teams and started wondering if I could hit the light pole down the left field line with a rock. So, I picked up a good rock and threw it at the pole…incredibly enough, I hit that pole dead center, also incredibly enough, the rock then ricocheted way over to the left and hit Dee's car right in the windshield, smashing it good. I couldn't believe it; first I couldn't believe I actually hit the pole, and secondly, how in the world did that rock bounce way over there and hit Dee's car? You never heard such silence from 16 guys…I guess they were both stunned at what happened and also waiting to see if Dee was going to whip my butt. I was too. However, Dee handled it much better than I thought was possible; he didn't beat me up, or threaten me or even try to make me pay for it—and I volunteered to pay for it. He said no, the insurance would handle it; I didn't actually know what insurance was or how it worked, but I was sure glad Dee did.

The name of our home town, Red Springs, was derived from the springs that surfaced at various locations around the city. One of the most popular of these springs was at Flora McDonald College. My mother went to college at Flora McDonald way back then, and my grandfather worked the gardens there until his stroke. It closed at some point and later became a girl's school, Vardell Hall, during my high school and college years (lucky us), and later still, it became a private local school for the Red Springs population, which it currently is. Flora McDonald had the only tennis courts in town in my youth, three of them. The first one had limbs from some oak trees overhanging it, so you couldn't hit lobs on that court, the third court was so rough and broken you really couldn't play on it, but the middle court was okay—for our purposes anyway.

Tennis was what we played when we couldn't find enough people to play baseball or basketball, but it was fun and very competitive, which I enjoyed. I really didn't know how to play, I was just quick and a good athlete, so I adjusted. I NEVER learned how to hit a backhand then, I would run around everything to hit only forehands—you can do that when you're fast and quick—until you meet a good player, like my friend Allen. He was good, forehand and backhand, he even played college tennis at Campbell College. I never beat Allen and in fact, had the one of the worst defeats in my short life against him. I was ahead of him 5-1 one set and got nervous, then, he started hitting every ball to my backhand and it wore on me. He won 6 consecutive games to win the set 7-5 and broke my heart. Sports and pretty girls can easily do that.

We played tennis in those days with white tennis balls and wooden rackets, at least the balls were white for the first couple of games, then they were just dirty—heck, we didn't care. When we'd get thirsty, we'd take our tennis ball cans and walk over to the spring and fill it up with good, cool mineral water from deep underground. Excellent tasting water, but it stunk like you wouldn't believe. Literally, you had to hold your breath while you went down the three steps to the spring and filled your can up. But, once you got out of there and drank that cool, sweet water, it was worth the trip. In my mind I can still smell that odor and taste that red, refreshing water…simple pleasures.

5

"It's not what you do, but how much love you put into it that matters."

Certainly everyone from my generation and older can remember where they were November 22, 1963 when they heard the news of President Kennedy's assassination. There are few memories so vivid that you never forget them: your marriage, kids being born, the death of loved ones, even the death of our President—you don't soon forget those things. They let us out from school early that fateful Friday afternoon, I remember on the walk home at John's Texaco on the corner of Main St., I watched the cars go by for a few minutes to see if I could spot one from Texas—I would have run to the police station if I'd seen one. Our world was seemingly so simple and naïve then...that day changed things.

As I wrote before, my mother was working at Fort Bragg at the time, so the President was in effect her Commander–In–Chief. She came home from work that day crying so hard we couldn't talk to her—she was devastated. That was a sad, sad weekend we all endured watching the funeral procession, seeing little John John saluting his dad, grieving for Jackie as she stoically, without crying, carried on through ceremony, dressed in black. Sad times.

Another sad time for my mom came with a sudden phone call one night. My mom, Anne and I were watching television when the phone rang and I answered it; an unfamiliar voice asked to speak to mama, so I gave her the phone. She listened for a minute or two then started weeping gently at first, then uncontrollably after she hung up the receiver. We knew someone had probably died, we didn't know who...everyone we knew was in reasonably good health. After several minutes, when she regained her composure, she told us our dad had died, Andy J. Hope was dead. Honestly, I didn't know how to feel, it totally surprised me that my mom cried like she did; somehow I thought he was totally out of her mind and life...I was mistaken.

We had not heard a word from Andy for about 15 years, mama tried a couple of times to track him down, but the lawyers she employed had no luck. I guess it was difficult back then with no computers and internet; it was also probable she just couldn't afford an all-out search. It was obvious he didn't want to be a part of our lives, even if she could have found him and somehow forced him to pay some child support, it would have probably been acrimonious and unsettling for us all. In retrospect, I think things turned out just like they were supposed to...the Lord always has a better plan for us, than we do for ourselves.

Even though I really didn't miss having a father that much (I was too busy having fun), I do remember times on the baseball field, or the basketball court, when I would look up into the stands to see if somehow, someway he had snuck into the game to see how his son was doing. I never saw him. Mama told us he was living in West Virginia at the time of his death and had been visiting his mother in California. He had left the Los Angeles area to drive back and decided to stop for the night in a little, tiny place called Tucumcari, New Mexico. A one stoplight town, with one hotel and not much of anything else. He went to bed that night and never woke up—42 years old and his heart just stopped. We found out later that his two brothers had also died early from heart attacks; one was 40 years old and the other only 38. Those things have a tendency to weigh on your mind from time to time, if you carry Andy Hope's genes in your body, which Anne and I do.

Anyway, at the time of the phone call, we didn't know any of these details, only that he had died (we didn't know where or how). He had recently remarried and we were told that his current wife requested strongly that we not attend his funeral or visit for any reason whatsoever. Okay. After a few days, it sort of faded away and life was back to usual; except for feeling badly for mama, I really didn't feel one way or the other about the whole thing. I was 19 or 20 at the time and had plenty of other things to worry about…trust me. So, the saga of Andy Hope was seemingly closed, except that it really wasn't. After his death, his mother contacted us and wanted to see us; she was forced to never contact us by Andy while he was alive, I guess for fear they would find him and make him start paying child support—I don't really know. Anyway, we had fond memories of Granny Hope and I really wanted to see her again. She would send me birthday cards with a $5 bill inside, how could you not love her?

Five years later a friend of mine, named Mike Boyd, and I worked all summer to save money for an epic 3 week west coast trip (which I'll describe a little later), before college started back—I was in graduate school at the time at Appalachian State University. My grandmother invited us to stay with her in California, it was the only way we could have afforded to go—a free place to stay. We had little money, so we decided to drive all the way from North Carolina to California without stopping—a grand plan. But harder than we thought. After two straight days of driving my little Volkswagen without stopping, we were completely worn out. We still had another day to go and knew we couldn't make it; so, we decided we'd stop and spend the night at the cheapest place we could find on Interstate-40. We saw a cheap looking hotel, got us a room, slept, and finally made it to L.A. and my granny's house the next day…she had a small little place, Mike and I had to share a double bed, but she treated us royally!

So much to catch up on, so many questions I wanted to ask; I didn't want to bore Mike, but there were things I wanted to know. One of the questions was what happened to him, how did he die? She explained it to me about him stopping at a little hotel and not waking up (we hadn't heard any of this before). I asked her where that had happened, and she said in a little place called Tucumcari, New Mexico. Mike and I almost collapsed…Tucumcari was the place we had stopped the night before to spend the night. There was only one hotel —a cheap one—and we spent the night there. I tremble now as I think about that coincidence. I'll say no more.

6

"Farming looks mighty easy when your plow is a pencil, and you're a thousand miles away from the corn field."

Now, a little about my mom, who died way too soon…57 years old. She was one of the most intelligent women I've ever known, as evidenced by how quickly she rose through the ranks of civilian employees in the Army to the post of base controller. She started at Fort Bragg, then, when Anne and I had left home, she received a promotion to Fort Lee in Petersburg, Va., then later another promotion to Fort Sam Houston in San Antonio, Texas. I was always very proud of her for what she had accomplished, for the type of person she was, and for how attractive she was—she was indeed a beauty. She always colored her hair as long as I could remember, I asked her one day, "Mama, what is the real, natural color of your hair?" She said, "The same mousy brown color yours is." Thanks mama. She wasn't trying to be cruel to me, that's just the way she was; I think she was so smart, that she was a little goofy and could say things at times, that either didn't make sense, or were downright weird.

She had several suitors while Anne and I were in school, but nothing serious; I'm sure her priorities at the time were to get us educated and taken care of. I think about that now and wonder what it must've been like for her, an attractive, intelligent woman from about age 25 up to about 40 putting her kids first, rather than her own happiness and social life. She had to be lonely, she had to be. However, she did have one constant companion…cancer. That cruel, unwelcome guest who comes to stay and WILL NOT leave. I'm not sure how old she was when she was first diagnosed with lymphoma, but I think it was in her early 30's. All I do know is that she fought that disease the rest of her life. The heartbreaking saga of chemo and radiation— losing all her hair, remissions, hair growing back; then, rewind and do it all over again. I don't know how many times she went through this cycle, more than I can remember, more than she deserved. I never heard her even once complain about it or ask "why me?" Not once. Oh, if you asked her how she felt, she would tell you that she was a little sick…that's all. A little sick to her meant throwing up all day long from the treatments and medicines they were giving her.

However, she always seemed to bounce back and had months where she was healthy and happy before the cycle started again. I remember one cycle where she had to be admitted to Duke for some serious treatments, I was 19 or 20 I think, had no money and no car and was a mixed up, lost and lonely soul. I missed my mama. So, one Saturday morning I set out to hitchhike up to Durham, from Red Springs, to see her in the hospital—I didn't really think this through. It was in the wintertime and got dark early; by the time I finally got to Durham and found the hospital, it was nearly 4:00 in the afternoon…it got dark at 5:30. I only got to spend an hour or so with mama before I figured I'd better leave. She was worried, but I told her I was fine…she didn't need anything else on her mind. It was not easy trying to hitch rides with long hair, in the dark in rural North Carolina. It seemed to me I walked more than I actually rode on that trip home. I finally arrived back home around 2:00 AM thanks to the kindness of some guy who took pity on me and drove me the last 25 miles to my house…out of his way, I might add. The Lord, seemingly, takes care of those who can't take care of themselves—like me. Thinking about that night reminds me of angels…I don't think I've ever met one, but I'm quite sure an angel would never actually tell you that he was an angel…would he?

As busy as she was at work, and as sick as she was at times, she still came to all our ballgames. Home and away games, she was always there and always supportive—she was a good mom. Later in her life, in her early 50's, she met an older gentleman and finally got married again. Bob was a great old guy and we all loved him…he loved my mom and treated her like a queen. He would get frustrated at times because Bob was extremely "old school"—coat and tie, proper manners, etc.; and mama could be a bit goofy, as I explained earlier. Case in point, I dropped by to see them one day after work, as I liked to do, and they were sitting in the living room watching a show on TV and eating a bowl of ice cream. I didn't like to stay too long when I visited, just to stop by, say hello and talk a few minutes. Mama always asked me if I wanted something to eat or drink when I visited and I always said "no, I need to be going." But, this hot summer day, that ice cream looked extremely refreshing, so when mama asked me if I wanted a bowl, I said "yes, that sounds great!" Well, mama looked at me said, "umm, we don't have anymore." Which I thought was funny, but, old Bob stormed out of the room, went to the bedroom and slammed the door. That was just mama…and that was just Bob. I loved that guy and still miss seeing him and talking to him.

One Thanksgiving, Anne was coming to visit us from Reno, so mama planned a big Thanksgiving dinner for us all. Now, mama was very smart, but she never really learned how to cook, or cared much about cooking. But this was special, so, she went all out…turkey, dressing, this, that, everything…this dinner was going to be first rate. She cooked and cooked, accepting no help from anyone; finally, she announced everything was ready and please come to the table. It looked glorious! All the various foods, the breads and that golden brown turkey in the middle of the table topping it all off. She was so proud. She asked old Bob if he would do the honors of carving the turkey for us and he was delighted to do so. Only problem was, he couldn't carve it…it was still frozen on the inside! Mama obviously didn't realize you had to THAW the turkey before you actually cooked it. Well, Anne and I thought it was just hilarious…not Bob. Again, he stormed off to the bedroom and slammed the door. But, he got over it, and we later had a great vegetarian Thanksgiving dinner. Oh mama…how I miss you.

7

"Courage is something you didn't know you had."

My high school years were filled with sports, I loved them all. I was fortunate and blessed to have some athletic ability, so sports came fairly easily to me. And, the friends I had loved sports just as I did; no need to go into details here; the story of my friends is covered in a previous book. We played whatever was in season, baseball, basketball, football, tennis, anything we could to compete with and against each other—it was marvelous. I never dated much in high school, I'd much rather be playing ball to be honest about it. I was only 17 when I graduated, the youngest person in my class (along with Michael Davis), so all the girls in my class were older than me...I felt awkward about that. Plus, until I was a senior, I was also short and skinny as well. Even into my junior year I was one of the shortest guys in my class. Then, between my junior and senior years I grew...too fast really, for a month or two it was weird, almost like I had lost some coordination. I went from 5'6" to 6'1" that spring and summer. I was a different guy on the outside, inside I was the same old guy who just wanted to play ball each and every day. I played everything available in high school...I liked it that the day football season ended, basketball started the next day and baseball started the day after basketball ended. I was indeed a sports junkie. And we were pretty good—our baseball team won the conference championship all four years in high school and our basketball team won the conference championship my senior year. Every summer, our baseball league teams would always win the championships, we had some great players, two of our pitchers signed pro contracts, Kenny Fowler and Norman Furmage—they had great arms and Kenny had one of the best jump shots I'd ever seen. I had some great matchups with him in pickup games, I always looked forward to playing great players. Norman was a great pitcher, he didn't have the arm Kenny did, but he knew how to pitch. Tragically, a few years after high school, he was killed in a car accident.

Looking back at those four years now, it all seems like a blur; hard to distinguish and separate each of the years...I just know I had fun. If I want to know any particular details I can always call Dickie and he'll tell me the story (whether it's factual or not—who knows? But he's always got a story to tell). Unlike some other friends I have, who will remain nameless, and who can barely remember what town they live in, right Larry? I do remember old Red Norris though, our summer league baseball coach; Red could hit the best grounders and pop-ups with his old fungo that I'd ever seen. Red had some contacts throughout baseball, he'd played professionally in his youth, and he parlayed that network into a college scholarship/grant for me at Elon College. Forever grateful for that, however, I was far too immature and naïve to be going off to college by myself. Lost in a sea of Yankees, actual Yankees from New Jersey, Maryland and Pennsylvania. In my group of friends at Elon, I was the only guy from North Carolina! Three guys to a room then, my roommates were from Philadelphia and Sea Girt, New Jersey. Strange dudes…but good guys, we became close. I would be remiss in my storytelling if I didn't mention their names now: Jeff Propert from Philly and Richie Beem from Sea Girt…great guys who influenced me—though I didn't know it at the time.

Jeff was a workout fanatic and he impressed me with his strength and resolve. He would run for an hour each morning before breakfast—he would never eat a meal with exercising first. Before dinner he would do 100 pushups and 100 sit-ups before he ate…he never changed this regimen; then he'd run again late in the evening or at night. He was amazing! Richie did not exercise at all, but he loved music and opened my eyes to all sorts of bands I'd never heard of before. He had a great collection of records and we'd spend hours listening to them…the Doors, Jefferson Airplane, Crosby, Stills and Nash—on and on I could go. A love of music I still have today, but that time frame was magical…the late 60's produced some of the most enduring music of all time, and Richie helped me understand it. Unfortunately, neither of my two friends helped me go to class…I was a slacker. We had fall baseball back then, and I also worked (part of the grant to help pay for school). Between working, which varied between painting the seats in the gymnasium, being an usher at some football games and being a cook and dishwasher in the cafeteria; and baseball practice—I didn't have time to go to class, so, mostly I didn't, and it showed in my grades.

I found out pretty quickly I wasn't as good a baseball player as I thought I was either…another freshman named Jerry Suggs played the same position I did, except he played a whole lot better than me. Suggs was very good; he made All Conference as a freshman. Consequently, I didn't play very much; my college career consisted of going 2 for 7 with a bunt single and a double over the first baseman's head. I did pinch run a couple of times and stole one base…that's it. I could see the writing on the wall, Suggs was just better than me and I wasn't going to play much…I was very discouraged, over-worked and homesick. However, I was one of the best egg crackers in the cafeteria…I could hold two eggs in each hand and crack them all at the same time. If some pieces of shell got mixed in, heck, that was okay, just gave the scrambled eggs some crunchiness and flavor.

After a year and a half at Elon, I had had enough; I was tired of working all the time, I was lonesome and I knew my baseball career was going nowhere. So, one day in the middle of the semester, I just decided to quit. I packed up my things, said my goodbyes and drove home. I didn't know what I was going to do, other than, I was going home. Home sweet home—where I belonged. I pulled into the yard, parked the car and walked in the front door and saw mama sitting there. What a sight, my home, my mama…I was so relieved to be there…for about 5 seconds! She looked at me and said "What are you doing here?" I told her I had quit and had come home; she said "Well, you're not coming here." What? Again, she said, "you're not coming here." I said, "but it's my home," "no," she said, "it's my home and if you quit college, you're not coming here."

Stunned, I walked back out to my car without a clue of what I was going to do; I kept thinking she would come out there and ask me to come back in…did not happen. After about 30 minutes of just sitting there, I started the car and drove away—problem was, I didn't know where to drive to. Then, it hit me, my cousin Joe (my hero), he'd let me stay with him—I was sure of it. So, off I go to Joe and Sara's house…in Mobile, Alabama. Of course, there were no cell phones in those days, so I just took off driving and about 12 hours later I arrived, unannounced and certainly unexpected. And as I expected, they took me in, gave me a room to sleep in and helped me find a job. After about six months, I discovered that working for minimum wage, with no permanent home, and no friends was probably not the best decision I had made. The only two good things during my stay there was the time I spent with Joe and Sara—they were so great. The second thing was that every other weekend, I would drive back to North Carolina to see a girl I was dating at the time…a very attractive young lady named Ruth Balance. I'd take off after work on Friday, drive the 12 hours, and arrive very early Saturday morning. Sleep all day and take Ruth out Saturday night, then drive back to Alabama Sunday morning. Girls can make you do crazy things like that.

After six months of this, I knew I had to continue my education if I was ever going to amount to anything. Mama finally relented and welcomed me back home, with the condition that I go back to school…and pay for it myself, since I'd thrown away my scholarship. Heck, I'd agree to anything to come back home…so I came and was very happy until reality set in and asked me "where are you going to school? And, how are you going to pay for?" Uh oh.

8

This, of course, was a very troubled time in American history. We were fighting a war in Vietnam that served no purpose, no one wanted to be there, and no one knew how to get out. This, so-called war did nothing but deeply divide our country and kill and maim thousands of young men—many of those who made it home with no apparent injuries carried unseen illnesses with them for the rest of their lives. Agent Orange related cancers, my good friend Frank Nicholson died from that, and post-traumatic stress issues affected untold thousands of young men for the rest of their lives. A dark and sad time in American history.

Obviously, the military needed bodies to send over there, and just as obviously, no one in their right mind would be volunteering to go to that insane place. So, we had the draft, and if you were drafted, you pretty much knew what was going to happen—you were going to Vietnam and then it was a crap shoot if you would ever return. If you were in college, you were exempt for a few years, but if not, you were immediately eligible...I was now immediately eligible. All sorts of crazy things pass through your mind...do I go to Canada, do I hop on a freighter bound for Australia? It was an insane time. The government came up with a draft lottery trying to make it fair—so they said. Each of the 365 days of the year would be put in a barrel (or something) and someone would pull out dates from the barrel to determine your draft lottery position. Each county and state had their quotas to meet, our county, as wonderful as it was then and now, had a hard time meeting it's quotas because of the nature of our population: 1/3 white, 1/3 Black and 1/3 Indian. And a lot of uneducated young men simply couldn't meet minimum requirements. So...you pretty much knew if they called your birthday in the first 250 dates pulled, you were going to Vietnam. Anything after that and you "might" be okay.

The lottery was on all the radio stations and TV that night; someone would pull a date out of the barrel and the announcer would say: Number 1 is July 14; then Number 2 is Oct 28, Number 3 is March 17...on and on it went. Since my birthday is in October, each time he said "the next Number is October..." all you could do was hold your breath waiting on the number. It was torture, with a capital T! Date after date it continued, number after number...100, 175, 200...at this point you were sweating bullets and so nervous you could not sit still. My number finally came at 305—I had survived! As I keep repeating, the Lord takes care of those who cannot take care of themselves. Thank you Lord for number 305.

Now that the draft was behind me, my top priority was getting back in college. Without the scholarship, I couldn't afford Elon, heck, I couldn't afford anything. I was as broke as broke can be. I had to turn my little red car in because I couldn't make payments any longer, and I had no money saved from my time in Alabama. Seemingly, Pembroke State University was my only and best hope of an education. I'd never been to Pembroke before and knew very little about it, plus, the semester had already started three weeks earlier. I didn't know what to do. My friend Furman and I would ride around in his little VW bug looking to pick up bottles to sell back to the service stations. This would give us a few dollars to buy gas and maybe go to a ballgame…I was at the bottom of a deep hole and didn't know how to get out. At least 3 or 4 more months before summer school started when I could apply for admission to Pembroke—if they'd even take me with my less than stellar resume from Elon.

Furman and I were sitting in my house one day, he was listening to my sad plight and my long road to nowhere when my good buddy decided to take control of the situation and save my sorry little butt from ruination. Furman was, and is, one of a kind. He can make you laugh at anything, and can tell stories that you know can't be true, but you believe him anyway—because of the way he told them. So, Furman says, look up the phone number for Pembroke, I'm going to call them. I said, "What can you do, school started three weeks ago, and who's going to listen to you anyway?" "Just get me the number" he said. So, I did. Furman called the university and asked to speak to the Registrar's Office…these were in the good old days when you actually spoke to a human being when you called somewhere. They transferred him over and when he got to the appropriate person, Furman said, "I'm calling from Governor Scott's office and I need to speak to the person in charge," the governor of North Carolina at that time was the honorable Robert Scott. I could not believe Furman had said that, and even more, that they didn't threaten to call the police on him for this impersonation.

Instead, someone else got on the phone, and again Furman said, "I'm calling on behalf of Governor Scott and he wants to know if you can do him a personal favor." Silence, silence, silence…then Furman says "yes, the Governor has a personal, close friend, Gary Hope, who wants to attend your fine university, he's aware school has already started, but is there any way you can go ahead and admit this fine young man as a personal favor to the Governor?" More silence…then, "okay…okay…okay…he'll be right over." And he hung up and said, "Let's go, you're starting school this afternoon! Just tell them the Governor sent you." As John McEnroe once famously said, "You cannot be serious!"

Well, it worked; Furman drove me over there, I went to the Registrar's Office and told them my name and that the Governor had sent me. They fumbled all over themselves getting the paperwork done, signed me up, got me in classes and told me I didn't have to pay until the end of the semester. After signing all the papers, I went back to the car and Furman and I whooped and hollered all the way back to Red Springs…what a day! I was back in college.

I started Monday morning, problem was, I had no car and no way to travel the 10 miles over to Pembroke. My first class was at 8:00 AM Monday morning, so at 6:45 I was out on the

Pembroke road thumbing. I thumbed over to school and back home and was only late for class one time that I remember. Usually, early in the morning there were a lot people traveling over there and most were pretty nice about picking me up—and I'm thankful for all those who took the chance to do that. As I've said before, those days were not as dangerous as it is today; however, my appearance may have scared away a few people unintentionally. When I left Elon, I decided to let my hair grow long and grow a beard—so, I did. In fact, at that time in early 1970 I was the only guy in Red Springs with long hair. It didn't mean anything, other than I was hoping some of the Vardell Hall girls might like it, and it was a mild protest against the war in Vietnam.

Thumbing home was altogether another issue. It ALWAYS took longer to get home—much longer; there were times I'd be out there 2-3 hours waiting for someone to have pity on me. But that was okay, something had changed in me, and I absolutely loved going to college now. I loved the classes and the professors I had, learning was fun and I looked forward to most of my classes—not the math classes, just all the others. I didn't like math, I thought it was senseless and useless then, just as I do now. Why would anyone (especially me), care if 2 times X divided by M = pi? What was the point? How did that EVER come into your life in any practical way? But I knew I had to have some math credits in order to graduate, so I took several math classes…the longest I ever lasted in any of them was about three weeks before I dropped the class. I'd take it next semester. Sometimes procrastination can be your friend.

As I started school I also figured out I had to get a job, riding around with Furman picking up bottles was not going to buy me many textbooks. There was a textile mill in Red Springs called Celluknit, I applied and got a job in the dye department on third shift (11:00 PM until 7:00 AM). We would load these huge rolls of cloth into a vat, or dye machine, to dye the cloth to the desired customer order…lots of manual lifting and loading. My starting pay was $1.65 per hour, I got $0.05 extra for working 3rd shift. Celluknit was about 4 miles from my house in the opposite direction from Pembroke, just a little too far to walk in a timely fashion; but not too far to ride my bicycle. So, that's what I did, rode out there about 10:30 or so at night and pedaled home after work in the morning. I just had to make sure I didn't take any more 8:00 classes; I wouldn't have time to get off work, pedal home, then hitchhike to school by 8:00. And it worked out pretty good, the only problems were in thumbing home after school around noon or 1:00…by that time I was terribly sleepy and tired. So, thumbing for an hour or two or three after I'd been up all night working was no fun whatsoever.

Soon, my charm and good looks got me promoted to third shift supervisor, that plus the old supervisor got arrested and put in jail. And, I got a huge salary increase to $1.95 an hour…Yippie Ki Yo Ki Yay! I had it made now, and I knew it. I was so happy out there that I convinced my good buddy Jerry to apply for the recently open second shift supervisor job. I told our manager, Jim Matthews, that I would personally vouch for Jerry; and after a short interview, he hired him that day. So, now we had our mentor, Spencer (a very smart, hard-working Lumbee Indian) on first shift, old Jer on second and me on third. We had that dye department humming on all cylinders.

I was actually making so much money now that I could afford to date a few Vardell Hall girls; my first true love was a Vardell Hall girl from Columbia, SC, named Becky Wayburn—a true beauty. I was mad about her, and she was mad about me—for several months it was pure bliss. Go to Pembroke, thumb home, get a few hours' sleep, do my schoolwork and papers, go see Becky, then pedal my bike out to Celluknit for 8 hours…then do it all over again. Your first love can keep you going strong. We had so much fun together, I knew we would get married one day—she did too. When school was out for the summer, Becky went home to Columbia…that didn't stop us. After my last day at work and my last class for the week, I would thumb down to Columbia for the weekend. Becky lived in a large house with a few spare bedrooms and I was allowed to stay in one of these…her dad was a good guy; he was a doctor there in Columbia.

It would have been about a three hour drive to Becky's house, if I had a car; thumbing was an entirely different time frame. I tried to leave home after school on Friday around noon or so, and start thumbing; since it was summer, the days were longer, which helped—it's no fun thumbing at night. I would usually get down there from 5:00 (if I was lucky) to about 8:00 (if I was unlucky thumbing). That gave us Friday night and all day Saturday and Saturday night together before I had to thumb back home Sunday. A couple of times that summer, she came to visit me in Red Springs for the weekend; we just knew we were made for each other. I took her over to Pembroke and showed her around, visited my friends and some relatives, walked around town together—just enjoying being together.

Up to this point, Becky didn't know what her future plans were; after graduating from Vardell Hall, she really didn't know what she wanted to do. I suggested enrolling at Pembroke, but her heart wasn't in college really. She loved jewelry for some reason and had found some school that gave you an associate's degree in jewelry repair and management—this was what she wanted to do more than anything. Her dad told her if she got that degree, he would set her up in the jewelry business…that really excited her. The problem was, this school was in Paris, Texas. Texas!!!

I hated Texas, first for what happened to President Kennedy, then for the Packers arch enemies, the Dallas Cowboys, now for taking Becky away. I'm not sure how I feel about Texas now…but Marky hates that state, so that's good enough for me. Becky and I started with letters back and forth every day…We were both lovesick. Long distance telephone calls were too expensive and email hadn't been invented yet; plus, there's something about a letter that's special—it's way more personal than an email. Find me one person in the world who wouldn't rather receive a letter than an email from someone special. Letters were great. This went on from September, October and into November, when I had saved enough money to go out to the dreaded Texas and visit her. I could catch a flight from Fayetteville to Dallas, then a little prop jet over to Paris.

Mama took me to the airport, I was nervous, excited and apprehensive—I'd never flown before—and I'd never been in love before. The memory that sticks with me is when the jet started down the runway on that initial liftoff, just how powerful that thing was. It threw me back in the seat, and then lifted off the ground so gracefully…it was truly an amazing experience. Even today when I fly, I'm amazed that something that big and heavy can actually get off the ground. The prop jet from Dallas to Paris was way different…shaky, bumpy, seemingly thrown about by the wind…I did not like it at all. But, when it landed, there was Becky waiting on me. It was worth it.

We had a grand and marvelous weekend together, but there was something unspoken and fateful in the air between us those few days. I think we both knew long distance romances seldom work out, we just didn't want to face it or admit it. Once I got back home, the letters became less and less frequent; from every day, to every other day, then a couple a week, then once a week, until my heart was completely broken. I knew what was happening and could do nothing to prevent it. For the next year, literally a whole year, I was despondent, did not care about seeing any other girls, or doing anything socially. I just went to school, worked and played ball. I would get the occasional letter from her, but we both knew it would never happen again the way it used to be. You only have one first love and it was hard to get over it…very hard. I prayed for things to be different, but it was what it was…Becky was gone and I was alone.

Fast forward about 15 years or so, and I had just gotten divorced from a wonderful woman…more on this later; it was all my fault by the way; more explanation coming. But, I was very lonely and heartbroken over this unfortunate state of events. Sitting alone in a little apartment I had, I started thinking about my first love, Becky. How nice she was, how beautiful she was, how much fun we had—how stupid I was to not doggedly pursue her till the end of time. How could I have let her get away from me? The more I thought of her, the more I couldn't stop thinking about her. Finally, I decided I was going to call her; but how? Certainly, she's probably married by now with a house full of kids, or moved away to who knows where…maybe even that God-forsaken place called Texas. All I knew was that I had to at least try.

I thought I'd start by trying directory assistance in Columbia, first I'd try her dad's name and get his number and see if he even remembered me and would be kind enough to give me her number. The telephone lady came on the line and said, "What listing please?" without thinking, I said, "Becky Wayburn," she said, "Hold for the number." What? She was actually in the phone book in her maiden name? Was she not married? Married and divorced and kept her old name? I couldn't believe it. I got the number and stared it for at least an hour. Should I actually call her? Really, Gary? How could I not? So, after much consternation and fear, I finally dialed the number…hopefully, I could explain who I was and maybe she'd remember me…it had been over 15 years ago, after all.

She answered the phone with "hello," I said, "Becky?"…she said "Gary?" The only word I had said was her name and she recognized my voice after 15 years! I wish I was smart enough to describe how I felt, but I can't; I don't know the words for that. However, we talked for almost 3 hours, then again the next night and the next night. Finally, we decided I'd drive down to Columbia the next weekend and visit…totally unbelievable!

She had told me she'd gained a little weight, but was working it off; I was blinded by hope and didn't pay any attention to her…after all, she was beautiful (15 years ago). When I pulled up in her yard and she walked out the front door, I was flabbergasted; she hadn't gained a little weight, she had gained a WHOLE lot of weight. My beautiful, beautiful Becky had turned into an old, fat woman. I'm sorry if that seems cruel, but, it was cruel. It broke my heart and I could tell she knew her appearance had surprised me. We visited and had a nice talk, but…

Sometimes, when you pray, and the outcome isn't what you wanted, you question the Lord…why didn't you answer my prayer? All those years ago when I prayed for Becky and me to be together, I didn't know it at the time, but the Lord did answer my prayer. He had a better plan for me in the future; I just had to wait 5 more years to fulfill it.

Back to the college years…with school, work and sports, I kept pretty busy, girlfriends would come later, hopefully. I had a guy working for me at Celluknit that I got to be pretty good friends with; I'll never forget him because he had a great name…Gene Autry Rogers. Now, I was the supervisor making $1.95 / hour and Gene was working for me, obviously making less than that. How come I rode a bicycle to work and Gene drove a new pickup truck to work? And a new Chevelle too? Now old Gene could not read or write, but I knew he was very intelligent and had a knack for making money. As Gene explained it, he did some farming…that was why he was working 3rd shift so he could farm in the daytime. Okay, this sounded reasonable to me, but sometimes you can tell when something seems a little fishy…I could never put a finger on it, but something about Gene was a little shady. He would never tell the whole story about anything, he would never quite explain exactly what he was "farming." All I knew was there was more than he was willing to tell. There was one thing Gene did explain to me that I have regretted ever since then, which was exactly how a chicken factory operated. He had a brother that worked in the chicken factory in Raeford and Gene asked me if wanted to take a tour of the plant. Sounded like a great idea to me, I loved chicken…who didn't? So, Gene's brother walked us through the plant with the blood and the smell and the sound; and of all the things in my life I wish I could forget, this is at the top of the list—but I can't forget it. And, ever since that day in 1971, I cannot bring myself to eat a chicken. And since I don't eat fish either, I'm now fairly limited in my diet; but really…fish? How can anyone eat that slimy, scaly, stinking varmint? I don't understand it really; my sister will eat anything from the ocean—ANYTHING! Stuff that doesn't even have a name, she doesn't care, the more exotic it is, the more she likes it. I don't know what's wrong with that girl.

I liked Gene and we became very friendly; I kept bugging him about his farming—what he farmed, where was his farm located, etc…finally, one morning after work he asked me to take a ride with him and he'd show me his farm. We took off towards Raeford, then took a left on a remote dirt road, then took another left on a weed infested rut of a road and kept driving until the semblance of road expired. At the end of the line sat, what looked like an old abandoned tobacco barn, except it had a big padlock on the only door and no windows either. We got out and Gene said, come on over, I want to show you something if you promise not to tell anyone what you see. I made that promise to him, but I'm telling his secret now—I hope the statute of limitations has run out on keeping secrets, heck, this was over 42 years ago, Gene, I hope you'll forgive me.

He opened up that barn door and turned on his flashlight, there was no electricity, and I saw these big gunny sacks nailed all around the walls of that barn. I don't know how many; 18-20 at least, maybe more. He says, "Well, what do you think?" "Think about what?" I say. He says, "Pick one out, any one, doesn't matter." So I choose one randomly and he goes over and takes it off the wall, lays it on the ground and opens it up. Nothing but $20's, $10's, and $5 bills…I didn't see any $1's, nor did I see anything larger than a $20, but it was stuffed full. He said this was his "bank," he couldn't read or write and didn't trust real banks, thought he might get cheated. I asked how much he had in here, he said "a lot." I left it at that. He told me no one else knew of this except his wife; why he trusted me with this secret, I do not know. We never talked of this again and were friends for several more years until I left Red Springs to go to graduate school. I hope all worked out well for Gene…I still never knew how he got all that money, and I quickly figured out, I didn't want to know.

9

"I've learned that even though I have pains, I don't have to be one."

I was really comfortable with my life now, I loved the college life and the learning—especially the learning. I had a couple of history classes that were fantastic—because of the professor, David Iliades. When he was lecturing, it was as if he were telling us a story, fantastic stories; so much so that when the bell rang ending the class, I was always disappointed. Actual history is so much more interesting and incredible than anything Hollywood could make up. Don Riklefs was another of my favorites, incredibly enough, he made Geography sound interesting—at least to me. He first planted the seed of a Master's degree in Geography in my mind, that's really how I ended up at Appalachian State, by his mentoring and urging.

And, of course, there were the ever present Vardell Hall girls…Never any serious relations with them however; just having fun and enjoying the times. I'm pretty sure I had the longest hair of any student at Pembroke—certainly in Red Springs; and I dressed for the times as well. Mama had gotten me a pair of combat boots from Fort Bragg; I painted them white and put a red peace sign on the toes. My way of protesting the war. There were plenty of organized protests and marches around, but with working and school and ball…I was too busy for that; so the boots were my personal form of protest.

Mama didn't seem to mind my appearance, nor my bizarre dressing habits either—if she did, she didn't say anything to me—she just loved me. However, the police did not love me…they harassed me to no end. One night I met my high school friend Walter Marley up town at John's Texaco, where we would sit on the hood of his car and talk—one of the great forms of entertainment in a small town. We were catching up on each other's college lives when all of a sudden, here come two police cars screaming into the parking lot with lights flashing. We didn't know what was happening. The police jumped out of their cars, yelled at us to get on the ground and surrounded us. They had us get up, one at a time, and searched us thoroughly (I'm assuming they were searching for drugs, even though they gave us no reason—certainly a long haired freak like me had to be selling drugs).

Finding nothing on us except a half empty Pepsi bottle, they then proceeded to search Walter's car. They even took the back seat out and looked under it, then they searched the ash trays, glove compartment, then the trunk. Finally, they took Walter's golf clubs out of the trunk and dumped them on the ground and searched his golf bag inside and out. Having found nothing, they didn't say another word, simply got back in their cars and drove away. I helped Walter with the golf clubs and straightening up his car, he fumed he would never come back to Red Springs again…and as far as I know, he didn't. I certainly never saw Walter again after that night, which was sad, he was a good guy. I was so sorry he was harassed just because he was hanging around with me.

In a previous book, I wrote about an old white hippie van I bought for $100…it didn't run long before in burned up—literally burned up. But before it did, I drove it around one summer; it was nice not having to ride my bicycle everywhere. One evening, as I turned the corner to come to my house, the police got right behind me and turned their flashers and sirens on. I pulled into the yard and they pulled in right behind me…oh Lord, here we go again. As I got out of the car, Mama came out the front door, smoke coming out of her ears; she laid a verbal thumping on those two policemen, threatening them with all sorts of legal actions for harassing her totally innocent son (well, I may not have been totally innocent…but I definitely was her son)! The next morning she went to see Chief Haggins, of the police, and stayed there quite a while…she never told me what she said to the chief…all I know is that the police never questioned me again, never stopped me again, never even waved to me again. Mama had made her point.

Finally, my boss at Celluknit gave me raise up to $2.00 an hour…I was happy. I had finally gotten to the point where some Vardell Hall girls, and Pembroke State girls were getting my attention. For a while, I was maybe partying a little more than I should have; maybe doing a lot of things I shouldn't have. One evening in particular, mama let me use her car and I was going to Lumberton to see some people—and quite honestly, I shouldn't have been going. But, you're young, you're adventurous, lots of things look attractive—when really they aren't; and you get caught up in things without really thinking them through.

The road to Lumberton is basically flat and straight, mostly farmland and woods. It had gotten dark early when I left home and there wasn't much traffic on the road; I was listening to the radio and looked down to change the station. When I looked back up there was a man with a rope, leading a cow across the road—DIRECTLY in front of me. All I could do was close my eyes and turn the wheel as hard as I could—there was no way I could miss hitting them—no way! I whipped the wheel to the left and slammed on the brakes as hard as I could, the car started spinning round and round—it was totally out of control. I don't know how many times I spun around, but when I came to a stop, I was facing back towards Red Springs in the middle of the road and another car's headlights were coming right at me. The man and the cow were now secondary to this car hitting me head on.

That car stopped and the car behind me stopped and they both ran over to me in my car to see if I was okay. Except for being scared to death and badly shaken—I was. When they asked me what happened I told them I had swerved to miss the man and the cow. "What man and cow?" they said. I explained about the man leading the cow across the road, that's why I had to swerve like I did. Neither car had seen any man or cow…we all got out and looked, we went to both sides of the road—nothing. There was fencing on both sides of the road as far as we could see in both directions—and, there was no gate in the fences and no holes in the fences. And no man or cow.

I am a sane, normal human being…I know what a man looks like…I know what a cow looks like. I did not imagine this, I saw that man and that cow as plainly as I've ever seen anything before. How do I explain what happened? I can't. Where did the man and cow go? I don't know. There is no rational explanation; but, I know what I saw. I should not have been going to Lumberton that night—I could have only gotten into trouble. I believe in angels…I believe they are all around us, guiding us and even sometimes helping us. I also don't think we ever know when we see an angel—I'm pretty sure they never announce themselves. I don't know what happened that night on the Lumberton road…I do know that I went back home, a little shaken, and did not go where I shouldn't have been going.

It took me awhile to stop thinking about that incident; it still comes into my mind from time to time, but I accept it now for what it was. As scared as I was that night, another incident frightened me even more. As I've mentioned before, one of the great pastimes in Red Springs was sitting around at John's Texaco, or Alvin's, talking with your friends. Sports, girls, sports and girls—any of those combinations worked just fine as topics of conversation. One balmy summer night a group of us were at Alvin's sitting on the hoods of cars shooting the breeze, seeing who was going to tell the most outrageous lie…having no cares in the world. Alvin's was a great place to congregate; it was at the corner of Main St. where you could easily observe what little traffic there was. There happened to be a small car wash next to Alvin's as well…it never did much business and we certainly didn't pay any attention to it—no girls were ever going to go over there and wash their cars at night.

The rest rooms at Alvin's were at the rear of the building; they were locked at night of course, but being gentlemanly we always went around to the back when we had to relieve ourselves and just watered the grass and weeds as best we could. As the lies were getting pretty ridiculous, I decided to make the trip to the back of the building to water the weeds. As I was zipping up, someone grabbed my shoulder and spun me around; four Lumbee Indian guys, who had just finished washing their car, had seen me go around to the back of the building and followed me. One quickly put a knife to my throat, while another one held from behind; the one with the knife said, "Jake, do you think I should kill him?" Jake said, "Nah, don't kill him, just hurt him real bad." This was not the reply I was hoping for. They did hurt me…but not real bad; they hit me and knocked me down and kicked me a couple of times and told me to stay there until they left. I did.

After I heard their car squalling tires as it left, I went back around to where my friends were still telling lies and described what had just happened to me. They didn't believe me! They hadn't seen any Indian guys, they didn't hear anything; Joe McPhaul did remember hearing a car leaving, squalling it's tires…but still, they didn't believe me. But, that's okay; my friend Jake didn't kill me that night—and he could have. So, no matter what my friends thought, I came out ahead…way ahead!

Anne, mama, & me

My friends, and me, were not fighters; I was never in a fistfight, never even close to fistfight. Oh, we would get mad at each other on the basketball court, but that was only temporary and usually only ended with a hard foul. There were some guys in our town who did fight, Randy Williams was feared by all—he did not care and would fight at the drop of a hat. But most of us just wanted to play ball, listen to records and lust over girls. The closest I came to an actual fight was when my old friend Furman and I went to the Blueberry Festival near Bladenboro one night. I don't know why we did that, it was a long way to drive…but we went. As you can imagine, there wasn't much to it; we walked around and quickly discovered that the pretty girls had also decided there was nothing to it, because they boycotted the Festival. So, we got a BBQ sandwich, some fries and decided to head back home. Well, old Furman ate his BBQ a little too quickly and it gave him indigestion and gas. Being the gentleman he was, he turned away from me when he had to belch real big, but unfortunately, he didn't see the old country boy red-neck on the other side of him. Furman burped in the guy's face. The old red-neck did not appreciate that at all, and was threatening to "kick your asses" all over the Festival grounds. Now, if I'd been Randy Williams, I would have fought that old boy. But Furman and me? No, we're athletes and lovers…and runners. We got out of there as fast as we could, got in Furman's little VW bug and didn't come close to slowing down until we saw the sweet, sweet sights of home.

Finally, I'd like to at least mention Vardell Hall and the girls we knew over there. Pretty amazing to have an all girl's school in our little town. Some of these girls were indeed half-crazy, but some were very nice and have turned into great women. No need to mention any names, but some were special friends and stayed friends for years afterwards. I cherish a lot of those memories, and some, I'd like to forget—just like life in general. Mostly, we just had some fun and some good times…which was very welcome while working full time and going to school. Enough said.

During my last year at Pembroke, my mom got a huge promotion to transfer to Fort Lee in Petersburg, Va. Great for her, not so great for me. This meant I'd have to find a new, inexpensive place to live when she moved; there were not a lot of choices in Red Springs. However, I did find an apartment next to Boots Paris's house (the place where my friend Allen lived for a while). It quickly became a gathering spot for my friends to hang out and congregate. They were welcome anytime and they knew it and basically came and went as the mood struck them. Somehow, between working from 11:00 PM till 7:00 AM and going to school during daytime hours, I had to work in some sleep time. It was difficult with so many people coming and going…but, heck, I didn't mind. Except for once when my friends got the best of me on a practical joke. It was winter time and got dark early, I had gone to bed when I got home from school about 2:00 or so. As usual, a group of my buddies were in the so-called living room of my apartment—they weren't loud, and were usually very perceptive to my sleep needs.

I would usually wake up about 7:00 or 8:00 at night before I had to be at work at 11:00—I didn't have an alarm clock, just a wall clock in the living room. On this particular night I was sleeping soundly when someone starting shaking me—one of my friends told me I'd overslept and that it was 10:30 and I only had 30 minutes to get to work! So, I jump up, throw some clothes on, run out door and speed off to work. I ran in Celluknit and looked at the time clock to see if I'd made it on time—and the clock read 7:45. My friends got me good! They changed the clock at my house to make me think I was late, when actually I was 3 hours early. I knew they were hee-hawing up a storm back at my apartment, it was not easy to get over on me—but they did. Now, I had to figure out how to get back at them—quickly.

There was no way I was going back to the apartment and give them the satisfaction of pulling off a major league prank, so my little mind starting working overtime. I came up with the perfect retaliation. I went back to my apartment—covertly—sneaking back to their three cars parked in the driveway, and quietly let the air out of one tire on each vehicle. Then, I went back to the plant and to my office and did some homework I needed to do—a very productive night for me. Good study time and three flat tires in my driveway! I never heard a word from any of my friends about that night…and I never mentioned it to them; but, they never woke me up early again either.

As I mentioned earlier, I had stopped cutting my hair and shaving…I was different, but not on the inside, I was still the same old Gary…just hairier. Some people took offense, like the time my friend Furman and I went to a high school basketball game in Pembroke one night. We paid our money and started walking towards the bleachers to find a seat, when an Indian man stood up and yelled "By God, there's Jesus! Let's crucify him!" Furman and I looked at each other, turned around, forfeited our admission money and got the devil out of there. But, those things didn't happen often, mostly it was the not speaking, from people who used to be friendly, that bothered me the most…but, people will be people—there's good ones and bad ones.

One of the good ones is my friend Jerry (who worked 2cd shift at Celluknit with me). He had fallen in love (I think) with a girl from Raeford and was planning on a nice, big, fancy wedding. When the plans started formulating, old Jer asked me to be one of his ushers at the wedding; didn't matter to him that all his other friends were very well groomed and I was a virtual wooly-booger. If it bothered him, he never mentioned it to me; he never asked me to cut my hair, or even shave—he accepted me for me—which was all I could be. Today, when I see pictures of myself at that wedding…well, old Jer was a good old boy.

During those college years I really developed an interest in music…good music as I defined it. I saw several concerts at various locations with various people; concerts I still vividly remember. Hillis, Robbie and group of us went to Charlotte to see the Rolling Stones—pretty amazing.

When the band took the stage, Mick Jagger was not there, then the spot lights turned toward the ceiling and here comes Jagger floating down from the ceiling in some harness, dropping rose petals on the crowd. Needless to say, the girls were going berserk, well, we all were...in the vernacular of the day—it was groovy. The same group of us also went up to Washington, D.C. to see George Harrison in concert. Very, very groovy! Except for a long opening set from Ravi Shankar, it was everything I'd hoped it would be—I actually got to see a real live Beatle.

I was also fortunate enough to see several other bands, including the Allman Brothers, Three Dog Night, The Byrds, Linda Rondstadt, Alice Cooper, The Box Tops, The Association, Foghat, The Eagles and The Beach Boys, just to name a few. The late 60's and early 70's produced some iconic bands whose songs people are still singing 40-50 years later. Wow!

Time was flying by quickly (as it has a tendency to do), I was now in my last year at Pembroke, contemplating what I would do next. My favorite professor, Don Riklefs, kept urging me to attend graduate school and pursue a Master's Degree in Geography. Two issues arose: first, there were not many schools offering Master's degrees in geography; and, second, how would I pay for it? He helped me with these issues and pointed me towards Appalachian State University, who had one of the top programs in the south. He helped me with the application process, the loan process, the grant writing, etc...if not for him, I would have never given it a second thought. He was a great guy.

Now, all I had to do was graduate from Pembroke. I'd made Dean's List, had a great GPA, and loved every minute of time I spent there—I truly loved my college experience at Pembroke. But, I hated math, and had dropped every math course I'd taken. The only thing left of me was to complete the math requirements. They might as well have asked me to fly to the moon. What I fine mess I've gotten myself into now: last semester in school, accepted into the Graduate program at Appalachian State and still needing that last unbearable, unfathomable, STUPID math class.

But, as so often happens to me (and you), the Lord, at times, takes care of those who can't seem to help themselves. And I so often fall into that category. That last year at Pembroke, I was dating a beautiful young lady named Lydia Thompson. Lydia was not only beautiful and very intelligent, but her parents were both Deans at the University. The subject of my math situation was a major topic at the time between me and Lydia. I commiserated my sad state of affairs. She offered to help tutor me in the class during summer school...but summer and math? Really? They go together like peanut butter and collards. One evening, Lydia invited me to dinner at her house with her parents, who were very nice. Of course, during the evening, the math problem came up and I obviously gave a sad, sad evaluation of my predicament. Her parents were very sympathetic and offered all kinds of sage, wise advise...for the normal person.

The next week, Lydia told me her mother wanted me to come by her office at the University, she offered no reason why, just that her mother wanted to see me. Okay. I figured it was going to be more of the same—tutoring, mentoring, blah, blah, blah...I was so sick of the whole idea of math. Dr. Thompson asked me to sit down and pulled out a folder from her desk; she didn't say anything for a couple of minutes, then asked me if one of the Geography courses I'd taken had a lot of statistics in it. Before I could answer, she said that looking at the course curriculum, she was sure that it did. I said, "yes ma'am." She said "that course really could be classified at either math or geography, so, in all fairness, I can change that course to show Math credits." She asked me if I was okay with this. Again, before I could answer, she thanked me for coming by and said she would make the appropriate changes to my transcript. I walked out, wondering what had just happened; and there was Lydia, smiling at me. She knew what her mother had done. Lydia, Dr. Thompson…I have never forgotten that gracious act of kindness; and wherever you are now, I hope you're both gloriously happy and content.

10

"Hard work beats talent, when talent doesn't work hard."

Now that my last obstacle for graduation was settled, I had to start focusing on the future…namely, graduate school at Appalachian State, but also, saving as much money as I could to pay for my living expenses in Boone. That meant I had to cut back on my expenses and luxury items this summer to save all I could…no more album purchases, no more hamburgers from the Dairy Ranch (still the best hamburger I've ever had—and I've had a lot), no concerts this summer, no beach trips. No, the only entertainment I could afford was the zero dollar kind…like going out to the Amtrak train tracks in the country, climbing up a sign that spanned the tracks (for signals to the train conductor), and waiting for the train to speed under you, feeling that rush of wind and heat as it sped under us…well, it was quite the rush. And, it was free.

Having made a little money now, I could afford a car; my mom wanted a new car, so she "sold" me her old car, which was a Volkswagen 411. They don't make those any longer, but it was a neat car; a unique 4 door VW that was fairly roomy and had a nice engine. The only thing I didn't like about it was the color—Carolina blue; but for the price, I could live with it. So, my next step was to pack up my meager possessions and my dog Barky (the best dog a boy could ever have) and start the next chapter in my life. Barky, however, would have to stay with Joe and Sara in King while I went off to school—no dogs allowed.

I had negotiated to stay at the Boone Trail Motel, in the downstairs apartment of the office. It wasn't a hotel room, it was just a little cramped apartment underground, with no windows—but it suited my needs and the price was affordable. It was about a mile from campus, so I could walk to school easily; little did I know then that the wind in the mountains blew in your face no matter which direction you walked and it cut right through any thin little coat you were wearing. We got our first snowfall in November and the cold was something I wasn't prepared for. But, the biggest shock to me wasn't the weather, it was the school. The Master's program did not play, it was not undergraduate work; they expected top notch quality papers and anything less was totally unacceptable. Only A's and B's were acceptable by the guidelines of my grants and terms with the school…anything less than that and I would be asked to leave. That's a lot of pressure.

I was given the job of teaching incoming freshman an introductory geography class, which really was nothing more than grading papers, and I worked in our map library and on a special project, which was building an 8' diameter globe. I worked on this globe with several other people for about 2 years and we never finished it—incredible how time consuming it was getting all the mountains the right height and the coast lines correct, etc., etc. But I sort of enjoyed the work, I made some nice friends there and we could all commiserate with each other on how the professors treated us—they always treat first year students terribly, then the second year, they ease up on you.

I was making enough money to pay for the tuition and the rent on my apartment, but that was it—very little was left over for anything else, including food. I quickly discovered how to hunt for bargains to feed myself…Campbell's tomato soup would be on sale every week or two for $0.11 a can; and I would buy 20-30 cans of it. You were supposed to add a can of water to the soup itself, but, I only used half a can of soup with the can of water to double my inventory. It made the soup a little thin, but, if it was hot enough and you were hungry enough, it didn't really matter. I ate more than a lifetime's worth of Campbell's tomato soup those two years in Boone. Luckily for me, one of my best friends up there was a guy named Mike Dula, who was married to a lovely girl and they liked me and kept inviting me over to their apartment for dinner—I never turned down these dinner invitations. I have tried several times to find Mike over the years, but have never been successful; again, my own fault for not trying harder.

About the only thing I really didn't like about living up there was doing laundry. Every time I went to the laundry place it was full of women with babies and other poor students like me. You had to wait on machines and I really had no patience for this…I found the best time to go was after midnight, then, you could get a machine, do your work and get out of there. I would wait till I virtually had nothing left to wear that was clean, including wearing my cleanest dirty shirts more than once. Then I would go to the laundry and stuff everything I had in one machine—sorting colors? No…stuff it all in and turn it on. I couldn't afford to dry the clothes, so I took everything back to my little apartment and hung up the wet clothes on door knobs, shower curtains, backs of chairs, etc., all over the place until they dried.

That first semester was a tough adjustment, but just like all things, you do what you have to do and move forward. Thankfully, I had one professor who liked me, Dr. Imperatore, a very fine man who guided me and helped me immensely. And, of course my friend Mike Dula and his wife Brenda; but I also had a girlfriend up there who made life particularly enjoyable. A cute little undergraduate who found me very charming, sophisticated, handsome and intelligent…those undergraduates are so naïve. But, we enjoyed each other's company…and, that's all I'm going to say, other than she was a very nice girl.

Besides sports, which I still played year round, including up in Boone, I had learned a lot of card tricks, which then evolved into all sorts of magic tricks. My classmates and friends loved them and I became known for the "amazing" feats of magic I could do (they were really not that amazing). My mentor, Dr. Imperatore, heard about my magic and asked me to show him some tricks—I did, and he was impressed. He got me in touch with a guy at a ski resort near Blowing Rock and this guy hired me to come in on Saturday nights to do a magic show for his guests. I was thrilled. He paid me $20 for my show, which lasted about an hour. $20! I had gone from

$1.95 per hour at Celluknit to $20 an hour at the ski resort. Thank you Dr. Imperatore, $20 a week really made a huge difference to my lifestyle.

I made it through that first semester with only a few scars and two A's and two B's…I was satisfied –not happy, just satisfied. Now it was home to my mama for the holidays and 3-4 weeks of no school and no working. The only negative was that mama was living in Petersburg at the time, so I couldn't see all my friends in Red Springs. I was planning on spending a few days with mama, then going down to Red Springs for a while…mama had other plans. Anne was also there, home from Wake Forest, when mama sprang the news on us that her old friend Maury, who was now living in Los Angeles, wanted to pay for mom to fly out there and see him over the holidays (he was still in love with her). Mama said she would come, only if Gary and Anne could also come (good old mama) we'd take the airfare money and all drive out there for about a week or so. Maury hesitated a bit, but the idea of seeing mama again was too much for him…he agreed, we agreed and off we went the day after Christmas heading to Los Angeles—city of angles, Hollywood, west coast, surfer girls, the place of dreams and stars. I had been to Florida before, and the beach, and the one plane trip to Paris, Texas—but California? Wow! We were all excited…well mama and I were excited…sometimes with Anne it was hard to tell how she felt—but she agreed and off we went in mama's Monte Carlo to the land of fruits and nuts.

We took turns driving and sleeping and made it all the way to Albuquerque, New Mexico before a snowstorm closed I-40 and forced us to get a hotel room—we didn't complain. I'd never seen mountains like the Sandia Range before…seemingly bursting straight up from the plain, no rolling hills like here in North Carolina, just straight up—it truly amazed the geography student in me. And, the buttes and mesas were incredible; I couldn't absorb the scenery quick enough, I wanted to experience it, breathe it, feel it, live it…I was hooked! The snow covered Rockies almost took my breath away, I never knew such beauty existed; it was mesmerizing and magical…I don't know the words to describe how I felt—help me Ed.

We spent the night in Albuquerque and in the morning the roads were cleared and off we went again. Mama, bless her heart, had one side trip she wanted us to take…the Grand Canyon! I knew of the Grand Canyon from geography…but I did not KNOW the Grand Canyon. I had no idea of the massiveness, the grandeur, the awesomeness and the heart-breaking beauty of that mystical place. I was totally unprepared for what I saw. I don't care how many pictures you see of the Grand Canyon, how many videos you watch, how much you read of it…you have no idea, your mind cannot grasp what you are seeing when you first walk up to that rim and look at it for the first time. I literally could not talk, nor could I hear, all I could do was breathe and try not to cry or faint. I was completely overwhelmed by the majestic beauty of that special place. And because of the recent snows, parts of it were still snow covered and even more beautiful…and there were very few people there along the rim to ruin any of the moments we had. Never had I experienced anything remotely similar to this; it was almost too much to take in…and none of us had a camera. I would never make that mistake again.

We finally made it to Los Angeles and to Maury's apartment, which I thought was very nice…it was still hard to fathom that I was in Los Angeles. Robeson County to Los Angeles was quite a stretch, not only in miles, but also in perception and reality. And I don't care how cool you think you are…LA personifies cool, they invented it, and they've mastered it. We were just trying to absorb some of it without gawking too much. Maury took us to a very nice restaurant that first night, it was at Marina del Rey, right on the waterfront, with valet parking and all the waiters had on white shirts and ties and had some sort of towel draped over one of their arms…are you kidding me? This was definitely not the Dairy Ranch. I could tell Maury wanted some alone time with mama, but nope; wherever she went…we went—sorry Maury. We did some sightseeing, the usual tourist stuff, but what had us all excited was the meeting with our grandmother that we had planned…my dad's mother. She was living in a suburb, El Monte, and we arranged to meet with her, the first time we'd see her since our trip to Tennessee when I was 5 years old. It was great! What a wonderful woman she was, so sad we lost all those years in between. Even mama was happy to see her and she made us all feel so special and loved. We were only there for a couple of hours, but I promised I'd be back…didn't know how or when; but I knew I'd be back.

Maury had a friend out there who was a part time minor actor, but this guy had some sort of connections at NBC, because he got us tickets to the Tonight Show, starring Johnny Carson—I loved Johnny, epitome of cool and funny, and a little mischievous. Our tickets were for New Year's Eve, bad luck for us I thought; no way Johnny was going to be working on New Year's Eve…but still, it would be very cool to go to the show. So, that day we went early and took the tour of the NBC studios and saw Lucille Ball walking around…that was pretty neat; and we saw Red Foxx's Bentley convertible in his parking space. The Tonight Show taped at 5:30 PM in those days, for broadcast at 11:00 PM that night—it gave them time to edit out any four letter words that happened to slip out. We got in line with our guest passes about 5:00, but when they saw our passes, they took us right in and sat us in the second row—the SECOND ROW!! The studio, which on TV seems rather large, was actually small; from our seats, we were no more than 20' from Johnny's desk and about the same from Doc Severinson's band. We had no clue how it all worked, who was going to be on the show, who would be guest hosting, or anything…we were just going to take it all in and be happy.

Soon, after everyone else was seated, all was quiet and Ed McMahon comes on the side of the stage and announces: "From Hollywood, The Tonight Show, starring Johnny Carson…and now, heeeeeeere's Johnny!" And Johnny walked out—let me repeat that—Johnny walked out! New Year's Eve and he was working. He came onto the stage and walked up to the front to give his opening monologue for the night, at that point, he could not have been more than 10 feet away from us…we could have almost touched him—did I mention we were on the SECOND row? After the applause died down, instead of going into his monologue, he announced that Jack Benny, his hero, had died and they were going to do a film clip tribute to Jack in place of the monologue—first and only time in Tonight Show history Johnny did not do his nightly monologue.

Well, it was still great; Johnny was there, but I guess on New Year's Eve it was hard to get many big stars on the show. Back then, the show lasted 90 minutes; so after the film tribute to Jack Benny, Johnny and Ed and Doc bantered some and told a few jokes, then he brought out his first guest, Roy Clark. Now, I liked Roy, star of Hee Haw and the Grand Ole Opry, and one of the finest banjo pickers and guitarist around. He played a few songs and they talked, then Johnny brought out his second guest, Madeline Khan. Who, you might ask; but in the 70's, she was a fairly well known television actress; then the last guest was Orson Bean—google him. Then, just like that, it was over…The band played, Johnny told Ed to take it easy on the partying tonight and walked off the stage. It was almost like a dream…had we actually seen Johnny? Those 90 minutes went by in a flash, then we were ushered out and drove back to Maury's. From Johnny to Maury…such is life in LA.

Later that same night, New Year's Eve, Maury had us tickets to the New Year's bash at a huge hotel downtown Los Angeles…how huge? The Ohio State marching band (over 300 musicians) was playing in the ball room—it was a rocking scene. There were several celebrities there as well, the only one I remember was Lorne Greene, he was "Pa" on Bonanza. The reason I remember him was because he asked mama to dance with him, and she did, for two dances—Maury didn't like it, but mama thought Lorne was handsome. Mama…Lorne Greene? Really? Nobody asked me to dance, but guys were hitting on Anne, she was (and still is) a good looking honey. This one guy in particular was laying all kinds of lines on her; the best one being that he was going to a party later at Elvis's house there in L.A. and he wanted Anne to go with him. Elvis's house…right.

Well, Anne was curious, but none of us really believed the guy; mama made him show his license and we wrote down his name and license number before she would let Anne go. Well, guess what? L.A. being L.A. means you never know what will happen…it was at Elvis's house for real. For the juicy details of that party, you'll have to call my sister at BR-549. Maury, mama and I stayed with the party at the hotel and rang in the New Year with the Ohio State marching band and a couple of thousand other Buckeye faithful. Maury was an Ohio State graduate and fanatical fan, so he was totally thrilled with the evening; mama was as well because she got to dance with the handsome Lorne Greene; and I, well…I was looking forward to going to the Rose Bowl game the next day with Maury—Ohio State and Southern Cal. No. 1 in the nation playing No.2 in the nation…the Heisman Trophy winner, Archie Griffin, against the hated Southern Cal Trojans…what a game it should be. And thanks to Maury, I was going (only because mama declined…did I tell you my mama was a good old girl?).

Maury and I went to the Rose Bowl game on New Year's Day, but unfortunately for Maury, Southern Cal beat his beloved Buckeyes; but what an experience it was. Over 104,000 people on a beautifully crisp, sunny southern California day. And, lucky for me that Maury brought a camera and photographed me sitting in the Rose Bowl at the game…the only picture of that entire trip that I have—but it was a good one. The next day, Mama, Anne and I packed up and started on the drive back home—memories we wouldn't soon forget; and for me, the door that had been opened to the wonders of nature and travel…a door that is still wide open.

11

"I don't know the keys to success, but one key to failure is to try to please everyone."

After the holidays, Anne went back to Wake Forest and I went back to Appalachian State; but I could not get the "west" out of my mind. The mountains, the deserts, the canyons, the whole experience had engulfed itself in my being…besides school, it was all I could think about. I'd be working in the map library and find myself studying the maps of the places we'd just visited, dreaming about them and what I'd seen, and trying to figure out how to get back out there. School was draining and hard and time consuming; whereas undergraduate school was fun and eye-opening, graduate school was drudgingly mundane and boring. However, I made good grades, all A's, but it was no fun—I didn't like graduate school and felt it had more to do with enduring, rather than actually learning. At this point I was just looking forward to getting the semester over and going to Red Springs for the summer. My old boss at Celluknit, Jim Matthews, told me he'd give me a job for the summer—I think he just made up something for me because he liked me; but it was on first shift and I was very grateful for that.

My goal was to save some money for school again in the fall, one more year in the graduate program, but I could not get the west out of my mind. I had a good friend at that time, Mike Boyd, and I was constantly telling him stories of how beautiful it was, and how I wanted to go back. Mike and I played on the same softball team and had several of the same interests at the time, so we hung around a lot together. Soon enough, I had convinced him that we needed to take a road trip out west. So, we started planning. We could take my little VW 411, with good gas mileage, camp out when we could and stay with my grandmother in El Monte. We only had to budget for gas, food and what little entertainment we could afford. My grandmother was thrilled I wanted to come back out there and was looking forward to seeing me again.

So, Mike and I saved every penny we could find and started planning our epic 3 week trip. We were leaving in August, just before school started back up again and had a rather aggressive agenda planned…we wanted to see it all and do it all. We afforded ourselves one luxury before the trip, the Eagles were in concert in Greensboro the night before we were to leave, so, we bought tickets to that and saw them give an outstanding performance. Instead of driving back to Red Springs after the show, we went to King and spent the night with Joe and Sara. It was hard sleeping that night in anticipation of the trip and from the excitement of seeing the Eagles in concert. Early the next morning, after very little sleep, we packed up the car and got ready to go; Sara had made us a huge pan full of brownies for the trip and had packed some sandwiches as well…we were ready.

Our plan was to drive straight through to Los Angeles, taking turns driving 4 hours at a stretch; it worked pretty good the first couple of days through Tennessee, Arkansas, Oklahoma and Texas. But after those two days we were wiped out and needed to stop, this is when we stopped in Tucumcari, New Mexico—which I have explained earlier in the book. After a night's rest we hit the road again and headed for that magical place I'd been before…the Grand Canyon. Mike had never been out west before and my descriptions couldn't capture what he was about to see. Needless to say, he was overwhelmed at the immensity of the place and its colors and grandeur. We walked down the Bright Angel Trail for a bit; certainly nowhere near the bottom, just enough to get a feel for it. Then we stopped at several of the overlooks and took pictures of everything that impressed us, which was everything we looked at! I still have all those pictures today—faded a little, but still glorious.

We next headed straight south for Phoenix, why we wanted to go there escapes me now; especially since it was mid-summer and my little car had no air conditioner. We got into the city around 7:00 PM one evening and passed a bank that had the time and temperature on a sign out front…it was then 113 degrees. But with the dry air out there, it only felt like 110. We quickly found a 7/11 and bought us a small cooler and a cold watermelon. Neither of us drank alcohol at that time; which really was a little unusual, I was 25 and Mike was 22 and neither of us drank anything but Pepsi's and Mountain Dews. We drove out of the city and found a nice overlook with a pull off and we cracked that watermelon open and ate it completely to the rind. Then, for dessert, we each had an ice cold Pepsi. Life was good!

We made the trip into Los Angeles and my grandmother's house in El Monte without too much trouble. Hard now to imagine how we found her place in the days before MapQuest, computers and GPS's…but we did. She was thrilled to have us stay with her and had a big dinner waiting on us; after three days of McDonald's, we were very appreciative. Mike and I spent the nights at my Grandmother's house and explored L.A. during the days, we wanted to do it all and were pretty successful at fulfilling our lists. We went to Disneyland, which we loved, we went to Venice Beach and ogled the pretty girls, we drove down Rodeo Drive and looked at all the Bentley's, Mercedes and Rolls Royce's. We did everything tourists normally do: Beverly Hills, Hollywood, etc., etc., we even met my old friend Maury one night for dinner. I had told Mike the story of the restaurant at Marina Del Rey, with the valet parking and the waiters, but we knew we could never go there—way too expensive for us. When I called Maury, he asked us what we had been doing out there and what we wanted to do; I told him all the stuff we'd seen and I was telling him that I wanted to take Mike to the restaurant at the Marina that Maury had taken Mama, Anne and me to—just to show it to him, not actually go to dinner there. But Maury says, "Hey, let's go to dinner there tonight…I'll call and make reservations and I'll see you there at 7:30." Wow! I surely didn't expect that, Mike and I had no dress clothes to wear, all we brought were shorts, tee shirts and tennis shoes.

We figured the least we could do was to at least buy a shirt with a collar on it, so we found a thrift store and we each bought a fairly respectable shirt and wore the cleanest pair of dirty shorts we had. When we met Maury at the restaurant, he gave us a bit of an "oh my gosh" look, but, we went in and the restaurant people never said a word. It was just as I remembered…all fancy and high class, with a wonderful (but expensive) menu. We all ordered steaks and desserts, it was one of the best meals I'd ever had, and Maury was in great form telling us all kinds of stories. Then, the bottom dropped out! When the waiter came back with the check and gave it to Maury, Maury said, "we'll just go ahead and split this three ways, is that okay with you guys?" Huh?? We thought Maury had invited us here and it was his treat, like with Mama and Anne. Oh my God, this meal had just blown our budget completely out the window; we were used to having a McDonald's dinner for a couple of dollars—MAX. Now, we'd bought a new shirt and just spent over $35 each on ONE DINNER! The evening was ruined. We drove home in silence, wondering how we'd recover from this.

As usual, my grandmother was waiting up for us, no matter how late we stayed out, she always waited up and had a snack for us to eat—she was so nice. There was one TV station out there that showed re-runs late at night, of the old Groucho Marx show "You Bet Your Life," and my grandmother loved Groucho. She would watch him and just giggle and giggle…it got to be contagious, Mike and I soon looked forward to getting back home and giggling and laughing with my grandmother and Groucho. Those are some excellent, excellent memories.

You'd think two young guys in L.A. would be checking out the bars and clubs and popular night spots; not us. We went to see the Dodgers and California Angels play virtually every night we were there. You could buy very cheap bleacher seats back then for just a few dollars. We loved it! I thought then, just as I do today, that Dodger Stadium is the prettiest ballpark I've ever been to; from the concourse area you could see downtown Los Angeles all lit up at night—it was quite a view. Angel's stadium was not as pretty, but cheaper—which we liked—and at every game, they'd announce that the owner was at the game, and old Gene Autry would then lean out of his luxury booth and wave to the crowd, which always brought a rousing ovation.

Well, eventually it was time for us to continue our journey; we truly hated to leave. My grandmother spoiled us both and we loved her company and home cooking, but the road was calling. I would not see my grandmother alive again; two or three years after this, she passed away. I flew out there for the funeral and spent time with some cousins and Aunt Betty, it was a sad time for us all, she was a marvelous and loving woman—I wish things could have been different for us all.

We pointed the VW north and started up the coast highway, maybe the most beautiful highway in the country, towards San Francisco. Our goal was to drive across the Golden Gate Bridge and explore San Francisco a little, our main goal was to go across the Bay Bridge to Oakland to see the A's play. They were in the midst of winning three World Series titles and had a great team—unfortunately, they had to play in Oakland in a dump of a stadium before lackadaisical fans. But we enjoyed the game, because with so few people there, we could walk down to right behind the A's dugout and see Reggie Jackson and Sal Bando and all those guys up close…very cool.

This was the last thing we had planned before returning home and ever since the dinner fiasco with Maury, we were really pinching pennies. We knew how many miles we had to drive and the cost of gas, so we calculated how much we had to have to get home. We found the cheapest, dirtiest hotel in Oakland to spend our last night—we knew we'd have to drive three days straight through to N.C., so we needed a good night's rest. We woke up early in the morning and started packing the car when the hotel cleaning maid called to us from the balcony on the second floor where our room had been. She asked us if we'd left anything in the room, we said no, we were okay; she then asked again if we were sure we hadn't left anything in the room. I looked at Mike, he looked at me—no, we were pretty sure we had everything...thanks anyway. Then, she pulled up her skirt and looked down at us and asked again if we were sure we hadn't left anything in the room...oh! Now we get it. Robeson county boys aren't that wary of the ways of the big city; no ma'am, thanks anyway—and off we went.

Back across country on the northern route, through Nevada and Colorado, should be some good scenery, at least until we passed over the Rockies, after that, not much to see. Everything was on track the first day or so, our money was short, but we could always scrimp by with food to make sure we got back. Then disaster struck. In the high desert of Colorado, virtually in the middle of nowhere, the car made a sudden loud boom, then stopped. We couldn't remember the last town we'd seen, nor even the last exit we'd passed; from looking at our map, it seemed the closest town to us was Grand Junction, Colorado...and it looked as though it was quite a ways off. We decided I'd hitchhike towards Grand Junction and Mike would stay with the car. I soon caught a ride and indeed it took about 45 minutes to get to Grand Junction. I walked up to a service station (which in those days, actually were service stations), explained my problem to the guy, he asked me if I had AAA, I'd never thought of it until then, but I remembered mama had given me the membership a while back...so, yes I had it.

The guy says okay, hop in and let's go. We drove in his tow truck back out to my car and Mike, the guy hooked up my car and towed us back the 45-50 miles to Grand Junction and they took my car into the garage and started work. People my age, in those days, did not have credit cards; nor did we have any checks, nor did we have any money...we did not know what to do. There was a phone booth there, so we decided we'd wait till they finished, find out how much it would be for the towing, the parts and the labor, then call either Mike's dad or my mom and see if either of them could possible wire us some money. After 3-4 hours, the mechanic comes out and says you're ready to go, some sort of gasket had blown a hole in something or other and they had to replace several things—all Greek to me; but we tried to nod and act as if we understood what he was talking about.

He took my AAA card and went in the office for a few minutes and came back out and said, "okay, $5.00 ought to take care of it." $5.00??? We did not want to question him, all we wanted to do was give the guy five bucks and get the devil out of there before he realized what he was saying—and we did just that. Once again, Mama had saved my butt...she was indeed a good old girl!

12

"God never does anything accidentally."

Finishing graduate school was next on my agenda, at this point I was pretty tired of going to school. Whereas college was fun, the Master's program was not fun…plus, I was living below the poverty line and staying hungry much of the time. My last semester at Appalachian I had to do internship teaching at Caldwell Community College in Lenoir three days a week. This meant using what little cash I could make from my magic shows to spend on gas to and from Lenoir. I was buying gas $2.00 at a time; it was all I could afford. The last course I had was a class on urban geography and it required a road trip for the entire 13 person class, it was the last thing I had to do to earn my Master's Degree. We were gone for nearly 4 weeks and received three credit hours—it wasn't worth it. The trip itself was great, the circumstances and conditions were terrible. The following story of that trip was written shortly after I returned; I'll let the descriptions speak for themselves as to my feelings on things in 1976.

Our trip starts from Boone, N.C. with 13 people (that should've been the first omen) in a 12-seat van. One professor, Ole Gade (pronounced Oly), twelve of us—one girl, eleven guys—poor Ole never had a chance. Our trip is to be a field study of the urban landscapes with comparative and differing references on U.S. and Canadian cities. The itinerary will take us to Washington, D.C., Philadelphia, New York City, Quebec City, Montreal, Ottawa and finally Toronto. We almost have a fight in the van before we leave N.C.—it's going to be a long trip. One of our two undergraduates on the trip, a fellow of Oriental heritage named Chin, insisted on reading—out loud—every road sign and billboard we passed—I mean every one. Fifteen minutes of this was enough for us to threaten his life, and at the very least, cut his tongue out that night. We didn't like the two undergrads—they didn't like us: nobody liked the girl, Kathy.

Why did she come on this trip anyway? One female spoils it all, no crude jokes, no lustful lying stories of romantic conquests, we have to employ a minimum of restraint and manners—we're not going to have any fun at all. Kathy is one of these liberal, feminist, pro-active, prissy, prudish, pseudo-intellectual, libertarians who always wore a skirt, but never shaved her legs—you know the type, everybody hated her guts—including Ole.

The rest of the group was mostly forgettable. I've certainly forgotten them, except for my two friends Steve and Mike. I will not use their last names, in case they want to deny that they were the two biggest potheads on campus—it's their business. They were also the two smartest guys in the graduate department. Steve was a genius; but, very weird, that's why I liked him. He was a professional student, had several degrees, wanted several more, just enjoyed the academic life. He had long black hair and a beard, about three shirts and two pairs of old, worn jeans—period! (No underwear). My other friend, Mike, was great…he was married and always dressed nicely. He looked like Charlie Daniels…big, heavy, scraggly-looking beard, great sense of humor—or, maybe he was just high all the time—I'm not sure. Mike was from a small town in the NC mountains, Steve was from NYC—we three made quite a team; the others were afraid of us, I think Ole was too, at least he knew that we knew that he didn't intimidate us, like he did the others.

The first leg of our journey sidetracked into the mining area of West Virginia, where we did some field work in a company owned town. I would never have thought this could happen in America…but it does. Our first night we camp at a KOA, this being a minimum expense trip, and arrive after dark, which makes it very difficult setting up tents and tarps. Upon hearing claps of thunder, we speed up. We finish, just as the rain is starting…we've covered two large picnic tables with the tarp, which is where we'll prepare our dinner for tonight. It is now pouring down rain, but all tents are up, we're dry and the hamburgers are cooking. Aside from our grill fire, there were no lights in the campground, the bathroom was about 30 yards away in the darkness. One by one we each made the dash through the rain and blackness to the toilets and back. Just as beans and burgers were nearing final preparations our other undergraduate idiot comes running back from the bathroom the wrong way. He smacks right into the lead guide wire holding up the tarp, the whole thing collapses instantly with us under it. The fire turns to smoke, choking us, the burgers fall into the ashes, the beans are turned over onto the ground and the fire is out…it's pitch black, pouring down rain and cold.

We salvaged some wet potato chips, pickles and soggy cookies; when we finally got the tarp back up, we were cold, hungry and mad; our first night was pretty miserable. It got worse. Being unaccustomed to camping, and being stupid, we pitched our tents in a low area which quickly became saturated—no, flooded is a better word. Ever try sleeping in a wet sleeping bag, in a wet tent, in wet clothes? A most unpleasant night.

We come into Washington, DC a disheartened group, but anticipating better and greater things. Our headquarters for two days will be the old Iranian Embassy, which is now something akin to a youth hostel. Very ornamental and attractive outside, a dump inside. Two other groups were staying there (one group was mostly girls, our luck was changing), making a total of about 40-45 people. The rooms had no furniture at all, you simply threw your sleeping bag on the floor. There were two operational bathrooms (two toilets—two showers) for 45 people—the first three people in the shower had warm water, the rest of us suffer.

We enjoyed Washington, it's a great tourist town, Ole would turn us loose late afternoons, all we had to do was be back before our first meeting in the morning. We also found there weren't too many people in line for the showers at 4:00 AM. In reviewing my notes from the this trip in 1976, a couple of things struck me as odd; first, we were told that public schools in Washington were 98% Black…that shocked me. Second, we visited the wealthy community of Reston, Va. where new homes were selling for the unheard prices of $49,000-56,000 (who could afford that?), and nice condos were selling for $25,000…in 1976, this all seemed exceptionally steep.

Three things I remember most vividly from this trip were: one, seeing James Schlesinger, former Secretary of Defense and future cabinet member, getting out of his car in our parking lot. Mike and I recognized him and went over to meet him. He was driving a beat up 1967 Oldsmobile, dents all over it, dirty—just like our cars. The other guys didn't know who he was, just Mike and me, and we talked to him at least 10 minutes; he was very gracious and funny while answering every question we could think of—including who really killed JFK (he didn't know). Second, we saw Ted Kennedy coming out of a doorway at the Kennedy Center as we were going in to visit. He was walking and talking to someone, so I turned around and followed him for about two minutes listening to him talk. Three things struck me about him: he really did talk with that Boston accent, he had a huge head, and I was standing three feet away from the brother of John F. Kennedy—it was awesome! Third, one night in travels around town we ended up on 14th Street…hookers, pimps, crooks and prostitutes of every persuasion were there—we didn't stay long, this was a little too much for a naïve, redneck boy from rural North Carolina.

We finally left D.C. and drove through Baltimore and into Philadelphia—since I have nothing nice to say, I won't say anything. We spent the night in Newark, N.J.—as bad as that sounds, it wasn't, we had fun. Don't misunderstand, Newark itself was the pits, but we found an old Greek restaurant and had a party there that night; those Greeks are okay with me, even if they do eat some weird stuff. Mike and Steve tried everything there, not me, if I couldn't identify it or tell if it was alive or dead…I wasn't eating it.

The next day surprised me more than anything else on the trip. We traveled into New York around Bear Mountain on the Palisades Interstate Parkway, it was beautiful. I was shocked. I thought everything this close to New York City was paved, polluted and prostituted. I apologize New York, this countryside reminded me of my own Blue Ridge Mountains, in fact, West Point is in a beautiful location in this area. We stopped for a picnic lunch along the Hudson River on the Palisades, which are steep cliffs 500 feet above the river. I won the rock-throwing contest into the Hudson.

Our base for the next two days was Vasser College in Poughkeepsie, NY, a most exclusive school for any well-bred, socially aspiring, debutante to attend. Why they let us stay there is a mystery. We found that Vasser costs $4500 a year (that was a lot in 1976), by comparison, my alma mater, Pembroke State University, cost me $176 a semester; and even though I never went to a debutante ball—I had a ball. We met some snooty-looking girls, who were there for summer school, we asked them to come over to our dorm that night for a party—they refused, our feelings were not hurt.

By this time on our trip, we were all on each other's nerves and we took out our frustrations on two people in particular, Kathy and the two undergrads (I refer to these two guys as one person). In some warped way, it was fun being dirty to these two. The undergrads were careful around us and made it difficult to sabotage them, but Kathy was so stupid, everything worked on her. She never could understand why, if she went to the restroom during a meal, her food always tasted salty when she came back. Or, why there was always something weird in her sleeping bag—why no one else's? And, why did all these street corner winos walk up to her and try to hug her? She was so stupid.

In New York City, Ole felt sorry for us and gave us a day off to explore the city on our own. We'd been looking forward to this, Steve is from Brooklyn and he's promised us a grand adventure. Steve, Mike and I start out early, we take a train from Roosevelt Island into Manhattan and it's already crowded, but I guess that's normal. People, people, people…old ones, young ones, Asians, Blacks, whites, businessmen, dope dealers, weirdos, wackos and us hicks all pressed together shuffling along. Nobody speaking to anyone else, no one even making eye contact with anyone else—absolutely anonymous, secular, existence multiplied a million fold. I'm too busy looking up at the tall buildings to notice much anyway, I hope a pigeon doesn't drop something in my mouth.

We went to the top of the World Trade Center towers, what a view! You can't see the dirt or trash from up there, just the incredible diorama that is New York. Steve takes us to Washington Square, where there's guys playing guitars, people dancing, roller skating, singing, playing chess, sleeping— it was pretty neat. We go to Chinatown and eat at some open air delis and finally make our way to Greenwich Village, which really excited Steve for some reason. He wanted us to be impressed— we weren't. We visited several coffee shops, saw some strange people, then left for a walk down Broadway and finally a ride to the top of the Empire State Building—very cool!

Along the way we noticed we were being followed by three overly-dressed young women. We noticed because they started walking very close behind us, crossing streets when we did, stopping when we did. Something wasn't right, but I couldn't figure it out—I'm not from New York, Steve was—and he finally took control. One of the three women asked us if we wanted a "date," when we heard it talk, we knew it wasn't female. Mike and I were stunned, Steve asked it if it wanted its teeth knocked out, they all wheeled around on their high heels and quickly vamped away—my first encounter with transvestites.

4:00, 9:00, midnight…New York never changes; crowds, cars, cabs, hustle, bustle, noise—it wore me out. We left New York City and drove out the length of Long Island, where it's rural and agricultural—again, a surprise to me. We passed through several small insignificant little towns and caught a ferry for the hour and a half ride over to New London, Connecticut. We visited the pretty little town of Mystic, which seemed like a nice place—I'd like to go back there and see how it's changed over the years. It was in Mystic that we convinced Ole that everyone was in the van (Kathy was really in the bathroom) and we left her behind. We only made it about 5 minutes before he realized her ingratiating voice was absent, but what a glorious 5 minutes it was. Ole blamed Mike, he was driving at the time and responsible for the head count—good old Mike took one for the team.

Rhode Island, Massachusetts, New Hampshire and into Maine we go, remnants of glacial scarring everywhere—we geographers love to talk like that. We stop for the day in Kennebunkport, Maine, this was before George, or "W" made it famous—we liked it. We leave the coast and head inland, northward…forests, lakes, nothing, wonderful and beautiful. We pass a lake that is over a mile long (we measured it), full of logs—huge, stripped, naked, drowned trees, half floating in this liquid storehouse. That sight even made Chin and Kathy quiet—for a few moments anyway.

It's getting cold as we near the Canadian border, I don't think we brought enough clothes—I know poor Steve didn't. We now face our biggest and scariest problem of the entire trip, the one dilemma we've been dreading for several days—how to hide Mike's marijuana from the Canadian customs agents. Do they search suitcases? Will they inspect the van? They won't search us will they? The van is extremely quiet as we pull in line to wait our turn at the checkpoint. Could it be there are others among us, besides Mike, that are feeling a little tense right now? Probably so.

The customs agents make us unload all the luggage, he walks in the van, shines a flashlight around, walks out and waves us through—this smuggling's a piece of cake. In Quebec City we quickly learn we are in a foreign country; everyone is speaking French, they probably can speak English, but refuse to, especially to Americans—and I don't really blame them. They're proud of their heritage and want to keep it; it's a struggle not to become Americanized. I empathize with their efforts to formally secede from Canada and form their own French-speaking nation. A government should be by the people and for the people—not imposed upon the people.

We stay in the heart of the old walled city of Quebec, which dates back hundreds of years. A youth hostel is our headquarters –and it is indeed hostile. Enough said. At this point in my life I was still not an alcohol drinker, didn't matter really, I was too broke to buy beer in the clubs we went to anyway—I just tagged along. Mike and Steve obviously had saved their money for these situations. The first place we went to was an old pub, where no one spoke English; Mike and Steve somehow ordered a beer, they brought them two beers apiece. We didn't know how to argue with them, so we just let it go. We went to another place (we were searching for exotic French dancers), same thing—they order a beer and they get two. This time Steve tries to argue, to no avail, they get the two beers. What's going on here, are they taking advantage of us, or is this normal? One final stop, order one—get two—this can't be a coincidence and by this point, I'm the designated walker in our group.

It's May 24th and there's still snow on the ground as we spend our last day in Quebec City—I enjoyed my visit there, but we're now off to Montreal, another large city…blah, blah, blah. At this point in our trip, we all wanted to go home. I had just broken up with my girlfriend, or I should say, she broke up with me. Yes, it's true, my charms, looks and grace could not keep the girl – she grew weary of long nights at Mike's house listening to Allman Brothers albums and watching plastic dry-cleaning bags burn and drip it's wax into pots of water, while trying to, but never quite satisfying the constant torment of the munchies –girls are so hard to please.

Ottawa, the capital of Canada, was a very clean city, but our meetings with planning boards, etc was boring us all—including Ole. There was a direct correlation between boredom and the severity of our nastiness towards Kathy. She could make it more fun for us if she would get upset and scream; but, she just thinks she's having bad luck. Listen Kathy, luck doesn't have anything to do with the washing machine overflowing with suds; or your hamburger coming without meat; or a fuse blowing in the bathroom while you're taking a shower—NO! These things take planning Kathy, we work hard at this, at least lose your temper once in a while, okay?

On the road to Toronto, my notes read, "glacial remnants, boulders strewn askew, stone fences, tills and drumlins," Tills? Drumlins? I guess I was trying to impress Ole with my geographic verbiage. I'm pretty sure I've never used those two words since then. We finally cross the border again near Niagara Falls; at this point we no longer care about border guards, in fact, we're all pretty insolent towards everyone. The U.S. customs agents check nothing, they just wave us through. We stay at Niagara Falls throughout the afternoon and get drenched on the boat ride at the bottom of the falls…it was pretty awesome down there, louder than the speakers at an Ozzy Ozbourne concert (I know, I've been there).

On through the dreary city of Buffalo, through the gorgeous Finger Lakes region of New York; but, who cares? We just want to get home and most of us sleep through the drive, we're even too tired to hassle Kathy anymore. One more night spent somewhere in Virginia and we're free. The school springs for rooms and dinner this last night, Ole supplies beer and wine (he doesn't care anymore either). After dinner we have a farewell blowout, we make truce with the undergrads—they don't trust us (they shouldn't). Kathy even becomes more at ease (maybe it's the wine), she joins us outside for libations, stories and lies and contributes to all three. Finally, about 1:00 AM, Mike, Steve and I decide to retire to our room to cap off the evening and the journey. Incredibly, Kathy asks if she can join us; as I'm thinking up a good excuse to say no, Steve invites her in. She is, at this point, feeling no pain. She flops on the bed next to me and starts giggling—she never giggles.

About 2:00 AM, Mike and Steve doze off, Kathy still giggles and is somehow almost fun to talk to. We talk, she becomes less and less inhibited, I'm beginning to see her a little differently now. Can I? Should I? Would anyone find out? She's certainly leading me in that direction. She turns out the light and slides over towards me…You don't really think I'm going to tell you what happened do you? With Kathy? Are you kidding me? No one would believe me anyway.

13

"Sometimes you have to stop thinking so much and just go where your heart takes you."

Tied up all my affairs at Appalachian, signed all the papers, said all my goodbyes, cleaned out my room at the Boone Trail Motel and packed my little VW for the trip home. The Boone Trail Motel, like most places in Boone, is on the side of a mountain, or hill; my car was parked on this hill and I hadn't been in the car for about 5 weeks, while we were on the road trip. I cranked it up one day to make sure the battery was okay and checked the gas tank (which registered full); I only had a handful of change left after closing out everything—no folding money at all, but I knew a full tank of gas would easily get me to Red Springs.

I cranked up the old VW, pulled out from the hotel onto US-421 south and instantly noticed that the gas needle went from full to ¼ full. I pulled over, tapped it, hit it, beat on it…but ¼ full was all it would register. Seemingly, parking on that hill sloshed all the gas to one end of the tank and fooled the register into thinking the tank was full. I knew my car got good mileage, but I was deeply concerned now about getting to Red Springs on ¼ tank of gas. Dang! But, having no alternative, I had to give it a try; so off I went, coasting as much as I could down the mountain. In those days, it was all 2-lane traffic, lots of stopping for slow cars and trucks and cars turning off—not conducive to good gas mileage. I was getting very concerned now. I had a little over a dollar in loose change; it would buy a couple of gallons of gas maybe.

The inevitable finally happened…I ran out of gas on I-40 in downtown Winston-Salem, right at the Cherry St. exit. If you're familiar with that part of I-40, you know there is no median, nor shoulder to pull over on. All I could do was coast over about two feet off the highway, which left about 4-5 feet of my car still on the roadway. Cars were honking, people were cursing—I thought Winston-Salem was about the rudest place I'd ever been. As I got out of my car, thinking what I should do, I looked downtown and saw a tall building that said "First Union," heck, if I remember right, I had a First Union checking account…maybe this was going to be okay after all. I hadn't actually used my checking account in months—or, was it years? But, by golly, I had one.

I walked the few blocks over to the bank and went inside right up the first available teller, she was nice middle-aged lady, first nice person I'd seen in Winston. I told her I didn't have my checkbook with me, but needed to cash a check and wondered if she could help me. "Sure," she said, "give me your name and social security number and we'll fix you right up." Great! I gave her the information, she walked away and came back a couple of minutes later with a not too pleasant look on her face. Uh oh. She said, "Mr. Hope, your account is overdrawn by $5.00, you need to pay us that money right now."

Crap!! Think, Gary. Ummm…"okay" I said; "let me go out to my car and get my wallet." I went outside alright, and ran away from that bank as fast as I could. I ended up at a corner with a phone booth; but who could I call? Wait a minute, Joe and Sara lived near here, up in King…they saved me before, surely, they would save me again. Fortunately, for me, they answered the call, understood my situation and told me they'd be right down to get me. As I've said before, the Lord often takes care of those (like me) who can't take care of themselves. So, I went to Joe and Sara's house, they took me in again, fed me, comforted me and talked me into staying and finding a job in Winston-Salem…Red Springs would have to wait.

Shortly after I moved in with Joe and Sara, her brother Jimmy moved in with us as well; he was living in Alabama and needed a change…so we were one big happy family. I got a job that first week, not one I particularly enjoyed, but it paid a lot more than what I was making—which was nothing. Seemingly, a Master's degree in Geography didn't impress a lot of people; why didn't I major in Business, or Economics or Finance so I could get a job when I graduated? Why? Because when I went to school, foolishly, I studied and took courses that interested me, that enlightened my mind that stirred my soul…not boring courses that would help me find a job after graduation. So, now I had to make the best of it. That first job was only a time filler till I found a better, higher paying job with Roadway Express, in the management training program.

In the meantime, Jimmy had been dating a lovely young lady who had a friend that was currently single and unattached and Jimmy lined us up a double date one cold winter's night. His date, Judy, was going to make a spaghetti dinner for us all at her apartment…this should be fun. My blind date was also named Judy and we had an excellent dinner and conversation…my date was indeed a beauty and I was attracted to her immediately. Jimmy had told these two young ladies that I was a fantastic magician, so they bring out some cards and ask me to show them stuff…and I did. As I mentioned before, I was not a drinker at all; nothing stronger than Pepsi's in my life to that point. However, they supplied wine with dinner and then wine after dinner and then wine during my magic show. I tried sipping it a little, then a little more, then a little more and by the time I was halfway through my card tricks, my head was starting to spin—not a good sign. Suddenly, I knew I needed to get outside quickly, I was getting ready to taste that spaghetti dinner again as it was coming back up. I barely made it outside before I fell to my knees and heaved in the fresh new snow on the ground. That patch of snow wasn't white for long. I don't remember much after that, I think Jimmy put me in his car and drove us home; I only know that I woke up the next day with a raging headache and a ton of embarrassment. What a first impression I had made.

Jimmy had assured me that my date, Judy, had indeed enjoyed herself and would like to see me again—why, I truly don't know. But I called her and we started dating, then we started dating seriously, then more seriously; I was now in love for the second time in my life. After a courtship of several months, we decided to get married in September that year, 1977. But before that, I had a better job opportunity come along with Pilot Freight Carriers, so I put in a notice with Roadway and built in two extra weeks before starting the new job so I could take a vacation—I knew it would be a year before I got another one. By now, wanderlust was truly in my veins and Judy and I decided to take a cross country trip to the west coast during those two weeks. I had a Monte Carlo that rode pretty smoothly, so I made the plans and figured out the route and off we went. I had to show her the magnificent Grand Canyon and the deserts of Arizona as well as the canyon country of southeastern Utah (maybe the prettiest landscapes in the world). We passed through Moab, which would be my first of many trips to that old mining town, surrounded by the most heartbreaking beauty there is, in a land that has no heart.

We finally made it into Los Angeles and I showed her some of the sights I was familiar with; we went to Disneyland and rode all over the city and area. One day we pulled up to a stoplight, in the right hand lane, of a four lane road; I looked over to my left at the car that had just pulled up beside me at the red light, and it was O.J. Simpson sitting in the passenger seat. This was when OJ was only famous for being a great football player and actor—not a killer. I started fumbling for the camera and telling Judy that OJ was there and trying to roll down the window, all at the same time. OJ saw me doing this as he looked over at me, and laughed—that's when I got his picture—which I still have.

We drove up the magnificent coast highway, US-1, to San Francisco, over the Golden Gate to the pretty little town of Sausalito, which my sister would live in for a few years, much later; we spent the night at the Sausalito Hotel, right on the bay. That building is still there, but it's not the Sausalito Hotel any longer. We drove over the mountains, through Reno and up towards Yellowstone and the Grand Tetons—two sights I had to see—and how awesome they were. Words escape me as to the beauty and grandeur of those places. On and on we went…all over the country. True, it was long and we got tired of driving, but Lordy, Lordy at the things we saw on that trip. Once we got back home, we started making plans to get married; we were working hard, visiting my friends occasionally and going to some concerts as well. We saw The Eagles in Greensboro and also saw Elvis in Greensboro a couple of months before he died. He was a little overweight, but so what? He was Elvis! The man who changed music in America, and basically the world; and the women still went crazy over him. It was truly a magical performance from the opening song till the guy announced "Elvis has left the building." When we heard the news he had died a couple of months later, it was hard to understand and to accept; it didn't seem possible that Elvis was gone.

We got married September 25 of that year, with my friends there with me: Jerry and his first wife, Allen and Janice, Dickie, Jimmy and of course, my best man, my cousin Joe. Mama had given us a wedding party the night before at a local restaurant and Anne may have toasted the champagne a little too much, I'm not really sure, but I do know she did not feel well the next day at the wedding. And I was a tad sleepy as well, I was working 7 days on, then 7 days off—at nights. So, I had just finished my week of working and had gotten off that morning at 7:00 AM. Everything was great, just as I hoped it would be. Judy was beautiful and wonderful and successful…a great career at RJR built on her hard work. We planned to honeymoon at the Outer Banks, a place I'd never been to, but wanted to see; so as I slept, Judy drove us off to the beach to begin our lives together.

14

We'd only been married a couple of years when Sara called us one afternoon, on the day of the ACC basketball championship game. Easy to remember the day you receive the phone call that tells you your hero and best friend had died. I won't go into the details; they are documented in another book, if you're interested. Needless to say, it was hard to get over. Judy and I had great memories with Joe and Sara…we almost froze to death at a Redskins/Falcons game in Atlanta; drove through a snowstorm to Charlotte, to watch Duke play Louisville (where we saw my friend Dickie and his wife Carol), and had season tickets to Wake Forest basketball games together—we had some grand old times. Joe was special and I miss his guidance and friendship and the security he gave me; he was truly one-of-a-kind.

My mom had transferred to San Antonio and was working at Fort Sam Houston at this time; Judy and I made a couple of trips out there to visit. You know my general feelings about Texas, but San Antonio seemed different; it was nice—it didn't feel like Texas. We enjoyed our visits there, I even enjoyed visiting the Alamo, even if I was a little disappointed that it was in downtown San Antonio—I thought that was a little weird. Mama was experiencing some difficult medical issues at the time…all results of the lymphoma which she could not rid herself of. The medicines she was taking were both strong and addictive, and she didn't handle them well. I am not, and will not, be judgmental with those issues—I truly have no idea what she was going through and the pain she suffered…but I know it was substantial. She, seemingly, could control her medicines when she needed to be at work; but, when we were there, she would over-indulge in the pain medicine and it made her goofy and almost unconscious at times. There were instances when we'd be at dinner and she would just pass out at the table—literally pass out. Sometimes, it was funny, other times it was downright scary! I was very concerned for my mom.

One December evening I was working the night shift at Pilot Freight and around midnight one of the clerks came out of the office and told me that John Lennon had been shot and killed. Shot and killed. Killed. John Lennon was dead. John was dead. Dead. Somehow, I made it through that night and got home the next morning to watch all the news shows documenting the tragic events; I taped them for 3-4 hours as I watched. I've never viewed those tapes since that morning, could not bring myself to endure those unspeakable moments ever again. I can't adequately explain how I felt (and still feel) about John; if I try, all I do is end up with tears…even as I write this, 34 years after those events, it's still emotional for me. Enough said.

Judy and I wanted to start a family, but, we were having a problem with conception; we went to several doctors and tried all sorts of things, but it just wasn't happening. We were happy, but we did want a child together as well. We kept up the travelling, it was in my blood and I wanted to see as much as I could see; Judy was a good sport about it all and never complained—though I'm quite certain she didn't love it like I did. We went to New York City and Washington one year; Arizona again and the canyon country. We were at Monument Valley at an overlook when an Indian rode up to us on his horse; he said he would ride out to the edge of the drop off, for us to take what should be a magnificent scenic picture of him on his horse with the famous Monument Valley "Mittens" in the background. Okay, we'd pay for it; as he started to mount his horse, Judy asked him what his horse's name was; you'd have thought she just cursed him. He said, "It's just a horse lady, it don't need no name!" Judy said, "Well how do you call him?" He said, "I whistle and he comes…he don't need no name!" And that was that.

We flew to San Francisco once and drove up the coast to Seattle, where my pretty little niece Casey now lives. Great memories of that trip, the Olympic Peninsula, the Redwoods, it was really amazing; we drove up Mt. Rainier as far as we could, we had dinner in the Space Needle and drove down the Columbia River gorge to see all the incredible waterfalls. We visited Aunt Mary, in Orlando, and went to Sea World, Disneyworld and all the other places there, but most importantly, just spent time with Aunt Mary. She was special. We kept trying for the baby thing to happen, times of the month, pills, etc., etc…but nothing seemed to work. We hadn't given up, but were getting a little discouraged with it. One night my Uncle Donald called us to chat; he was more like a long lost brother than an uncle to me. Uncle Donald and his wife Pat had three children, Donnie, Tammie and the youngest and prettiest, Brenda. Well, Brenda was about 19 years old and had already had one baby and was now still unmarried and pregnant again. Uncle Donald had urged Brenda to give up the unborn baby for adoption since Brenda couldn't afford the baby she already had. When he told me that on the phone, fireworks started going off in my head…I got Judy on the phone with us and we told Uncle Donald that we would love to adopt the baby; it's what we were hoping for and would keep the baby in our family.

We called Brenda and had a great conversation with her, she was thrilled that someone from our family would want to adopt her baby. Judy and I drove down to visit her in Dothan, Alabama and meet with the social workers who interviewed us. Brenda was just as sweet as she could be, heck, we wanted to adopt her as well. Finally, everything was done, all the papers were signed and now we only had to wait for the birth…it was not an easy wait. She was actually overdue and every phone call brought your nerves on end. Finally, on February 6, 1982 a beautiful little girl entered the world in Dothan. We got the phone call and drove down there early the next morning, straight to the hospital, straight to Brenda's room and stood there while they put that precious little baby in my arms. Unless you've ever held your newborn child in your arms, you cannot understand the emotions overwhelming you at that moment.

We had the name picked out (really I picked it out, Judy liked it fortunately), Shelley Christine Hope. Shelley was from a character in a book called "Trinity" I had read; and Christine was for

Chris Evert. We stayed there all day and fed little Shelley and held her while she slept and cried; we talked with Brenda, who handled everything exceptionally well. Everything was fine health wise and the hospital okayed us leaving the next day…we did not get much sleep that night. We put a pillow on the console between the two front seats and that's where we laid little Shelley for the ride back to North Carolina. Obviously, this was in the days before car seats and seat belts were mandatory. She cried almost the whole 12 hour drive back home…oh my God, what had we gotten ourselves into—we could not get her to stop crying. We arrived home around midnight, totally exhausted, but had promised to call Sara when we got home; so we did, and she insisted on coming over and seeing Shelley. Finally, Shelley fell asleep, we fell asleep and our new lives had begun—NOTHING would ever be the same again.

The months went by in a blur, everyone came by to see Shelley—Judy's parents, mama, Anne visited, aunts and uncles and friends, all were so happy for us and our beautiful little girl—and she was indeed a beauty. Judy took three months off from work to stay home, and on the seven days I was off, every other week, I took care of her when Judy went back to work. Changing diapers and preparing formulas became our daily rituals…And we loved it! I don't think there were two more happier people on earth; or a more photographed baby on earth—I went a little overboard there—but she was sooooo pretty. Every time we went out, people would stop us and comment on how pretty Shelley was, people kept urging us to take to TV stations and get her in commercials, or to professional photographers for magazines. But no, we were happy just the way things were.

Mama was still in San Antonio at this time, but came to visit us fairly regularly; she loved Shelley and doted on her. I could tell her health was not good, the medicine usage was more extreme and happening too often; I knew she was in pain. I don't know how many times she'd been in the hospital for chemo and radiation, recovered somewhat, then repeated that horrible cycle again. I HATE cancer and especially what it did to my mom. I truly wondered how she got by on her own in San Antonio and did her job like she did; she was one of the smartest, most intelligent women I'd ever known; but this cancer thing was beating her down…and winning. Soon, it became apparent she could no longer work and she was granted a full medical retirement by the government; she was just over 50 years old…she was still young!

I had to fly out to San Antonio, rent a big U-Haul, load up mama's stuff and drive it all back to North Carolina—that trip was no fun…no fun at all. My boss at Pilot, Jimmy Harris, had never been anywhere except to Florida once, and he volunteered to go out there with me on our next 7 days off, if I paid for all the expenses. I was very grateful to do that, I knew loading up all the furniture and everything would be quite an ordeal. But, we loaded up the truck, got ready to go and ate our last meal in Texas at a Mexican restaurant—my first trip to a Mexican restaurant; I learned very quickly the difference in hot sauces. We made it back okay and stored mama's stuff, she was going to move in with Judy's mother until she could find a place of her own…I'll always be grateful to Judy's mom for that gracious act of kindness. We got mama settled, sort of, and continued onward with our blissful lives raising our little girl…live was good.

***

But even in our new baby life, the west was calling me, urging me, pulling me like the tides in the ocean…we had to go back. So, little Shelley, less than a year old, Judy and I go back to the Grand Canyon and Arizona; this time to the less frequented North Rim—I had to break Shelley in right. She did great on the airplane and the travelling and we had a grand old time; at least I did. Judy was so nice and agreeable to accepting the wanderlust in my heart…I can never thank her enough for that. Back home our lives were idyllic, and I don't know how we could've been happier—we loved our lives and our little girl with all our hearts. At this point in my story, I'm going to skip over some things that are personal and no one else's business but mine (and Judy's). Bottom line is that we separated and soon divorced—it had absolutely nothing to do with Shelley or financial matters. And, Judy was, and is a wonderful woman and mother; it was basically my fault. And that's the end of the story.

15

"God does not play dice."

Anne had graduated from Wake Forest and had gotten a job coaching women's basketball at St. Mary's College in Joliet, Illinois. Sara, Judy and I visited her there once…we didn't actually see much of her, she was so busy working and working out—she had begun to get interested in bodybuilding—serious bodybuilding. But we had a good time anyway. We toured around Chicago and Judy and went to the play "Beatlemania," as if I needed a mania. Anne would come visit us at times during her bodybuilding phase and would literally eat nothing more than a couple of leaves of lettuce. Sometimes if she got up too quickly from the couch, she would almost pass out. I thought it was very weird at the time. She once brought a guy home with her on a visit, a very nice guy named Tim (you have to be careful of those one syllable names). Tim had finished in 5th place in the Mr. Universe contest—he was HUGE! At meals, I couldn't stop myself from staring at the muscles in his arms; each time he picked up a fork or spoon his muscles would just ripple up and down his arm—it was truly amazing to see.

There was a low level tennis circuit tournament held back then at Tanglewood and I asked Tim if he wanted to go with me one day. Sure, he said, sounded like fun. We got there a little late and had to wait till the first change over before we could get into the stands. Did you ever dream of being invisible when you were a little kid? Well, that day, at that moment—I was invisible. When this huge hulk of a man walked in that place, every eyeball in that stadium fell on him…I could've walked out there naked and not a soul would have noticed. This guy was so big he couldn't buy regular clothes, he had to buy bolts of cloth and have his clothes specially made for him. I'm sure old Tim was a workout fanatic, but I'm also positive old Tim indulged in some steroidal type of medicines as well…human beings cannot get that big naturally—NO WAY! But, he was a very nice guy, with a great sense of humor and I liked him…but my sister really needed a two syllable name—she would have to wait.

I'm not real sure of the sequence of events, but my sister started entering bodybuilding tournaments, finishing 3rd, then 2nd, then finally winning the Miss America Bodybuilding contest. She made Robeson County proud. She also landed a new job at the University of Nevada-Reno as women's basketball coach and Athletic Director. Reno would be her home now for many years, a place I enjoyed visiting…a nice place. She settled in Reno quickly and started her career in full swing; having been a beauty queen in high school, college athlete, and bodybuilding champion, she was in much demand at the single bars and dating scenes in northern Nevada. But, I knew my sister; she dated several guys, but her career was a little too important to her at the time—so I thought. When we heard the news she was going to get married, I was shocked! What sort of guy could convince Anne Hope to marry? And this guy wasn't even from Robeson County.

His name was Steve McGranahan, a truly great guy…good looking and friendly and successful. They married and went on a Caribbean cruise for the honeymoon; near the end of the cruise they were walking on the dock back to the ship, after some shopping, and Steve walked off the pier and fell into the ocean. Anne thought he was just kidding around…but he wasn't. Steve was sick. When they got back home, he went to see doctors and was eventually diagnosed with testicular cancer…and it didn't look good. Amazingly, Anne had become pregnant—given Steve's condition, it was truly a gift from God. Steve started with the chemo and radiation and all that goes with fighting this hated disease, but the cancer would not be denied.

***

Casey Elizabeth McGranahan was born into this world on March 17, 1987; red-haired, big-eyed and beautifully healthy. Steve died a few months later. Cruel cannot describe these turn of events. Many things in life don't seem fair, we don't know why things happen as they do; fortunately, my sister had (and still has) great faith in the Lord. He knows why things happen, and He has told us that all things work together for the good of those who love the Lord. One day, we'll know why Steve was taken so early, we'll know why my mama suffered so much and why my friend Bill is slowly dying of that dreaded C word. And why my hero Joe, simply died while driving down the road one day. Until then, all we can do is trust in the Lord, and know that He has a much better plan for us—than we do for ourselves.

It was a difficult period for Anne; her family so far away, now widowed with a newborn baby and full-time job requirements, including travelling to recruit basketball players to Reno…a place many parents did not want their precious little daughters to go. When parents think of Reno, they automatically think of gambling, prostitution, drugs, etc., etc…it was a miracle Anne could convince anyone to go to school there. After some time (a long time), Anne started seeing some other gentleman…Pat, Nick, Tom, John, Ray—do you see a pattern here? One guy sort of measured up a little, even though he was a bit swarthy, Ray was a good tennis player—really, an excellent tennis player; and Anne had taken up tennis with the same sort of determination and passion she did with the bodybuilding. And, being just like her brother, she was competitive and a good athlete and tennis was a good fit for her—she became good very quickly.

One year I met Anne, Casey and Ray out west, we visited Joshua Tree National Monument and climbed all over that gorgeous place…really a hidden desert treasure. We then made our way to Wickenburg, Arizona to a Dude Ranch/ tennis camp. We were only interested in the tennis. First night there, it was getting near dark, but Ray and I decided to hit some balls while Anne and Casey unpacked everything. We only had time to hit a little, then play one set…I beat Ray 6-

4 that set. I remember it well because it was the last game I won from him the rest of the week—not the last set, the last game! Next day, he beat me 6-0, 6-0; couple of days later, same thing 6-0, 6-0; forget this, I only played Anne the rest of the week. But, that one day, I did beat Ray; and Ray had recently won his local tennis club tournament by beating the assistant pro there, who had been a minor league professional and had beaten some journeyman pro, who had at one time in his life, beaten the tennis pro Peter Korda, who had recently played at Wimbledon and was a top 10 player in the world. So…if you do the math and apply all algebraic and geometric formulas to it…I could've played at Wimbledon—it's possible!

The four of us made another memorable trip to Arizona the next year—I enjoyed visiting my little sister and little Casey, we had fun together—she had forgiven for most of the pranks I played on her growing up. Anne had an athletic conference to attend in Flagstaff, so we met there and Ray and I decided we would hike to the bottom of the Grand Canyon that week. First, we wanted to visit there and let Ray check it out and take little Casey with us. We had a fine old time at the canyon that day, unfortunately, a few of the pictures I took of Ray holding Casey by the arms over the canyon rim should have been hidden from my sister better than they were. Ouch! But little Casey loved her Uncle Gary and would do anything he said…Ray didn't really believe this, so to prove a point, I pointed to a lump of dirt on the ground (a little lump of dirt—not big), and said, "Casey, eat that lump of dirt." And she did…and she liked it! Good old Casey.

Early the next day Ray and I dropped Casey off at a babysitter we'd found in Flagstaff, while Anne went to her conference. Grand Canyon—here we come. Ray and I were pumped, down to the bottom, dangle our feet in the cold 49 degree water of the Colorado River and hike back up, all in the same day. No problem, we were fairly young (sort of) and in good tennis shape; and we had our supplies with us for the trip down: an orange and a Diet Pepsi. Hiking down the Grand Canyon is amazingly easy…it's ALL downhill. You're taking in the majestic beauty of the place, whistling, telling jokes, singing songs—life is good! We started our journey at the rim, which is over 8000 feet elevation. The canyon is over a mile deep there, so we ended up at the river 5000 feet lower than where we started. Early that morning, the temperature was in the low 60's…at the bottom, in the middle of the day, it was about 90 degrees. Our Diet Pepsi's had been long gone by the time we got to the river, but, we each still had an orange. We had noticed the faces and demeanor of some of the hikers going up as we were coming down—they didn't look too good; but heck, they weren't in as good a shape as old Ray and me—not by a long shot!

We took off our shoes and put our feet in the water for a few seconds…the water was too cold to stay in very long, it was coming from the bottom of the hated Glen Canyon dam—over 600 feet tall; the water at the bottom of that sucker is dark and cold and dead. After telling a few more jokes and eating our orange, we were ready to go. It had taken us about 2 ½ hours to get down, so we figured it might take us 4 hours to get back up, since it's all uphill. Plenty of time before it got dark. Think about going to a football game and sitting on the first row of the stadium…then, think about climbing up those steps after the game—it's a long way up, your legs get tired, you get out of breath; but a minute or two and you're done. Multiply that by a thousand!

Every step is uphill…let me repeat that: EVERY STEP IS UPHILL. We started off fine, then we started taking breaks every 10-15 minutes, then every 5-10 minutes, then every 2-3 minutes. My legs were like wet noodles, my lungs were burning, I was parched and thirsty and hungry—mostly, so thirsty I'd have drank ocean water if I'd had it. There are no water fountains in the Grand Canyon, no snack machines and no mercy of any kind. A brutally heartless place for those who take it for granted and don't prepare—like me.

I soon lost all concept of time, I knew the sun was getting very low and I was nowhere near the top. Ray asked me if it was okay if he went on ahead and tried to get to the top; he said he would bring some water back. I knew I was slowing him down, I couldn't help it. Every step was a struggle and I was beginning to lose the struggle…and I knew it. After Ray left, I tried to make it a few steps to a rock, sit down, catch my breath, then move to the next rock. As the sun started to go down past the rim, I absolutely knew I'd never make it up—and, at that point, I didn't care. All I cared about was sitting down, closing my eyes and resting—I thought of nothing else. And that's what I did. I found a rock off the trail, leaned up against it and passed out.

Next thing I remembered was a bright light shining in my face, and hearing some gobble-de-gook language. I wasn't sure if I was on Mars, or in heaven, or…uh oh; not there! Then someone started shaking my shoulders and I could make out the faces of three young men with backpacks, shining a flashlight on me. Turns out they were Germans, who spoke virtually no English; but they had water and shared it with me and took turns holding onto me as they guided us up the canyon to the top. I don't know if anyone else passed by me without stopping or not, nor do I know how long I was there before the Germans helped me; but I do know I'd have never made it out of that hole without the help of those German guys.

They helped me to the top, I walked off the trail, puked and sat down. Ray found me and went to get me something to drink—a Diet Pepsi (why a Diet Pepsi Ray? Why?). He helped me to the car and laid me down in the back seat, gave me the soda, which I drank, then threw up again—in the car. Ray was not happy…I didn't care—I just didn't want to die at that point. He drove us back to Flagstaff, much later than we'd planned on; we knew Anne would not be happy with us coming back in the dark and leaving Casey at the babysitter's all day. Maybe she would have pity on me because of my condition, but old Ray knew he was going to get an earful. Back in Flagstaff he woke me up and said, "Gary, what street is the babysitter's house on?" Huh? How would I know, I thought he would remember that, he was the one driving. Let me tell you something—Flagstaff looks much different at night than it does in the daylight. We drove round and round, up one street and down the next and nothing looked familiar. Well, if the canyon didn't kill me, Anne surely would for losing her daughter. Finally, we found the house…the babysitter was very unhappy with us and we had to pay extra, but at least we had little Casey, who was happy to see us. Back at the hotel…Anne was not happy to see us. Well, she was happy to see Casey—but Ray and me…oh mama. Fortunately for me, I threw up one more time and passed out in the bed; poor old Ray endured the rest of the night alone.

16

"Inside every older person is a younger person wondering what the heck happened."

Around the mid to late 80's I started playing a lot of tennis; I'd never really played seriously before, just as something to do in between baseball, basketball and football. But, I couple of guys I worked with played and acted as if they were good. That's when the competitive thing stirred in me. I bought a tennis racket and started to play—still couldn't hit a backhand, but I knew I could probably beat these two guys just on athletic ability alone. I was right. But, I also knew that to play better players, I'd have to learn to hit a backhand. So, I just made up my mind I'd keep hitting the backhand as much as I could, even if it cost me from winning (which it did many times), I had to learn to hit it. I was fortunate to have a couple of tennis courts right beside the condo I lived in at Raintree. I'd play there when I could, but I'd play anywhere I could find a match really; then one day this young girl was out there practicing serves by herself. I went out and introduced myself to her and asked if she wanted to hit some balls…she did, and that started a great and wonderful friendship and partnership for us both.

Her name was Amy Franklin, she and her new husband Robert, had just moved here after their marriage because Robert was starting law school at Wake Forest. Amy worked a part time job, but mostly had a lot of free time on her hands while Robert was at class or studying. So, we started hitting balls almost every day; we didn't play much because Amy was just starting out, but she was a great athlete and so eager to learn. She had played college softball at Clemson and could throw a softball harder than I could. This motion was natural for her serving—and she developed a good one, and being 6'1" helped her as well. We played and played, she'd be out there waiting on me to get home from work and we'd hit balls for hours. Even when I played other guys, she'd wait for me to get back and hit balls with her as long as I could. Those were fun days, Robert was a great guy as well, although not much of an athlete; and they invited me and Shelley (when she was staying with me on weekends) over to their condo for dinner and snacks all the time. Shelley was the darling of the neighborhood and thought that everyone at the complex loved her and was her best friend—which was pretty accurate.

One day I saw the notice in the newspaper for an upcoming tennis tournament in Winston; this really excited me, I wanted to start playing good players and test myself further. I signed up for my first tournament over at Hanes Park and since they had never heard of me, I was assigned to play the No. 1 seed in the tournament, a guy named Francis Barker. I had no idea who he was, but figured he must be some stud of an athlete and very good player. The day of the tournament, I went to the court and saw a short, balding guy with a beer gut standing there. He had no tennis bag, like I did, he didn't have 2 or 3 rackets, like I did, he didn't have a water jug, like I did, nor a towel, nor anything else—he only carried a single racket and a can of balls. This was the No. 1 seed? An overweight, short, balding guy?

He beat me 6-0, 6-0 and it wasn't even that close. He ran me ragged, side to side, drop shots, lobs, he made me look silly. I learned a very valuable lesson that day—NEVER judge someone by their appearance, and…I needed a lot more practice. So, practice I did; I played every day, usually twice a day on weekends…I'd play anyone, anytime, anywhere—plus, all my hitting with Amy. I changed my phone answering machine to say, "If this call is about tennis, leave me a message and I'll call you back; if it isn't, just call back later." I was serious now. I eagerly waited for the next tournament to test myself again and hopefully not get as humiliated as before—but, I had to test myself. Fortunately, I didn't have to play Francis Barker in the first round; I won that match, then two more matches before losing in the quarterfinals to a very good player, Bart Williams.

I joined a USTA league team, which introduced me to more and better players and soon I was making a name for myself in Winston tennis circles. The next year our tennis team won the North Carolina state championship, with me playing No. 1 singles. We would go on to win three consecutive state titles, all with me as the No. 1 singles player. Then, I started advancing further in local tournaments, I'd regularly make it to the semi-finals, then, I started making it the finals of tournaments. The first tournament I won was very special to me, one of the proudest days of my life. Amy was improving as well and we entered some mixed doubles tournaments together. We were a good team, Amy had a great serve and being so tall, she was very intimidating at the net. Her ground strokes weren't very good, so, I'd cover most of the court and station Amy at the net—with this formula, we were good.

One summer we won the Winston-Salem, Forsyth County Open mixed-doubles tennis tournament, beating a guy and girl who both played on the Wake Forest tennis teams. Individually, each of them was much better than either me or Amy—in singles, they would've killed us. Our strategy was to hit EVERY ball to the girl—the guy was just too good to mess with. Soon, the girl began to struggle and the guy began to berate her and yell at her. We could see tears in the girl's eyes on the changeovers…but this was war. We kept it up, every ball to her and she began to crack under the pressure of having to hit every ball and her partner yelling at her. We eventually won 7-5, 6-4…I felt so sorry for the girl, but ecstatic for us. The sorry guy didn't even shake our hands, instead, he just walked off the court without the girl and left.

I made it to the finals of another tournament at Hanes Park and was scheduled to play Francis Barker in the finals. I had not played him since my humiliating defeat earlier. Without going into the details of the match, I won in two sets. Maybe my most gratifying match ever, to see how far I'd come, I was proud of myself. Francis was the top seed in this tournament as well, and when it was over, the Winston-Salem Journal's tennis writer, Mary Garber, came to interview me…I was tongue tied and really don't know what sort of babble came out of my mouth.

Anne came to visit me one time during the Winston-Salem, Forsyth County Open tennis tournament; I'd told her about it, so she scheduled the trip so she could play in it—it was "open," which meant anyone could play. She won it! And the other women players were not happy that a "ringer" had come in from out of state and beaten them all. I lost in the finals, which was a bummer, but what a week it was…we had a ball.

I brought Shelley with me to a lot of tennis matches, but her main enjoyment was the nice pool at the condo. She would stay in the pool from the time she got up, till I made her come in; she was everybody's friend. She go have lunch with Amy, go for snacks with Paula Ceresa, eat pickles with Bob Jones—she was so cute and pretty that all my neighbors wanted to entertain her. One late summer afternoon, nearly everyone had gone in for the day except one young lady on the other side of the pool from me, who was just laying out, reading a book and relaxing. Of course, Shelley assumed this girl wanted to be her friend, so she started to talking to her—no one else at the pool but the girl and us. Soon, Shelley swims over and walks up to me and says, "Dad, that girl wants to know if it's okay if she gives me cookie?" Just to mess with Shelley, I said, "What girl?" She said, "That girl over there," I said, "Oh, you mean the fat girl over there?" (she wasn't fat, just a little chunky). Shelley, says yeah, that girl. I said, okay, so Shelley walks around the pool to the other side and says to the girl, "my daddy says you're fat, but I don't think you are." Oh my God! Should I try to act like I'm asleep or what? Another lesson learned…be very careful of what you say in front of your children.

Another day at the pool, Shelley had made friends with these two little girls who were new to the pool, I hadn't seen them before, but they were having a blast playing with each other. People were always coming and going at the pool, so I didn't pay much attention to who was coming in or leaving; I just kept my eye on Shelley. I was watching her when suddenly she stopped what she was doing and started staring at the entrance to the pool. I looked over and this woman who was on crutches came in the gate; the woman had only one leg. She was the mother of the two little girls Shelley was playing with, so she came up to the edge of the pool to say hello to her daughters. Shelley still had not moved. After the woman spoke to her girls, Shelley dog paddles over to the edge where the woman is and says, "did you know you only have one leg?" The woman handled it well. You never know what kids are going to say.

Since my divorce I had the good fortune to meet and date several lovely, intelligent and wonderful women. Some fairly seriously, some not. I dated this one woman, who was a P.A. (no reason to name names here) off and on for 3-4 years; she asked me to marry her a few times, but I always sloughed it off. She was very nice and we enjoyed our time with each other, but I knew I wasn't in love with her that way. That relationship ended rather abruptly when she caught me in a lie. We had made a date earlier in the week to have dinner Saturday night, which was pretty normal for us. However, I had met a new girl (a psychologist it turns out) who was very pretty and fun to talk to. This psychologist calls me Saturday afternoon and asks me if I want to have dinner with her that night; before I realize what I'm actually saying, I agree. After I hang up the phone, it hits me that I now have two dinner dates for tonight—uh oh. I struggled with this for some time, but, finally I decided I'd just call the P.A. and tell her something had come up and I had to keep Shelley that night—couldn't be helped. She totally understood and we made plans to do something Sunday afternoon. Perfect!

I picked up the psychologist and asked her where she wanted to go...she said, how about Mexican? Great, we had several Mexican restaurants to choose from, so off we go. Walk in the door and the waiter says, "follow me"; I see the open table he's taking us to and as we arrive, I glance at the table next to us...yep, you've guessed it by now—there is the P.A. with a couple of her girlfriends having dinner at the same restaurant, at the same time as we are. What are the odds of that? Of all the restaurants in Winston, at the exact same time??? She never said a word, she just stared a hole in me the entire dinner. Without a doubt, the worst dinner I've ever had. Another lesson learned—lies will eventually catch up to you—some sooner, some later, but, you'll get caught...trust me.

17

"God said, 'I am your Creator. You were in my care even before you were born'."

As my cousin Linda once told me when I was complaining about the scarcity of really attractive, intelligent women—Gary…you're no Prince Charming. Sort of hurt my feelings a little, but I guess she's right. However, I (nor anyone else), should ever settle for anyone unless you are their Prince Charming and vice versa. That was the problem I was having; I dated several very nice, attractive, intelligent and successful women; but they just weren't my Princess Charming. I liked them, had a great time with them and enjoyed our companionship (most of the time). I was asked by at least three of these women if I wanted to marry them—I didn't. Most of the time, it was not the answer they were hoping for. Then, when I was working at Pepsi-Cola, I met a young lady who was different; my feelings for her were stronger than I'd expected and had realized before. Her name was Kathleen and she was from Indiana, but was working at our local Pepsi plant for a one year training program.

I had seen her in the offices, but never thought of asking her out…I didn't even know if she was married or not. After a few months, one of the guys who worked for me told me that Kathleen had seen him in the break room and had asked him about me…was I single, or seeing anyone. That was weird. I forget the details now, but eventually I asked her to dinner, she accepted and we had a great time. Kathleen was very attractive, smart and fun to be with and I could tell my feelings for her were more genuine than with any of the other girls I had been seeing. As the weeks and months passed, we grew closer and closer and the conversation always came back to the point of what would happen with us when her contract was up and she went back to Indiana. Neither of us wanted to face that question initially, but as the deadline drew near, the thought of marriage started to enter the equation.

The night before she was to go back to Indiana, we decided that she would go back and I would think about what I wanted…she had made it perfectly clear to me she wanted to get married. She wanted me to "think" about it. Well, when she left, it took about 4 hours for me to decide…yes, I did want to marry Kathleen—she was the one. Again, this was the time before cell phones, 1988 to be precise. I waited until I thought she would arrive back in Indiana and called her, she was thrilled to hear my decision and told me she was going to tie up some loose ends and drive back to Winston-Salem in a couple of days. She had about a month before she was to start her new job at Pepsi in Indiana, so in the meantime she would explore transferring permanently to Winston. She told me to figure out the logistics of getting married—she preferred us driving to South Carolina and doing it the next weekend. In those days, you only needed 24 hours to get married in South Carolina…the laws in North Carolina were much then different then.

Plans were being made, excitement was high, and I couldn't wait for her return. She came back to Winston Friday evening and we planned to drive to S.C. early the next morning and get married; I had called some place and arranged everything. We got up Saturday morning and packed my car for the trip; we got in, I put the key in the ignition…and I couldn't turn it. I didn't hear any voices, but somehow, I knew this wasn't the right thing to do. I could not turn the ignition on. She asked what was wrong…I had no answer, I didn't know what to say. This woman had just driven 17 hours the day before in hopes of marrying me—because I asked her to. Now, I couldn't even talk to her or explain why I couldn't talk to her. After 10-15 minutes of silence, she got out of the car, took her suitcase and put it in her car and drove away.

I didn't know if I was happy or sad; if I'd made a terrible mistake, or a great decision—I had no idea. I counted the 17 hours it would take her to drive back and then tried calling her…she never answered any phone calls for the next week. After a couple of weeks, she did answer and told me not to call her anymore—and she meant it; so I didn't. As I keep repeating, at times the Lord helps those who cannot help themselves; He has a much better plan for our lives than we do. I didn't know it at the time, but the Lord had a much better plan for me a couple of years down the road.

So, I played tennis and travelled when I could, which was a lot. I took Shelley and met Anne and Casey in Orlando at Aunt Mary's one year. I went to Zion National Park for the first time and Yellowstone for the first time—totally incredible. I visited Yosemite with my cousins Gail and Linda one November; it was an Indian summer day out there, warm and hardly any visitors to hamper our sightseeing—a very great day. I made another hike to the bottom of the Grand Canyon, much better prepared this time, I had a backpack with water and food; but make no mistake about it…hiking down a vertical mile, 8-9 miles distance; then hiking back those same 8-9 miles uphill all the way is very, very, very tiresome. I made it, and, luckily had a room at the Grand Canyon lodge, right there on the rim; I came up the last steps, walked the 50 feet or so to my hotel room and fell into my bed until the next morning. The canyon had beaten me again.

Back home, it was just me and Shelley and tennis—and I was happy with that. I took her everywhere with me, football games, basketball games, visits to my friends…I truly loved my little girl and loved spending time with her. My friends here kept trying to get me to have professional photographers take shots of Shelley and get her in commercials and such…my friend Bob Jones must have taken hundreds of pictures of Shelley, he really loved her. At a Wake Forest football game one year Shelley scared the daylights out of me; she wanted to go to the bathroom at halftime, so I take her to the doorway and let her go in and I stand there waiting on her. Problem is, she doesn't come out! 5 minutes, 8 minutes, 10 minutes…I'm in pure panic mode now. I know I didn't miss her coming out—what was going on? At those times, all sorts of weird and crazy things run through your mind. I finally found a female Wake Forest usher, told her what had happened, described Shelley to her and asked her if she would go in the restroom and see what was happening. She did and came out the door at the far end and was waving to me…I hadn't seen that door at the far end!

She told me there were no little girls in the restroom, she had checked all the stalls, halftime was over and the restroom was empty—no Shelley. I immediately sweated through my shirt and wondered how in the world I could tell Judy that I'd lost our daughter. The usher found a policeman and told him what was going on…the policeman started calling everyone on his walkie talkie, asking if anyone had seen a little girl. Finally…finally, a Wake Forest employee notified us that she had a little girl with her named Shelley Hope on the complete other side of the stadium! I ran as fast as I could, still being terror stricken, and found Shelley playing games with the ushers—she was having a blast and didn't want to leave all the ushers, who of course, fell in love with her. How she got to the other side of the stadium, I'll never know; but I knew I'd never let her go to the bathroom alone again either.

During the late 80's, tennis was a very popular sport, unlike today. Winston usually had an invitational tournament, either at Tanglewood or at Wake Forest every summer. I went to all of them. I saw the greatest of them all play—Rod Laver (well, he actually just hit some balls, but it was awesome); my friend Amy even got his autograph for me on a plastic cup—which I still have. I saw Michael Chang, Andre Agassi and Pete Sampras play when they were teenagers, before they became famous. You could tell, even then, without a doubt, Agassi would be a star. Obviously, no one had ever heard of him at that time, but when they introduced him and he walked out on that court with that long blonde, two-toned hair and he flashed that smile at the crowd…I would have bet right then and there that half the women in the place peed on themselves. He was so charismatic that he had the crowd won over before he ever hit a shot…then, he hit that forehand of his. I'd never seen a human being hit a tennis ball so hard and have it go in the court—it was truly amazing. I took at least 20 pictures of Agassi that day, which I still have; I didn't take any of Michael Chang or Pete Sampras. Agassi was the star of the show, more so than Brad Gilbert, who was ranked No. 4 in the world at that time.

We saw Johan Kriek play just after he won the Australian Open for the second time, and Grand Slam winner Stan Smith as well as many other prominent players…tennis was good then in Winston-Salem. Amy and I would go to most of these matches together, then go home and play tennis all evening. It was good times. Greensboro started hosting "exhibition matches" at this time as well, bringing in big names to play. We saw Pat Cash play there the same year he won Wimbledon, we saw John McEnroe play Bjorn Borg (my tennis hero), Boris Becker played Vitas Gerulaitis —who had the greatest tennis line I've ever heard. Jimmy Connors had beaten Vitas 16 times in a row, when Vitas finally beat Connors one day…at the post match interview, they asked Vitas how he felt about winning the match and he said with a straight face, "Nobody beats Vitas Gerulaitis 17 times in a row!" Classic.

18

"There are two great questions in life we all must answer: What is worth living for? And, what is worth dying for? The answer to both, of course, is love."

Mama had recently married Bob Colvin, whom I've described earlier; in 1988, and they both started having health problems. Of course, mama had them on and off for the past 25 years or so—but this was different—it was more serious, and so was Bob's. They both ended up in Forsyth Hospital at the same time; Bob was to undergo a triple by-pass heart operation, while mama was battling the same cancer thing she'd been fighting for a quarter of a century. Bob endured his operation, but had a tough time recovering from it; mama was another story altogether. It seems as though her kidneys were failing due to all the chemo and radiation she had undergone. After all the years of fighting the lymphoma, it was her kidneys that failed her in the end. The doctors told us there was nothing that could be done and it was just a matter of time—a short time. This is not the type of news you wanted to hear about your 57 year old mom.

The last two or three days, she would drift in and out of reality; most of the time not making any sense at all. But then, suddenly, you could have a rational conversation with her for a few minutes. I don't think she knew what was happening or what the final diagnosis was. Anne came home from Reno to be with us and we stayed at the hospital day and night, visiting both mama and Bob. On September 5, Labor Day, Anne, Sara and I were all in mama's hospital room...we knew she wouldn't last much longer. Her breathing started to become very labored, when suddenly she took one last deep breath and it was over. My mama had died. I can't write anymore about it.

I went back to work the next week, I was still a dad and a brother and an uncle...but I was a lost and lonely soul. Bob eventually recovered as well and went back to the now lonely apartment they had—he too was a lonely soul. His daughter, Nancy, a very great and wonderful woman, lived in Philadelphia, so Bob had nobody here but me and Shelley. I know he was very lonely, as I was. Robert and Amy kept urging me to get out and date, but I didn't have it in me. Shelley and tennis were enough to keep me happy for the time being.

After the New Year, sometime during the spring, I had gone to bed one night in my condo and was fast asleep, when something woke me up. I distinctly heard the sound of footsteps in my bedroom at the end of the bed. Unmistakable, the sound of someone walking on a carpet, with no other sound in the house—the air conditioner wasn't running, the refrigerator wasn't cycling on—not a sound in the world but those footsteps at the end of my bed. I was terrified! By now, I was sweating bullets and wondering what to do…I decided to pretend like I was still asleep, and if all this person wanted was to steal something, then let them have whatever they wanted and just leave. Certainly, they had either a gun or a knife, whereas I had nothing but fear.

But, they didn't go anywhere else in the house. They just stayed at the foot of my bed and walked back and forth. I was pretty convinced by now they would harm me—why? I didn't know. But, I didn't know what else to do but pretend to be asleep and see what happened. After a few minutes of this, I heard the person walk out of my bedroom, towards the living room and kitchen. By now, my sheets were soaking wet with perspiration, but I laid as still as I could and waited to see what would happen next. I heard no more sounds, I heard no doors open for the next 15-20 minutes; eventually, I summoned enough nerve to get up and investigate. Slowly and carefully I made it out of the bedroom and into the living room, kitchen and other bedroom…nothing had been taken or touched as far as I could tell. My front door was still locked, dead bolt and all; and the sliding glass door at the back was also locked, with the broom stick at the bottom in place. There was no physical evidence of anyone at all being there. But, someone had been there; someone had been walking at the foot of my bed for several minutes—I was as wide awake as awake can be. I heard the unmistakable footsteps over and over, back and forth.

I have my own explanation for this, one I'm sure no one else will believe. I know from the Bible, that once you enter heaven, you don't come back to earth—it just isn't done. But I do think my mama engaged an angel to come back and see if I was okay; and I think those footsteps were the angel sent by my mama to check on me…and in essence let me know that I was being looked after…that she was always going to look after me. I'm not asking anyone to believe this—I don't care if you do or don't. I just know what I know.

Eventually, I did start dating a little, nothing serious, just something to do. I dated a couple of Amy's friends and some other people that I was introduced to—I'd rather have been playing tennis. For the most part, they were okay, some were too weird for me; some, I was too weird for them…it's hard to find someone compatible when you're nearing 40. You get too set in your ways and don't want to change…just like my friend Dickie is now. I was beginning to think that either I was too picky, or that all the good woman were taken, but I was fairly certain there was no one out there for me. This one was too fat, that one was too skinny, this one had fat ankles, that one was too dumb…on and on it went; maybe I was too picky. But, dang, I wasn't going to settle for someone knowing I'd be unhappy with them—I'd rather be alone than do that.

One of my neighbors at the condo was a nice older lady named Bootsie, she worked at the bank I went to as well. Bootsie and I became friends at the pool through Shelley, who was friends with everybody out there. She started telling me she knew someone she wanted to introduce me to, a woman who came to her bank and seemed to be really nice. Week after week, she kept on urging me to call this girl, all summer long. We all knew how blind dates went, seldom were they good. Finally, I relented and told Bootsie I'd call her up and meet her. Not for an actual date however, just a meeting over coffee or a Pepsi maybe…easier to make an escape that way; this was not my first rodeo.

So, I met this young lady, Susan Carter, at TJ's Deli there on Country Club Road. Bootsie was right, Susan was very attractive and friendly. We both had travelled a lot, she overseas and me in the US and we talked and talked about places we'd visited and wanted to visit. And, we realized we'd both lost our mothers recently, the same year really. I thought Susan was beautiful, smart and fun…I was just hoping she liked me as well. She had told me she was getting ready to go on a three week trip to Australia with her two nieces, in a couple of weeks. So, I decided to call her the next week and see if she wanted to go out before she left on her trip. Fortunately for me, she did and we had a great time on our one and only date.

She left for Australia with her nieces and I was left behind, really smitten by now. I decided I could not let her forget me during these three weeks; she had left me an itinerary of her trip, so every few days I would wire flowers or a telegram to the hotel they were staying at in Australia. I made a full time job of "wooing Susan." They finally came home and we arranged to have dinner at her house, she'd brought some presents back and wanted me to see the pictures and stuff she'd bought. We stayed up all night talking and way late in the night—or, early in the morning as it was, she said, "why don't we just get married!" With no hesitation at all, I said, "okay, Great! When?" She said she started school in a week, so let's do it next weekend before school began…okay with me.

So, after all this time and all the years of dating, all it took was TWO DATES with the right woman to know I was at the right place. She wanted me to meet her family and a couple of family friends before we married, so I did at a restaurant in Greensboro…they grilled me pretty good, but were generally nice, just a little wary of the quick decision we'd made. One of the friends there was a Quaker minister, Wally, who agreed to marry us the following Saturday—we just had to go meet with him one afternoon before the wedding, which we did. Things were moving quickly, but for us, we KNEW it was the right thing…how did we know? I can't explain that…we just knew. One final detail…she insisted I call her dad and get his okay. Oh me! She spent hours telling me how terrifying her dad could be, how strict he was, how tough he was, how very stern and demanding he could be. She had me thinking Hitler had come back to life! When the call finally came through, he was just the nicest man I'd ever talked to and was thrilled for us both…I think the fact that he himself had just recently gotten married after the death of Susan's mom, was a big factor in that. But, bottom line was that he was happy and wished us all the blessings in the world…and, now he had someone to take care of Susan!

Our Saturday wedding, on August 18, 1990, included Bob and Shelley, plus Martha, Clarence, Wendy and Robyn and Susan's close friend Carleen, plus Bootsie who had introduced us. As the ceremony ended and we were eating some wedding cake, the phone in Susan's condo rang (we were married in her condo); it was a former boyfriend asking her out on a date. Pretty bad timing for the guy—she explained she had just gotten married and had to decline his offer. He had just dated her before the Australia trip…I'm sure he thought she was making an excuse not to date him. But it was a done deal now…there was only one stipulation, we had to go to Charlotte on our honeymoon night (the only night we would have since school started Monday). Susan had committed to go to her 20 year high school reunion in Charlotte the night of our wedding. So we went. I didn't care…I'd have gone to the moon for her. When we finally made it back to the hotel room, we were starved, so we ordered a Domino's Pizza to be delivered. We then had several phone calls to make…telling Anne and Jerry and several other people that we were married. Most of them thought I was joking with them, until I put Susan on the phone to verify—they just couldn't believe it. Heck…it was hard for us to believe as well.

After things got settled a little bit, we decided to put both condos up for sale and find a house we liked. Trying to market two condos, getting used to living with each other and Susan getting used to having Shelley around on weekends was quite an adjustment for all of us. Being that our honeymoon was only for one night at Susan's high school reunion, she decided to surprise me with a cruise that November—a belated honeymoon. Since I'd never been on a cruise before, I was really thrilled about it and totally looking forward to this new adventure. We flew to Miami, and boarded a Royal Caribbean ship, which seemed HUGE to me…I was totally amazed at everything on board: the swimming pools, the bars, the restaurant, the magnificent theaters, all the entertainment, the casino, the midnight buffet. No Toto, I was not in Robeson County any longer!

After the New Year, Susan and I flew out to see Anne, we knew she was having a difficult time because her relationship with Ray had ended; ended because he was not the person we all thought he was. He was still swarthy, he just wasn't a good man—not by a long shot. Anne took this hard and we wanted to support her, so we went. When we got there, we decided to go to San Francisco, Monterey and Carmel for a visit…my first visits to these unique and charming little towns. Anne was pretty despondent, but we made the best of it. After we came back home, we decided that Susan should go back out and help with Casey for a few days while Anne went on a business trip she had planned. I guess Casey was around 4 at the time and I don't think she'd ever had her hair cut. I remember Susan calling me one night, Casey screaming and crying in the background as Susan was trying to comb out the tangles in her hair…I was so glad I was in North Carolina! They somehow made it through, Anne returned and Susan came home…she was such a trooper to volunteer for that, but, it's the kind of woman she is.

19

"Jesus + nothing = EVERYTHING"

In the spring of 1991 we decided to start house shopping; we found a realtor and told her the price ranges we were comfortable with and she started making us a list...a long list of possibilities; I thought it would be fun seeing all the houses available. I was wrong. The first house the realtor took Susan to visit, she fell in love with it and called me at work and said, "I want this house!" I said, okay, don't you want to just visit some others to see what's out there? "No, I want this house, I don't want to look at any others." Okay, she gave me directions to get there, I went out, but I already knew the decision was made...she wanted that house, and that's the house we were going to buy. We made an offer, they countered, we settled on a price and boom, it was done. We would close the deal next Friday.

We lined up financing, got the lawyers all settled and had everything taken care of, just the formality of meeting on Friday to sign the papers at Piedmont Federal. I was working at Pepsi at the time and went in Friday morning to tell my boss I needed to leave a couple of hours early that day to sign the mortgage papers on our new house. He looked startled and upset...why would he be upset that I was buying a house? He told me sit down and started to talk, but sort of choked up and had to compose himself; Pepsi had just sold our plant to the parent company and all current management people were out of a job as of the end of the day. The management would be run out of Charlotte Pepsi, which meant over 30 employees (some of them with over 40 years tenure) were out of a job. Shocked, does not describe the actual feelings I had. I left his office and saw our accountants and bookkeepers and personnel people, all sorts of managers, crying and weeping out loud. I could not believe what was happening.

I went back to my soon to be ex-office and called Susan...how in the world was I going to explain this to her? What should we do? Go ahead and buy the house? Keep one of the condos? My head was spinning. That phone call to her was not pleasant; she raised even more questions. We had less than two hours before we were to sign the papers on the house. I drove home in a daze and we hugged each other and talked; she came up with a great idea—let's call her dad and see what he recommends, he's a smart guy and I trust him. He asked us several questions about our finances and after hearing everything, he suggested we go ahead with the purchase; he was confident things would be fine in the long run—I told you he was smart.

So, we went to Piedmont Federal to sign the papers and try to look happy, like new home owners should—it was difficult. During the signing process, he asked if we were still employed with the school system (for Susan) and at Pepsi, for me…well, technically, it wasn't 5:00 yet, which was the end of the day, so yes! I was still employed at Pepsi…for at least 45 more minutes. Everything signed, we left and drove to our new house and walked in…one scared school teacher and one scared, unemployed husband.

I really wasn't desperate to find a job, we had made enough down payments on the house to where our monthly payments were not going to kill us, or prevent us from living comfortably. I knew something would come along and didn't want to take a job quickly and then regret it. We settled on just taking a beach trip that summer, staying at a cottage that Barbara owned at Myrtle Beach. That was fun, then we drove over to Atlanta to watch a Braves baseball game; good old Susan, always indulging me. Our only problem was that after the game, we couldn't find our car; we must have come out of the stadium on the opposite we parked on. We walked and walked and walked…nothing; we even discussed hiring a cab to ride us around. Well, we finally, frustratingly found it and headed back home wondering what the end of the year would bring for us.

I saw a job advertised that looked interesting, finally, and applied for it, interviewed and was hired at B/E Aerospace, here in Winston-Salem, as Traffic Manager. The only job I had applied for since Pepsi. That indeed made Thanksgiving and Christmas much merrier and happier in our little family. I was still into tennis big time and won a few tournaments, as well as our USTA team winning the state title once again at the 4.5 level, again, with me playing at No. 1 singles. The regional tournament that year was being held in North Carolina at Pinehurst—the previous year it was at Chattanooga, Tn., which I enjoyed visiting. Pinehurst in July and August is hot! This year was no exception, they tried to schedule the matches in the mornings to beat the heat, but by 10:00 or so, it was steaming hot.

Our team was doing well and was in good position to win the regionals going into the second day. I was scheduled to play the second match, starting around 9:30 or 10:00. It was already approaching 90 degrees, with high humidity as well—typical weather in the summertime in North Carolina. The guy I was playing was good, he hit everything back and had a funny serve that got me off balance in the first set, which he won in a tie-breaker 7-6. I quickly figured out how to return his serves and easily beat him the second set 6-1; I knew (and he knew), that the third deciding set was all mine; he could not beat me off the ground. I won the first three games easily, making it 3-0 and we changed ends of the court; I sat down, took a drink of water and when I stood back up, seemingly, every muscle in my body started cramping. I couldn't move my legs or torso, and fell flat on my face, screaming from the pain of the cramps, which were from my shoulders, down my back and into both legs.

I was scared, and everyone else was scared…none of us really knew what was happening to me at the time. There was a rescue squad truck nearby and luckily they got to me quickly; I had passed out for a few minutes and when I awoke, they had IV's in both my arms, and they were loading me in the ambulance. They took me to the emergency room, checked me out, kept the IV's in and made me keep drinking fluids. I stayed there till about 10:00 that night, when they released me to go back to the hotel with the team. Obviously, I forfeited my match (which stunk, cause I was beating that guy bad), and our two doubles teams lost, so we didn't win the regionals. But, I was alive and sort of well, had a new job, a new wife, a beautiful daughter and a wonderful family—I just wish I could've beaten that guy!

I wanted to surprise Susan in August for our one year anniversary, I thought of all sorts of things, but couldn't come up with something unique, that she would remember. We just did the cruise, we'd been to the beach, we'd been to the mountains; as I was racking my brain for ideas, I looked up and saw a hot air balloon float by—Bingo! I found a company in Kernersville who did hot air balloon rides and called them up; it was fairly reasonable, so I made us a reservation on our anniversary, Aug. 18. Susan knew nothing of this until we woke up that morning and I surprised her with it—I don't know how she really felt, but off we went. What struck me about the ride itself was that since the balloon was going with the wind, inside the little basket while we were floating, it was completely calm. You could've lit a candle and it would never have flickered. It was quite a view and we enjoyed it –at least I did; only the landing was a little tense, but it was worth the views, the experience and the memory.

We were still trying to support Anne and Casey, all alone out in the wild, wild West; we decided we would go out there again and visit over the holidays, this time, we'd take Aunt Mary with us. She'd never been out there and it would be good to all be together. This was when the diabetes was starting to affect Aunt Mary and she could only move around with a walker, and then only slowly and for short distances. We got her out there and had a nice family visit at Anne's house; Aunt Mary wanted us to take her to one of the casinos to play the nickel slots—she'd saved a bag of nickels and couldn't wait to donate them to the local Reno economy. We drove her right up to the door and the staff there helped her get out of the car and found a wheelchair to transport her into the main casino lobby. She took her walker with her to move around from machine to machine, so she was all set up. I parked the car out in the parking lot and we all settled in at the slots for a fun afternoon.

We decided we'd stay till about 4:00, then leave and go to an early dinner somewhere; I'd been checking on Aunt Mary all afternoon and her bag of nickels was nearing empty, but she was having fun. My mom had taught her to switch machines often if they weren't paying off, so she'd put a few coins in one machine, then struggle with her walker and move to another machine, trying for better luck. I told her we were ready to leave in about 10 minutes and went to find Susan and Anne; when we got back to Aunt Mary, she was yelling at us "I won! I won!" She had hit a minor jackpot and won over $100 in nickels…these were the days when the nickels actually poured out of the machine—unlike today, when all you get is a printed card. Let me tell you, $100 in nickels SOUNDS like a lot of money as it drops out of those machines. She was stuffing nickels in her pockets, her pocketbook, her coat and had the biggest smile on her face. She kept telling us over and over how she did it as we made our way out to the parking lot and the car…how she watched for a machine to become vacant, then took it over when the other person left it, and then hit the jackpot. We heard that story three times on the way to the car—she was so excited! In fact, she was so excited, that none of us noticed until we reached the car at the far end of the parking lot, that Aunt Mary had WALKED all the way out there WITHOUT her walker and kept up with us as if nothing was wrong with her at all. I had to go back into the casino and retrieve the walker for her…amazing what the mind can make the body do, even more amazing, what a big sack of nickels can make the body do!

For the life of me, I cannot remember why, but Susan and I decided to go to Cancun, Mexico that year. We flew down and stayed in a hotel on the beach and it was all very nice. My only memories of that trip are the VERY strong drinks they mixed for us at a bar—we could not drink them; how white and sandy the beaches were, and getting an earache on the plane ride back home. It struck me that if the waiters had not all been Mexican, you would have certainly thought you were in Myrtle Beach…that's what it felt like. Another place we visited was one I'll never forget, the Grove Park Inn in Asheville. We went there over Thanksgiving and it was great! A place we'd return to many times over the years. At Thanksgiving, they had the huge Christmas tree lit and decorated in the lobby—at least 20-25 feet tall. The walk-in fireplaces were blazing, there was a Ginger Bread house contest on-going, and people from all over the east coast had brought in their ginger bread houses for the competition. We enjoyed sitting on the balcony out back, under heat lamps, taking in the view of the Blue Ridge Mountains…what a great place to visit. We would definitely be back.

Anne and Casey seemed to be doing well now, as we entered 1992; Casey had come to love gymnastics and was taking lessons virtually year round. Susan was teaching the Highly Academically Gifted students, which was her passion, and Shelley was a happy, healthy, beautiful 10 year old…the apple of her dad's eye. She had recently discovered soccer, with her friends from school; her team played Saturday mornings and Susan, Judy and I went to the games. Most games revolved around all the players following the ball, kicking at it and really accomplishing very little. There wasn't much scoring and even less action, but, I think Shelley liked it, and it

Anne and Casey

was important to get involved in things, regardless of how boring soccer matches actually are for the parents. Anne was starting to date this one particular guy pretty steadily, Nick. My sister can be pretty darned stubborn at times, or maybe she's just blinded by the obvious facts, and determined to tempt fate yet again. So, I tried to stay on the sidelines…me and my friends and family—Gary,

Shelley, Casey, Susan, Larry, Dickie, Jerry, Allen, Sara, Aunt Mary, Martha, Clarence, Wendy, Robyn, Conrad, Barbara...all of us multi-syllable names, we said nothing. Don't be prejudiced Gary, maybe the gods of fate will be kind this time. Or, maybe not...we'll see.

20

I was hoping that since I loved traveling so much, especially out west, that my daughter would as well. I decided to take her and Susan out to one of my favorite places—Yellowstone. What a marvelous destination to initiate them both into the grandeur of the American west…Susan had not been here either. We flew into Salt Lake City, rented a car and headed north. The first place we'd stay would be in the beautiful little town of Jackson Hole, Wyoming, next to maybe the most scenic mountain range in the United States—the Grand Tetons. The Tetons rose abruptly from the plain to over 14,000 feet and would take your breath away when you first saw them, snow-covered and reaching to the sky. But Shelley's most enjoyable moments were in the top of the bunk bed at the hotel we were staying…for some reason, she loved crawling up there and staying as long as she could.

We toured around the Tetons and the lakes before heading up to Yellowstone and our next lodging at the Roosevelt cabins in the north end of the park…and they were indeed rustic cabins. We watched Old Faithful erupt with all the other tourists and then decided we'd climb a small hill on the other side to watch if from a different view. This was the best place, no other people, and we could watch the eruption from on top, rather than at ground level. Yellowstone is full of so many geysers and mud pots and all sorts of geothermal activity, truly a magical place to visit. We were traveling in the park one day and a herd of buffalos was blocking the little road we were on, so we pulled over to let them pass, and I got out of the car to take a few pictures of these gigantic, 2000 pound creatures. They could be very intimidating and deadly if you got too close to them; people keep forgetting these are wild animals that can gore or trample you very, very easily. I've written about this before, but they scared Shelley so bad, she jumped in the back seat and wet her pants.

In northern Wyoming in early June, at over 8000 feet elevation, it can get pretty cold at night. The Roosevelt cabins, where we were staying, had no heat and only one little light bulb hanging from the ceiling. When we got to our little cabin about dusk, it was starting to get cold; by the time we went to bed, it was really cold. Susan and I had a small bed, that barely held us both and Shelley had a tiny little single cot…each of the beds had a worn sheet and thin blanket. It was cold! We slept in our clothes to help, but really, it didn't help; the walls of the cabin barely kept the wind out, it did not keep the cold out. Susan and I finally dozed off when we were awakened by Shelley, who was crawling in between us to get warm…my poor little girl was freezing. So, the three of us hugged together in that little bed and tried to sleep…never were we happier to see the sun rise in the morning, when we could get up, go the little café and get some hot coffee and cocoa.

Towards the end of the week, Shelley and I went on a raft ride down the Snake River, through the heart of Yellowstone—Susan deferred, since she did like anything to do with water, except drinking it. We saw two things we'll always remember, first, as we were approaching a small island in the river, the guide pointed out a moose who was standing in the water and grazing on the grasses from the island. The guide told us to be very quiet, that moose were unpredictable and could be dangerous. I'm guessing the river was about 4 feet deep at that point, maybe more, it was hard to tell; anyway, the moose was standing there with the water up to its torso, just staring at us as we approached. When we came about 15 feet from it, he started walking in the water towards us…the guide then says, "Everybody start rowing!" The faster we rowed, the faster the moose ran after us; we couldn't get away from him, but he couldn't get any closer to us well, because the water was getting deeper. It was huge, we were sitting in our little raft (which held 8 of us) and this moose was towering over us, with these massive antlers, running after us, for God knows what reason—I guess we got too close to his island. We finally got some distance between us and it gave up the chase…totally unbelievable.

Later on that same raft ride, the guide was pointing out some eagle nests along the river, when suddenly a cormorant dove straight down in the river in front of us, grabbed a fish in its talons and lifted up in the air—it happened so fast, we weren't sure what we were seeing initially. Just as it rose about 25-30 feet above the river, an eagle came up from behind it, turned upside down and grabbed the fish out of the clutches of the cormorant. Our guide was shocked…he had been on this river for over 20 years and said he'd never seen anything like that; it was truly amazing. What a way to end our week in one of the most incredible places on earth.

Back home in Winston-Salem, we were settled into a pretty good life, we liked our house and our situations. Susan has a great family, starting with her dad, a truly great man, Conrad Carter, his wife Barbara Carter, her sister and her family, Martha, Clarence, Wendy and Robyn. Bob was still living in Winston at the time, but I could tell he wanted to move back near his daughter Nancy, in Philadelphia. Plus, his health was not getting any better and I think he was just lonely—who could blame him? Susan decided to join Old Town Baptist Church, where I was a member, and give up her Methodist heritage. She got dunked by our pastor, Wade Dellinger, joined the choir and fell right into the Baptist swing of things. Wade was a great preacher; he could recite passages of scripture and give facts and stories all without the benefit of any notes from the pulpit. I always liked it when a preacher spoke to you, rather than reading to you…Wade could do that.

Susan and some other women friends of hers from the choir, started a Women's Ensemble singing group, headed up by the choir director and assistant pastor, Phil, who seemed to be an upright, conservative Christian man. Phil also helped the pastor with some counseling sessions for church members. The story goes something like this…Phil had been offering marriage counseling to a husband and wife for a couple of months; and it didn't seem to be helping them. Finally, the wife confronted the husband and told him she might be interested in another man—Phil, she thought he might be "sweet" on her as well. The husband, looked back at her and said, "I really don't think that's going to happen, since I'm the one having an affair with Phil right now!" I'm pretty sure that's not the answer she was hoping to hear…neither was it the answer the church wanted to hear. Phil resigned, left his wife and children, moved in with his new "boyfriend" and left church wondering what in the world had happened.

Susan was a gifted teacher, and appropriately honored as such, by being nominated for various Teacher-of-the-Year awards. I was working six days a week at B/E Aerospace, sometimes seven days a week, but we were happy; I still had the tennis bug and played a lot. We went to Shelley's soccer matches, visited our families, Uncle Paul made sure we had a Townsend family reunion every year and soon, Susan started hosting the reunion at our house. Before long, Susan was more a part of my family than I was; but, that's Susan, easy to love. The Yellowstone trip was great that June, but we wanted something else this year as well. Susan's history of travel was as much internationally as mine was domestically…she'd not only been to Australia, but China, Japan, France, Egypt, Germany, Switzerland and England, among other places…England…hmmm. The Beatles, the Stones, Big Ben, The Beatles, Tower of London, Buckingham Palace, The Beatles—I wanted my first overseas trip to be memorable (I'm not including our 51st and 52cd states — Canada and Mexico), overseas meant "over the sea," the pond, the big water. England it was, and we made plans to go…and little Gary was truly excited.

21

"The thing about smart people is that they seem like crazy people to dumb people."

Air travel is really amazing…we board a plane in Charlotte, eat a few snacks, watch a movie, take a nap, and boom—we're in London, England! We rode the train from Gatwick to our hotel, The Royal Lancaster, which was across the street from Hyde Park. First thing we did was take a nap…flying all night is hard. After we woke up, we walked across the street to the park and watched a cricket match; which is a game the English play only to certify they are indeed English—and you're not. There were several other oddities that let you know you're in England; first thing I noticed was that there were no trashcans anywhere—I mean anywhere! Yet, the streets and the park were clean. We learned that because trash cans made ideal hiding places for I.R.A. bombs, especially in airports, train stations and parks; they quite smartly did away with them. I totally understand that. What I didn't understand then, and don't now, is what is ever going to happen with Northern Ireland? The British don't really want it…the Republic of Ireland doesn't really want it; and the two religious factions there hate each other's guts—not an ideal commentary on their views of Christianity. Another thing that was hard to get used to was crossing the street; of course we knew they drove on the left side over there. But what we could never quite figure out, was which way to look first (left or right) before you crossed the street. Seems simple, but it was perplexing to us, and we never did really make the adjustment…you'd let your American genes take over while walking, then start to cross the street, and the next thing you knew, some taxi was almost running you down.

The English were enjoying a heat wave while we were there—good for them, bad for us. When it's hot, Americans want something cold to drink, preferably with lots of ice. Forget that! They didn't have any ice in the pubs we went to, and if you asked for ice, all you got was that "stupid Yank" look, so we endured the lukewarm beer. But, it's England Gary, not America; do we really want other countries to be like us…to become American clones? Do we want to visit foreign lands only to see a bunch of fat people on their way to Wal-Mart? No, by God! We want the English to be English, and the Irish to be Irish, and the Australians to be Australian, and the French to be…well, I might be carrying my argument one country too far. Stay British, stay Irish, stay Italian…please.

I wanted to visit the hallowed grounds of the All England Lawn Tennis and Croquette Club in Wimbledon while we were there. It was opening day for Wimbledon that Monday, I knew it would be impossible to get in, I only wanted to go there, take some pictures and visit some gift shops. We took the train out to the little village of Wimbledon, got off and started walking towards the tennis, when I noticed a tennis player walking up ahead of us with his coach. It was Peter Korda, ranked No. 5 in the world at that time; we hurried up behind him and tried to listen to what he and his coach were discussing. But, they were speaking in some Eastern European tongue that made absolutely no sense at all to me—I couldn't come close to identifying what language it was.

Korda went in the player's entrance and we stood outside taking a few pictures of the grounds and the ticket booths, which all had long lines of people waiting to get in…except one. At the far left side there was one booth with no one in line, that was weird. Susan obviously thought that booth was closed, but I saw a woman sitting in it, so I went over to it and asked her if she was selling tickets. She said "yes, how many do you want?" Incredible! "Two," I say; then she says "which court do you want?" I reply "Center Court!" "No" she says, "really…want court do you want?" I asked her what was available, and she said how about Court # 2? Great, I'll take it. We walk around the grounds for a while, taking it all in—it was beautiful—just as you'd expect; then we make it over to Court No. 2 and the usher looks at our tickets and says, "follow me." We do, and go down to the second row at mid-court! The second row!! I could almost reach over the rail and touch that famous grass. What dumb luck we'd fallen into. We had no idea who was playing, nor how many matches were planned there that day; we were just happy to be there whoever was playing.

The first match was with Jim Courier who, at that time, was the No. 1 ranked tennis player in the world! The second match was with Monica Seles, who was the No.1 ranked women's player in the world, and the final match was with Jimmy Connors, who was playing his last match ever at Wimbledon. How could anyone ask for more than that? After the first match, I went and got us some strawberries and cream, because, that's what you do at Wimbledon. By mid-afternoon it was around 90 degrees and sunny; we were hot and thirsty—but we weren't leaving (Susan sure spoils me). After the second match, I went to a concession stand and saw some Cokes in a cooler…very unusual. I got two and they felt sort of cold, maybe. When we opened them, the Coke fizzed and spewed out—the can was a little cool, but the soda was not. We tried to drink a little of it, but hot soda on a hot day is not very refreshing.

After the matches, we walked around some more, bought tee shirts and other junk and finally made our way back to the train station. We got in a half empty car and sat down and I looked over and two women tennis players were sitting across from us, talking and giggling with each other—Mary Joe Fernandez and Gigi Fernandez. Mary Joe was ranked in the top 5 in the world and Gigi was ranked in the top 3 in the world in doubles. What a day, Susan let me stay as long as I wanted to, never complained once about the heat, nor grumbled about watching over 7 hours of tennis…she's a good, old girl!

We did all the things you should do in London: see the Tower of London, Piccadilly, take a tour boat on the Thames, cross the Tower Bridge, go to Buckingham Palace, Big Ben, and

Parliament...we did it all and loved it. I don't know how, but Susan has a great sense of direction, she always knew which way to go, which train to take, which corner to turn at—we were never lost; whereas, I never knew where we were or how to get anywhere. One of my favorite places there was the British Museum—go there if you can. Mummies from Egypt, 2000-4000 years old, manuscripts from Shakespeare and original, handwritten music and lyrics from the Beatles...the place was totally amazing.

There were also two places I wanted to visit outside of London; Windsor, where the Queen has her "weekend" home, and Dover—I wanted to see the "white cliffs of Dover," made so famous in WWII. Windsor was about a thirty minute train ride out and it was gorgeous, Windsor Castle was better than Buckingham Palace, in my opinion. We ate lunch at a little café there in Windsor, with a view of the castle; traditional English fare of roast beef and Yorkshire pudding—it was wonderful. Inside the castle grounds we visited St. James Chapel, where several members of the royal family are interred...I stood on Henry VIII's tomb—that was a weird feeling, one of the most famous men in history, and I'm standing on his tomb. We walked around and visited all we could, the Queen was there at the time, so there were some places you couldn't go into, but, it was very, very neat. I asked several English people in shops if they knew exactly when England stopped being ruled by Kings, and started being ruled by Parliament and the Prime Minister? None of them knew—and I asked a lot of people.

Sunday, we took the train out to Dover, on the east coast. It's famous for the "white cliffs" which was what Allied pilots were looking for on their way back home from bombing runs in Germany. When they saw the cliffs, they knew they were almost home. I was disappointed (I shouldn't have been), they weren't white at all, sort of a creamy color and not that impressive looking. Oh well. What did impress me about Dover was that everything was closed on Sunday—no pubs open, no restaurants, no shops—everything was closed and we were hungry. Too bad for us.

The next day, we checked out of the Royal Lancaster Hotel and boarded the train north to Scotland, I was really looking forward to this. Susan hadn't been to Scotland before, so it would be new for us both. The train went up towards the west coast of Scotland, the train ride was very smooth and very smoky! I'm pretty sure Susan and I were the only two people on the entire train not smoking. Men, women, teenagers, conductors, waiters—everyone smoked; and they never quit smoking, one cigarette after another. Finally, gagging and coughing and reeking of stale smoke, we got off the train in the quaint, little village of Oban, Scotland—what a pretty place. Right on the Irish Sea, surrounded by low mountains, lakes and heather covered hills...a prettier place would be hard to find. We walked around Oban, ate scones, drank tea and marveled at the long-haired sheep grazing at an old castle on the outskirts of town.

I can't remember why now, but we wanted to take the ferry over to the Isle of Man, in the Irish Sea. It was raining a little when we left the harbor, then it started raining harder, then harder; and by the time we reached the island it was hurricane type rain—hard and sideways. We docked, Susan and I got off the boat, walked for about 30 seconds in a complete downpour, turned around and got back on the boat. I don't remember much of our 30 second visit to the Isle of Man; only that my raincoat was woefully inadequate. We made it back to the harbor, then to the hotel to change into some dry, warm clothes and visit a pub or two before dinner. I had made up my mind I was going to try Haggis for dinner tonight; a traditional Scottish meal, made from all the junk left over after they make the lambchops and mutton and everything else edible from a sheep. They take these leftovers, stuff them inside the linings of a sheep's intestines and boil them with spices. I fulfilled my Scottish ancestor's requirements and ate this meal…now I understand why my ancestors left Scotland and went to Ireland—to get away from the haggis!

We enjoyed our stay in Oban and were looking forward to travelling to Glasgow the next day. We should've stayed in Oban longer. In Glasgow, we took a tour bus around the city, with a guide pointing out all the scenic and historic sites…I didn't take a single picture—no, not one. Glasgow struck me as being a working class factory town, gray, dull and uninspiring; at least we'd only planned on one night here and were off to Edinburg the next day. As the train pulled into Edinburg, we were completely overwhelmed by the majestic Edinburgh Castle, sitting on top of a massive volcanic peak, that thrusts upwards in the middle of the city…absolutely awesome. Whereas Glasgow was dull, Edinburg was lively and very attractive…the San Francisco of Europe it was called.

For some reason we couldn't figure out, the Queen had followed us up to Scotland, from Windsor, to visit her Scottish home, Holyrod Castle. If she wanted to meet us, all she had to do was ask; Susan had met her mother once before at a play in London, so we were assuming Elizabeth also wanted to meet us—but, we were so busy seeing the sights, we never received the invitation—her loss. If you ever get the chance…go to Edinburg, you'll be glad you did.

Back to London and one last night in the Royal Lancaster Hotel before our trip back home…did I mention that the Beatles stayed in the Royal Lancaster when they first came to London from Liverpool? In fact, I'm pretty sure I stayed in the same room John stayed in…I'm special that way. I loved England and Scotland (notwithstanding what they've done to the Irish over the years), but what's in the past, is in the past. The Queen now enjoys visiting the Emerald Isle and feels bad for the way the British treated us over the years…I'll accept that.

What a year 1992 was…Yellowstone, England, Scotland; for some, that would be a good decade. But we were just getting started. Susan and I had in common a wonder of the world and different cultures, experiencing different peoples and different sights—we couldn't get enough of it. Rightly or wrongly, our goal was to save enough money to take off again on some wonderful adventure; to actually spend our retirement money now, while we were in great health and had the lust and desire to travel and go places. We made the conscious choice to do this. We could have saved our money, as most sane, responsible people do; gone to the beach a couple of times a year—maybe the mountains; and saved a great deal of money. There are times I wish we could have done that, maybe it would have allowed me to retire from work—but, I think—retire to what? Retire from what? Life?

Susan can answer for herself, but after that first cross-country trip with mama and Anne, the die was cast for me—I only had to figure out how to achieve my goals and go to the places most people only dream of. Plus, I honestly didn't think I would ever make it to retirement—and I still might not. Why save all your money and do nothing, then die with a full bank account? That would be the essence of a wasted life, in my opinion. My dad died at 42; his two brothers died at 40 and 38; my mom died at 57…No matter how healthy you are (or think you are), your genes are your genes, and you're stuck with them for better or worse. So, with that being said, I'm pretty sure Susan and I will never have much money, but oh my gosh, what memories we have, the places we've been, the things we've seen—what a fairy tale life we've led. I truly wouldn't trade those experiences for all the dollars, euros, pounds, francs, lira, pesos and rubles in the world.

And 1992 wasn't over yet. We had enjoyed our honeymoon cruise so much that we wanted to take another one, maybe someplace different. We found one leaving from Los Angeles going down the Baja Peninsula between Christmas and New Year's, stopping at Cabo San Lucas, Mazatlan and Puerta Vallerta. Royal Caribbean's "Song of America" was our ship and we truly enjoyed the stops and the beautiful towns along the way; especially Cabo San Lucas, truly a beautifully scenic place. We took a shore excursion inland, by bus, to a remote village in the mountains, where we were supposed to enjoy an "authentic" Mexican meal…by authentic, I'm assuming they meant bland and boring—but the scenery was nice. In my opinion, you really can't have a bad time on a cruise unless you try to. It really doesn't matter where you go, cruises are fun…the scenery may change (as we'd find out on later cruises), but it was all good fun, good food and good entertainment. Royal Caribbean does cruises right!

22

My little girl turned 11 years old in February, 1993; if you have children, you understand how time flies with them and the extreme brevity of their youth. She was now enjoying lots of activities at school, such as soccer and basketball and volleyball. Whereas the soccer matches were a little boring for me to watch (but aren't all soccer matches boring to watch?), the basketball and volleyball games were great fun. Shelley was a pretty good athlete and had developed a good outside shot in basketball. Susan, Judy and I went to her games, cheered her on and tried our best to stay away from the other parents who screamed at their daughters and the referees with unabashed abandon. It was embarrassing for us, and for their own daughters on the court to be subjected to some of the torrents of abuse some of these parents inflicted on all those around them.

We continued to host our family's reunion at our house—Susan made everyone feel special and took care of everything. There wouldn't be many years left where all the remaining aunts and uncles would be in good enough health to attend. Anne and Casey couldn't come this year, but we had over 30 others who did—it was a fun, but tiring day…I don't know how Susan does it.

In early spring I heard the news that Paul McCartney had scheduled a tour date in Charlotte at an outdoor amphitheater. I was going…the question was, who else was going with me. Susan was in and Martha and Wendy surprised us by wanting to go as well. I think Martha secretly had a crush on Paul when she was growing up—but didn't we all? We drove to Charlotte in great anticipation—we were actually going to see a real live Beatle—it had been over 22 years since I'd seen my last Beatle—I was ready. The show was grand and very exciting, the fireworks display during "Live and Let Die" were extraordinary…it was truly a night I wouldn't forget.

Susan and I had been telling Jerry and Wandre how much we loved our cruises, and we finally talked them into going on one with us to the Caribbean this summer. Once again, we went with Royal Caribbean, on the ship "Nordic Empress," from July 5-9. We enjoyed our stroll through the straw market in Nassau and down the streets visiting all the shops. There was a parade, for some reason, down the main street in Nassau while we were there. Bands were marching and playing, people were dancing, they were enjoying this event in true Bahamian fashion. Susan, Jerry and I took it all in, it was very festive, fun and loud. What about Wandre, you ask? She was shopping for jewelry and missed the entire event…in fact…she didn't believe us when we told her a marching band had played its way down the street. The girl is a serious jewelry shopper.

We went to all the shows, played a little blackjack and slots, stayed up for the midnight buffet, went to the Captain's dinner, had our pictures taken with him (Susan grabbed his butt—she says by mistake, and she's sticking to that story). We went ashore at Royal Caribbean's private island and laid out by the ocean, had a few beach drinks and enjoyed the cookout; Jerry was fortunate enough to be in the hamburger line behind a young lady wearing a thong; I think it was his first real life "thong" experience, I'm not sure. But what I am sure of, is that he came back to our table with only one hamburger—he didn't bring Wandre one…blame it on the thong. The thong experience would come back to haunt him again a couple of years later.

Back home, back to work, back to school for Susan and Shelley…basketball games, volleyball games; life seems to happen so fast, at times you wonder where it all went. Susan took her 6th grade class on a field trip to Birmingham, Alabama to visit the Space Camp there; she brought Shelley along on the trip. We were making every effort to involve her in everything we could, we wanted there to be more than just the every other weekend thing in her life with us. I'd noticed that a few years ago, she stopped holding my hand when we went anywhere together; little things like that were announcing that she was growing up a little too fast for me. One troubling thing, that would make a big difference later on, was that she seemed to believe everything her little 11 year old friends would tell her—but hardly anything Susan and I would tell her. A very troubling trend that would have dire consequences a few years down the road.

I was still playing tennis, but not as frequently as I was before, (not my decision); it seems as though tennis, as a recreational sport, was fading from the social consciousness. People simply weren't playing tennis as much anymore; I know several of the guys I played with had sort of become "weekend" players and it was becoming hard to find regular games any longer. Robert had graduated from law school and he and Amy had moved to Charlotte, some guys had knee problems or physical problems and quit playing and some others had moved onto golf. It became very frustrating trying to find people to play with. And, tennis is different from most other sports in that you just can't play with anyone; it's no fun playing with someone at a different level than you are. With golf, virtually any two players can play together and still have fun, because in golf you mostly play against par and against yourself, whereas in tennis, you can't do that; a good player won't have fun playing against a beginner, and vice versa. Plus, tennis is a hard sport to learn and enjoy…you have three tennis balls, you hit them into the net, you have to walk up there, pick them up, hit them in the net again, pick them up—it really isn't fun for a beginner. What is fun is to find someone who is good, and hit the same ball back and forth 15-20 times (or more), before it goes in the net. It was becoming increasingly hard to find those types of players.

We decided to visit the Grove Park Inn again over the New Year's holiday, this time with our friends Jerry and Wandre. They loved the place as much as we did and we had a grand old time. We visited the Biltmore Estate on a very cold and windy day, I kept my ticket, it cost us $51.90 to get in then—much more these days. We rang in the New Year with hats and horns and dancing at the Grove Park, looking forward to what would lay ahead of us in the coming year.

1994 started with Susan being nominated for the NCAGT Outstanding Teacher of the Gifted Awards. Martha and Clarence and her Dad and Barbara all met us at the awards banquet in Charlotte. We were all very proud of her, especially her dad, and we had a fun night honoring all the nominees. We still kept busy with Shelley's basketball games and the life of a 12 year old…The last year before the dreaded teenage years would begin. We all knew the horror stories Bob's daughter Nancy had been telling us of her daughter, Meg, and what she'd been through when Meg was a teenager and had become rebellious. But, all children are different and all circumstances are different; really, all you can do is the best job you can, expose them to the church and Jesus and lead them as correctly as you know how. We've all known preacher's sons and daughters who were wild as hellions; and, we've known kids from broken homes, drunken parents and drug infested environments, that have become very successful and great people— bottom line is that everyone is different, and everyone will make decisions about their own lives and eventually will be the only ones to answer for their actions—good or bad. Parents can only lead them so far…in the end, each person will be held accountable and responsible for the decisions they have made. End of sermon.

We had the Townsend family reunion at our house again this year and Anne and Casey were able to fly in from Reno to attend. The aunts and uncles were still relatively healthy and we had a house full of people. Casey was 7 years old and loved visiting us; during the reunion, Casey came running up to me and said "daddy, can I have something to drink?" Oh mama! Shelley heard her call me daddy and I could see the change in her facial expression immediately. She stormed off, went inside the house to her room and closed the door…she was jealous. She didn't want anyone else, including Casey, to call me daddy; I was HER daddy, not anyone else's. Susan and I finally coaxed her out of her room and tried to explain things a little to her; but, she was going to be a little pouty the rest of the day.

Susan, Shelley and I met Anne and Casey in Florida again at Aunt Mary's house in June. By then, Shelley was okay and we had a fine time at Disney and Epcot…and an even better time visiting with Aunt Mary. This was a quick little trip, I was planning a bigger one for later in the summer—Arizona and Utah. I wanted to share with Susan some of the things I'd seen and visit some other places I'd read about and wanted to see. I was really looking forward to this.

We flew into Phoenix to rent the car and then left as quickly as possible—no further explanation needed. Our first stop was in Sedona, a beautiful, quirky little town, deep in the red rock wilderness. We just loved the scenery and ignored all the "new age" junk usually associated with Sedona; from there we went up to Prescott, Arizona, which being over 5,200 in elevation, was a welcome respite from the heat of Phoenix. Our next stop was the Grand Canyon, my seventh trip here in the last 18 years, but I wanted Susan to experience what I had; however, we weren't prepared for the human explosion there. People, people, people everywhere, I had never seen it like this before. We went to several view points, but tried to stay away from the main crowds—it was still beautiful—just congested, I won't come back here in the summertime. I wanted us to hike down the canyon some (not all the way), we picked a less traveled route, the Kaibab trail, rather than the Bright Angel trail, which I'd done twice before. We walked down for a little over an hour, then came back up…great views, this trail followed a ridge line, which was different from the others. It was a good day, but we were ready to leave the crowds. I really wanted Susan to see the most beautiful man- made lake in the world, so we left the crowds and drove up to Lake Powell, my third trip there. The lake is the product of a massive dam on the Colorado River at beautiful, yet now lost forever, Glen Canyon. Before we leave here, Susan and I will take a raft ride from the bottom of the dam, down the Colorado River for about four hours. I wish we could've taken this raft trip years ago before Glen Canyon was flooded—what a loss— certainly, the most awesome, scenic canyon that no one will ever see again, just so the good people of Phoenix and Los Angeles can have the water they don't deserve. Really, how stupid can men be to build huge cities in the middle of deserts, with limited water supplies? Calm down Gar…it'll be okay.

However, Lake Powell is awesome, incredibly blue waters set amid the reddish sandstone of this heartbreakingly beautiful country. We took the tour boat trip out on the lake to the far end where we got off the boat and made the short walk over to Rainbow Bridge—a huge sandstone arch, over a hundred feet tall. The Navajo thought if you walked in the arch's shadow, you would die; so we took no chances. Only took pictures and marveled at a truly marvelous sight. The lake had changed somewhat from my previous boat trip here…before it was fairly remote and the lake had very little traffic on it and not much around it. Now, however, there were hotels and restaurants and marinas and gift shops all along the shore; and, water skiers, houseboats, fishermen and the pesky, interminable jet skiers, buzzing all around us. Good thing you're not around to see these eyesores Ed…it's pretty sad.

Before we left the Lake Powell region there was a remote spot I wanted to visit that was still under the radar for most people…Antelope Canyon. I'd known of it for years, but had never been able to arrange a visit—now was the time. It is located on a Navaho Indian reservation near the Arizona/Utah border, which means you just can't drive up to it, it's on Navaho property…thus private. You must arrange a tour with a Navaho guide taking only a limited number of people on each trip. The so-called canyon, is actually a split in a vast rock wall; the wall is about 80-100' tall, and the crack in the wall ranges from 6-12' wide—this crack or split winds on for about 200 yards. Since it's so tall and the split is only about 10' wide from top to bottom, sunlight does not reach into the depths of this canyon until the sun is almost directly overhead. Maybe an hour or an hour and a half at best, is it light enough to see, the rest of the day it's dark, pitch dark throughout the entire maze. But, Lord have mercy, when the sunlight enters and starts bouncing off those rounded, contoured, smoothed, sandstone walls, it is like no other colors you will ever see on this earth…reds, pinks, yellows, oranges, and every salmon-colored hue in between—a French impressionist's dream; something out of Timothy Leary's mind, or Salvador Dali's imagination!

We arrive there, with our guide, about 11:30 in the morning; we see the split in the wall, which is about 8-10' wide at the opening, and it's very dark inside. The guide tells us to wait while he takes a flashlight and a large stick and goes it to scare all the rattlesnakes out…which is where they go to escape the Arizona heat. I have no problem waiting. 15-20 minutes later he comes out, tells us it's safe and that the sunlight is now beginning to enter the slot canyon…we are excited. We were in there the entire time it was light enough to see, somewhere over an hour I'm guessing—it was so surreal, time got away from us. I used up every bit of film I had and cursed myself for not bringing more (the days before digital cameras). I really shouldn't be telling anyone about this place, but I'm guessing that maybe only 3 or 4 people will ever read this, so it's pretty safe the word won't get out…this amazing place needs to be kept out of the tourist mainframe, and remain what it was that glorious August day Susan and I were lucky enough to visit.

I wanted to find a photo shop and have my film developed immediately, but Page, Arizona didn't offer those services at the time; so, Susan ushered me into the car and off we went into the vast unknown of northern Arizona and southern Utah. Land of broken cliffs and broken hearts, mazes that can render a man senseless and defenseless; land of no water, no vegetation, no life, nothing flat, nothing living, nothing dying…mother's: don't let your children enter this country; certainly their hearts will be broken by this heartless, deserted, misunderstood scrabble of land.

We take the long road eastward, around the Grand Canyon, finally crossing the Colorado River over a bridge 1000' above the river—the next crossing spot is 150 miles downstream. We make our way over to the more remote north rim of the Grand Canyon, which is about 1000' higher than the south rim: still spectacular, whether you're looking from 8000' or 9000'. One day, I would like to do the "rim-to-rim" hike from one side to the other, before I get too old, or lose the desire to inflict pain on myself, whereupon, I'll just sit in my lazy boy recliner, eat ice cream and Doritos and see how many ballgames I can watch before nodding off into old age oblivion. Let me continue my story here before melancholia completely takes over.

I wanted Susan to see Zion Canyon…why? Because it's spectacular and not on the main tourist grid. It doesn't have the traffic and crowds that the Grand Canyon does…it's more remote and wild. And, because I'd been there before and I wanted to share it with her—selfish reasons. If you want a description of Zion…too bad; go see it yourself; get out of the car, walk the trails, climb the mountains, ford the streams, let the Virgin River wash away your cares and troubles— at least for a few days.

We eventually make our way back around to Monument Valley…you know the place, you've seen it hundreds of times on TV and in the movies. It's the classic western setting; John Wayne made about 100 movies here. It's the place where an old Indian once told Judy that his horse ain't got no name—it don't need one…it's just a horse! From Monument Valley (where I bought an amazing piece of Indian pottery for $39) to Canyon de Chelly, we had covered all we set out to see; and had a ball doing it. As we arrived in Flagstaff, the last night before flying home, we passed through a late afternoon thunderstorm and as it cleared, there was the most beautiful "double rainbow" I'd ever seen; as we neared the hotel, I jumped out of the car to capture this amazing image…and I did. I couldn't wait to get back home and see what it looked like on film.

When I had it finally developed, it looked as amazing as I thought it would, so did the McDonald's sign right under it that I never saw!

The year ended on a sad note: Bob died in December. He had moved back to Philadelphia to be near Nancy and his grandchildren; we missed him, but knew he was lonely and wanted to be around his family. His health had not been good for a couple of years, and after the move back, he really started having problems. My last phone conversation with him was telling, he said, "Gary, I'm tired, I'm just ready to go." I knew what he meant, and I knew we'd better get up there soon if we wanted to see him before he dies. Susan and I made flight reservations for the next weekend. Nancy would pick us up at the airport and take us directly to the hospital. When we arrived, she was there waiting on us, and upon looking at her—we knew. Bob had died on our flight up there, he just wanted to go home, to be with mama again and to be with the Lord.

23

1995 saw my little girl turn into a teenager…Lord have mercy on us all. Shelley had become one of her school's best athletes and most important players on the volleyball and basketball teams; and she was almost as tall as her mama and Susan—amazing how fast they grow up. It wouldn't be long before she wouldn't want anything to do with me, so I tried to plan some things for us to do together that she might remember. She'd always gone with me to Wake Forest basketball and football games, but I could tell that no matter how much I wanted her to enjoy these events, it was just not her thing. I hired someone to give her tennis lessons, which she didn't like, and other physical things, but swimming was about the only outdoor activity she was interested in. We did go on a canoe trip together down the New River, which I thought was pretty cool; I think she was just happy when it was over. I found out quickly that it's not easy to entertain a teenage girl. Seemingly, her friends were becoming more and more important to her, and her parents less and less—I guess that's normal, but it does hurt your feelings a little.

Susan went on another school trip to Russia, she enjoyed these trips taking kids from her school to foreign countries; somehow, she had come to really love Russia. She had met a lady over there that painted the hand-made matryoshka dolls herself…sometimes using only one horsehair to paint the delicate parts of it. Susan would order some from her, and the lady would have them ready for her when she arrived in Russia—they are all very well done and attractive; and Susan has quite a collection of them. I missed her when she was away on these trips, but she loved it so much, I never complained or said anything. She truly loved teaching and being involved in these trips; they offered her the opportunity to visit places most of us never see…Russian, Korea, Scandinavia, as well as the more popular places like England and Denmark.

Uncle Paul had the reunion at his house again, and maybe for the last time, all the uncles and aunts were relatively healthy. It was always nice to see the cousins every year, but it was mama's brothers and sister that made it so special. I've written before how these people were (and still are) my heroes, the things they did and accomplished in their lives is truly amazing, yet they never talk of it or discuss those events—as great as they may be. I would be truly neglectful if I didn't mention their names here, for they had a major impact on my life: Branson Earl Townsend, parachuted into Normandy on D-Day, 1944; G.C. Townsend, Jr., winner of the Silver Star in the Pacific; Alfred Paul Townsend, WWII vet and probably the best man I've ever known—ever; Charles Donald Townsend, Korean War veteran and a wonderful man; and my

Aunt Mary, who loved me almost as much as my mama did. All of them and my mom, born of Grover Cleveland Townsend and the beautiful, sweet as cotton candy, Ida Elizabeth Townsend. What an enduring legacy they have all left behind…I am truly blessed to be a part of this family.

Susan and I had a busy summer planned; somehow, I had a little money available and it was burning up my pockets. But first, Jerry and Wandre had invited us to join them for a long weekend in Hilton Head, S.C. Why not? I hadn't been there before and it was always fun to see Jer and Wandre, even if we did nothing but sit around and talk. Since Wandre and Susan were both in the school system, they could converse with each other non-stop, they didn't need us around, except to pay the bills at dinner. So, old Jer and I were free to discuss man-stuff…ball games, thongs, running, the lives of our friends (Dickie, Larry, Allen, Bill, etc.), or anything else in the world—except WORK. We kept that four letter word where it belonged…in the closet. During these man talks, we solved nearly every world problem, and nearly all of Dickie's problems…sadly enough, neither Dickie nor Presidents, nor Prime Ministers paid any attention to us—their loss.

There's usually one destination that all Americans would love to visit, but sadly, never do: Alaska! The last frontier, the frozen wilderness, wild and wonderful Alaska…how best to observe this majestic landscape? Cruise ship of course! You may read this and think I jest, but no, if you investigate, you'll see that almost all Alaskan cities are on the coast (there are a few exceptions, like Fairbanks, but not many). Plus, the inland mountain ranges come right up to the sea, leaving few level spots to actually build cities. And, mostly, there are no roads between the few cities; it's either boats or planes if you want to travel. So, cruise ships make perfect sense to visit different locales and see the majestic mountain ranges from the comfort of your stateroom or, your friendly ship bar (my choice).

We set sail on July 2 for the Alaskan cities of Skagway, Haines and Juneau and Ketchikan, plus stops in the Misty Fjords and Glacier Bay…doesn't that sound groovy? Glacier Bay! The first thing I noticed about Alaska was the snow covered mountains in view all the way up the coast; if you never left the ship, you'd still have amazing scenery. In Ketchikan, we pulled into the docks and there must have been 60-70 eagles perched on the docks and floating around the sky; I've never been this close to them before…huge, majestic birds. It was cool and drizzly in Ketchikan, which leads the U.S. in annual rainfall totals; but we enjoyed our walks up and down the muddy streets and shops there.

In Skagway, we took a train ride into the interior, across the Canadian border, and into the wilderness; it was less than thrilling. However, the helicopter ride we took from Juneau up to a glacier was fantastic. They dropped us off on top of the glacier, then flew away and left us up there for about an hour and a half. We had these "glacier boots" to wear to help grip the ice so we wouldn't fall, or worse yet, fall into one of the deep, blue crevasses all over the glacier. Back in Juneau, we walked all over this capital city, past the governor's mansion and down most of the streets, which still have many Russian Orthodox churches sitting around. I liked Juneau, a cozy little town, easy to walk, right up against the ocean and the mountains.

On each stop the ship made, one of the shore excursions was some type of fishing trip—obviously, we didn't do that, but some people from our dinner table did. If you caught anything, mainly salmon, the ship's cooks would clean it and prepare it for you that night at dinner; which they did at our table—we did not partake. However, we did take a float plane trip into the interior that was fantastic. First time I'd been on a float plane and for some reason, I thought it would be rough taking off and landing—in fact, it was the opposite. It was much smoother than regular flights, I honestly couldn't tell when we left the water taking off, nor could I tell when we landed back on the water—it was that smooth.

That plane trip took us over the mountains, into the interior for about 30 minutes—nothing but mountains everywhere you look—all mountains with these little lakes between the peaks. The pilot pointed out one tiny little speck to us and said that's where we're going to land. What? From our vantage point, it looked like a mud puddle…we kept circling, getting lower and lower, but the water never did seem like it would be large enough for us to land on—I was a little concerned. We finally made the dip towards the lake, surrounded by trees, and we landed so effortlessly and smoothly, I had to look out the window to actually believe we had landed. The pilot glided to a stop and turned the engine off and the quietness overwhelmed us.

There were 8 passengers on the little plane and we could actually get out and walk up and down the pontoons of the landing gears. No traffic to hear, no ambient noise of any kind, it was surreal how quiet it actually was. When I spoke to Susan, I felt as though I was disturbing nature. The pilot told us that because we were so far inland and below the mountain peaks that he had no radio coverage from our location. I immediately thought what would happen if the engines didn't start back up? How would we call anyone to help us? How would they ever find us? Flying above the mountain peaks, this little lake (which turned out to be not so little), was just a speck in the landscape, certainly our little plane would be impossible to see. The land in Alaska is so BIG, that you lose any sense of scale you have as to how big things actually are.

We stayed floating on the lake for 15-20 minutes or so, then piled back in the plane; the pilot lifted off again effortlessly and circled back around the unnamed lake one more time, and then back to the coast and the ship we flew. An amazing trip, it seems unfair to describe this experience in only a couple of paragraphs, but I'm not capable of translating into words the memories and scenes of that trip…I wish I could.

We walked around the little town of Haines and visited some shops there, we heard a clerk in one store telling a group of us that the day before, he saw a bear and a moose get into a fight out in front of his store. Ordinarily, you'd never believe anyone telling a story like that; but in Alaska—I believe it. Our trip continued through the Misty Fjords and into Glacier Bay. I truly don't know if global warming is happening or not—I'm not going to debate the issue with anyone, because I don't think anyone else knows either—not for sure. However, if something is happening and the world is warming up, I'm glad I got to see Glacier Bay while it is still glacierized. An incredible sight that takes your breath away! The cruise ship approaches very slowly, because there are icebergs all over the bay itself—some small, some large. The large ones could severely damage the ship and its propellers, so we proceed with risk. Remembering from high school, icebergs are only 10% visible, as many icebergs as there were, certainly beneath the ocean had to be absolutely cluttered with ice. I wanted to get closer to the actual wall of ice that was the glacier, but the ship couldn't risk that, there was too much ice in the water. Maybe next time we could get closer (in a few years, we would!).

Usually, on a cruise ship, the ship itself and all the activities are the main attractions: the dinners and food, the midnight buffet, the fantastic shows, the night clubs, the casino, the pools, the bars, etc., etc. As I've said before, the only way to not have a good time is to try not to. However, on an Alaskan cruise, the scenery is the star—by a good, wide margin. I knew we'd do this trip again and I was already looking forward to it.

Alaska was grand and I loved it, however, the west was still calling me; a thirst I couldn't quench, an itch I couldn't scratch…almost as though I was addicted to it and could only truly breathe when I was there. I wanted to experience some of the things my literary hero had experienced and somehow transfigure his words and passages into my life. To do this, I needed to get out to southeastern Utah, the most beautiful place in the world, escape the prison a car can often be, get on my own two feet, see the landscape up close and personal. Drink water from a forgotten stream, scrape my knees on the sandstone, skin my arms and legs on juniper and pinyon pines, let my ankles bleed from cactus needles—leave some of my DNA there for eternity. This is what I had to do…how would I do it?

Red Rock and Llamas, Inc.—that's how. A small outfit that would take us into the remote, wilderness areas in and around, Escalante, Moab and Boulder, Utah. Carrying your supplies for a week on the backs of llamas and what you could carry yourself—bare essentials: food, tents, sleeping bags, water purifiers, and in my case, a camera. The trip I wanted left in October from Boulder, Utah and went into the vast wilderness areas surrounding the Escalante River basin. The closest towns would be at least 50 miles away—as the crow flies, 100 miles driving distance. My birthday would fall in the middle of the trip—what better way to spend it than being surrounded by the eternal beauty and nothingness of this broken, creased, burnt and magnificent landscape.

I met Steve, our guide, and my two companions for the trip in the little town of Boulder, where we, and the llamas, would be transported by Steve's wife to a remote drop-off point. My two companions were a married couple from England (Nigel and Margaret)…we each had a llama assigned to us and we could not pack more than 75 pounds on the llama's back—everything was weighed and inventoried—better to be sure, than to get out there and realize we forgot something. The llamas were, for the most part, very agreeable and easy to handle; we were told that the reputation they had for spitting was overrated, but they greatly deserved one for kicking their back leg out—they did not like anyone standing directly behind them and would lash out with their rear leg with debilitating force. I took heed. The llamas, as with the Navaho horse, had no names, however, I thought my particular llama was a great beauty and thus I named her Doris, after another great beauty—my mom. Doris and I hit it off immediately, as soon as she let me know who the boss was—HER! We walked when Doris wanted to and stopped when

Doris wanted to, ate when Doris saw something yummy, and urinated and defecated when Doris had the urge—usually at most inopportune times.

We hiked most of the first day, only stopping for lunch, finally arrived at our camping spot in late afternoon—how far we'd hiked, I had no idea; I only know Doris and I were tired and hungry. We pitched tents next to 10' long pool of water that had accumulated in a sandstone depression; Doris and the other unnamed llamas could freely drink of this water—not us. It had probably been left there by summer thunderstorms and was black and scummy looking. We got out the water purifiers and started the slow process of making potable drinking water—it took about an hour to get one quart of water. We had all emptied the canteens we'd brought during the hike, so we were anxious to get some water available; the first hour got us one quart, split four ways—the taste reminded me of the spring water we'd had at the tennis courts at Flora McDonald college, back home…smelly, but very tasty.

We erected our tents and Steve got the small grill fired up, plenty of juniper and pinyon wood lying around, the scent of those two woods burning is sweetness to the senses. Most western states have beautiful Indian summer days in October, no rain, clear sunny skies and around 80 degrees in the daytime. But, when the sun goes down, with very low humidity and relatively high elevations, it gets cold fast. Within 15 minutes, we go from warm and comfortable, to jackets, gloves and toboggans. Steve has a fire pit started and we gather around it to get some warmth from the meager flames and eat our dinner for the evening. There's lots of things I never thought of that camping in the wilderness implies. First, there is no bathroom…we had a 3' pit we dug in the ground, which we all used; and a plastic bag to put the used toilet paper in—when camping in the wilderness, the only thing you leave behind are footprints. You carry everything in and you carry everything out—no matter how nasty it may seem. Then, the little things such as no water to brush your teeth, no showers, no mirrors, one small pillow and no pad to lay your sleeping bag on—sandstone is hard—trust me.

It got dark around 7:00 PM and after dinner and talking for a while, we each go off to our own tents, which we set up quite a ways from each other to allow for a little privacy—especially for Nigel and Margaret. We tied our llamas to a tree near our tent so they wouldn't wander off during the night…Steve was concerned with mountain lions attacking them if they were left alone. We had no flashlights or candles (weight restrictions), just laying on sandstone, in the dark, from about 9:00 at night until the next morning is not a lot of fun. I know I slept some, but I also know I didn't sleep much—it was hard. At some point during the night, when all was as quiet as quiet can be, Doris sneezed! Having never heard a llama sneeze before, I wasn't sure if a mountain lion was attacking us or if Big Foot had invaded our camp—it scared the daylights out of me. I peeked out of my tent and saw Doris looking back at me, and she sneezed again; and I could have sworn I saw her smiling at me…maybe it was just the moonlight. Steve would not let me tie Doris up too far from my tent, mountain lions, so I endured the entire week, listening to Doris sneeze, then smile at me…her way of reasserting herself as boss.

After waking up and warming up, we would hike all day to some remote, incredibly, indescribable, canyon, or plateau, or scraggly, rocky, thorny, place that very few human beings have ever seen. The hard, cold nights and sand in your food, sand in your nose, in your mouth, in your bellybutton and everyplace in between—was worth it, for those views. We hiked down canyons where the canyon walls fell straight down into a stream—no side banks to walk on, so we sloshed through the little streams; the water coming up to mid-shin level—sometimes higher. We were tracked by a mountain lion through that canyon (we saw his tracks on top of ours), we tried to immerse ourselves in some places where the water had pooled –just to get some of the grime off, but the water was so cold, it was hard to do. By now, we were used to each other's odors and we didn't really care. We saw age old pictographs and petroglyphs, found pottery shards and few arrow points—but left everything just as we found it—per Steve's instructions—and rightly so.

I celebrated my birthday without announcing it to my mates…it was my special day and I chose to spend it with the red rocks, junipers, cactus and Doris—it was a nice birthday present to myself. I remember every day we hiked there, I remember the nights around the fire, listening to Doris sneeze, eating Steve's wife's homemade cookies and seemingly always waiting for our water to pass through the purifier. Golden memories…I wouldn't trade that trip for anything, except maybe a softer bed.

Steve's wife met us at the end of the week, we hugged each other and promised to stay in touch—we didn't; again, my fault for not making the effort with Nigel and Margaret, they were a very nice couple and made the week better just by being there. I took my grimy self and my nasty belongings, packed them in the car and headed to Las Vegas to catch my flight home in the morning. A long drive, but filled with beauty, if you knew where to look. As I was driving down a lonely stretch of two lane in the remote Utah back country, I spotted a small herd of deer way off to my right. They were running as a group toward the highway, several hundred yards ahead of me; I slowed down a little to observe them longer, but they never slowed down—I didn't see anything chasing them and have no clue why they were running as they were. As bad as I was at math and geometry, I could easily tell that their course and my speed would soon intersect at the highway, if they didn't change direction. I started blowing my horn and flashing my lights, they kept on coming; I slowed, they kept on coming—I sincerely believed they would change their course and veer off. It was broad daylight and no trees to obscure their vision…but they kept on coming. At the last moment, I thought they were going to stop, but they didn't, a couple ran right in front of my car, one leapt over the hood, its hooves hitting my windshield and the last one ran smack into the side of my car, knocking the side rearview mirror off and putting a good dent in the door. I flinched and screamed, only to look in the rear view mirror to see that deer rolling over and over down the road. I stopped and ran back to the deer, it was obviously dead, I could not believe what had just happened. How could they not see me, honking my horn and flashing my lights? How could this have happened? It took me quite a while to actually stop shaking, I didn't stop thinking about it for weeks—I can still see that deer rolling over and over in my mirror.

As the sun went down that night on my drive to Vegas, the moon rose right in front of me. The largest, brightest moon I've ever seen; it was as though the moon had entered earth's atmosphere. Maybe it was the low humidity and clear skies of remote Utah, but all I know is that I had to put on my sunglasses for a few minutes that night, driving into that incredibly bright moon. I finally made it to Vegas about midnight, got into my room at the relatively cheap Circus Circus, and took a LONG, hot shower. It took quite a bit of scrubbing and washing to get Utah off my skin; fortunately, it would never wash out of my mind.

24

"Dream until your dream comes true."

Early in 1996, my uncle G.C.'s wife died; Ginny and uncle G.C. had 6 children and lots of love in their family. Aunt Ginny's main topic of conversation was her health, and she loved to tell all who would listen about every ailment and pain she had, or had ever had. I'd known her from my earliest memories as a kid and she was always the same…honestly, we never knew if she was really sick, or she just liked the attention being sick afforded her. However, when she died, Uncle G.C. was indeed heartbroken…I can't imagine the lonely feelings he must have known then. She was the first of our immediate aunts and uncles to pass away; we wanted to ignore the fact that everyone was getting older, that health problems were more serious now—we wanted things to always stay the same; but life isn't like that. Death is a part of life and we would visit this part of our lives many, unwelcome times in the next few years.

As a side note to this story, today's date (the day I'm actually writing this) is Saturday July 26, 2014, I had a heart attack this past Wednesday, July 23…obviously, I survived. More on the details and drama surrounding this day when it comes to the year in question. But, I wanted it noted, just in case I don't make it to that year in this narrative—you'll know why I didn't finish. I've always felt a little invincible, (which is pretty absurd given my family history), but I always thought I'd live for a great, long time. I've always been competitive and usually won at everything I tried—I had no reason to believe life would be any different…until this past Wednesday. Things are different now, my life's views are different, the way I feel is different; I might even be a little scared.

More later…onward in 1996; the year started with a big snowstorm in January, we had lots of limbs down, we lost power for a few days—pretty severe for N.C.—but we survived. Susan made another school trip to Russia, and we all continued attending Shelley's basketball and volleyball games. For Shelley's birthday, I was taking everyone out to dinner at a nice restaurant, Judy, Susan, Shelley and a friend of hers, Lynn. I went over to Judy's house to pick them all up and take a few pictures and my little girl had on makeup! Not just some makeup…a LOT of makeup; the lipstick made her lips look twice as big as they should be; I'm guessing, she thought if a little makeup made you pretty, then a lot of makeup would make you gorgeous. It was a struggle to keep my comments to myself and not ruin her birthday…but you should see those pictures now!

Another family reunion at Uncle Paul's and except for missing Aunt Ginny, everyone else was fairly healthy. In early spring we met Jerry and Wandre in Pinehurst for a long weekend. There, we formulated a great plan for an awesome adventure this summer...we would all go to California and explore that wonderland together. They'd never been before and wanted to me to make all the plans and arrangements, which I did. So many places to see, so many things to do; the problem was picking out which things to bypass...we only had one week. We flew into LA and stayed there overnight, checked out Hollywood, Rodeo Drive, ate some chocolate hot dogs, walked around Venice Beach and out on the pier, but we were really interested in leaving the city and travelling north. I'd told them how beautiful Highway 1 was on the drive up to San Francisco, and we wanted to spend some time in and around Carmel Bay.

We had a car with a GPS onboard, first time I'd ever seen that, or experienced it—we loved it. Up the coast we went, stopping at the fantastic overviews of the Pacific from the heights of the Coastal Range Mountains...very easy to use up several rolls of film on this beautiful scenery. As we neared Carmel, we stopped at a restaurant called Margueritaville, what better way to cap off our drive than to taste the namesake of the restaurant. We each ordered a tall one and before we knew it, we were all giggling and sloppy and pretty much unable to even to walk to the restroom. We never found out what they put in those drinks, but Lordy, were they strong. After we sobered up a little, we drove onto Carmel that afternoon to find a little place on Carmel Bay that had recently become famous in a Visa commercial...The Seven Gables Inn. Located right on the bay front, the Inn was fantastic, each of our rooms had a "gabled" window overlooking the ocean; exactly as we had hoped it would be. We stayed there three nights (and wished we could've stayed more), breakfast each morning was a feast of traditional items along with fresh fruits and juices and muffins. There would be a fruit plate on our table with varieties ranging from strawberries, cantaloupes, to blueberries, kiwi, mandarin oranges and watermelon. The problem was that the watermelon was always prized by me and Jerry both and we would each try to arrive at the breakfast table first to get the prime pieces of watermelon—without seeming to be obvious about it. I know Jerry well, and I know he would give me the shirt off his back if I needed it—and I would do the same for him—except when it came to watermelon!

The third, and last, morning there Jerry beat me down for breakfast and had the most luscious piece of watermelon on his plate when we arrived, the only piece left was a tiny chunk of half melon and half rind...DANG! Beaten again. Suddenly, I came up with a fantastic plan, knowing Jerry's proclivity and admiration for thongs, it was certain to be successful. As we finished saying grace and thanking the Lord for all He has blessed us with, I looked over Jerry's shoulder, out the window, (at nothing) and said, "Great day in the morning, Jer, look at that girl in the thong!" He jerked his head around so fast you would have thought Linda Blair was in control of his body—as he was searching for the non-existent thong, I stole the watermelon from his plate. Never have I had such a sweet piece of fruit in my life—before or since. Sorry buddy, but you've gotta do what you've gotta do.

Jerry and I went for morning runs along the waterfront while the girls got ready, we toured the amazing Monterey Bay Aquarium, had dinner in Clint Eastwood's Hog's Breath Inn pub, walked the beach at Carmel and shopped in the quaint little shops there. We went to Monterey and visited Cannery Row and I bought about a dozen John Steinbeck novels—it was a glorious, fabulous three days, capped off with the most amazing little drive you'll ever have—the 17-mile drive in Carmel-by-the-Sea. (it's actually only 13 miles long, but who's counting?). This drive takes you through the world famous golf courses, including Pebble Beach, where we walked around and bought some shirts and souvenirs from the club house. Jerry bought a gorgeous Pebble Beach jacket and wore it handsomely for several years. I walked out to the first tee and imagined what it would feel like to actually play golf on this little piece of heaven. Green fees this day in 1996 were $350…it would be worth it.

We hated to leave the Monterey Peninsula, it was something special; but we had scheduled to meet Anne and Casey in San Francisco for the July 4 holiday, so we grudgingly and sadly packed our bags and said adieu to the Seven Gables Inn and what John Steinbeck called "the greatest meeting of land and water in the world." I have no argument with that. San Francisco was, as always, gorgeous. We drove over the bridge and visited Sausalito and drove the little winding road up to the overlook of San Francisco, with the Golden Gate Bridge in the foreground…I won't try, because words can't describe it. We met Anne and Casey and all took a boat ride in the bay, past Alcatraz Island, out under the Golden Gate and back again with amazing views of the city. We capped off that night on the waterfront with the most incredible 4th of July fireworks display I'd ever seen. The next day, Anne and Casey went back to Reno; we shopped along waterfront and piers, had dinner at a restaurant at the end of a pier and watched the sun set through the bridge and sink down into the vast Pacific ocean as we sat and gazed in wonder.

I have to break the timeline of this so-called life story once more…my good friends Larry McRacken and Bill Coleman just came to visit me (Sunday, July 27, 2014); Larry drove from Jacksonville, NC to pick up Bill in Cary, NC and they both came here to Winston Salem to visit me and see how I was from the heart attack adventure. That's the kind of friends they are. And, Bill is dying from pancreatic cancer…the doctors have told him he has less than 3 months to live…he's in pain physically and emotionally, yet he had Larry drive him two hours down here to see how I was doing, eat lunch, then drive back—all while experiencing severe back and stomach pain from the cancer. And, for Larry it's been a 4 1/2 hour one way trip to get here. I am not worthy to have friends this good, certainly don't deserve it; but am extremely grateful and humbled that I do.

It reminds me of when George Harrison was dying from cancer at a clinic in Switzerland; he was flat on his back and couldn't lift his head off the pillow, days from death when Ringo visited him to say goodbye. After spending the afternoon together, Ringo told him he had to leave to catch a flight to Boston, where his daughter was having brain surgery the following day. George tried his best to lift his head off the pillow, looked Ringo in the eye and said, "Do you want me to come with you?" That's Bill, that's Larry, that's Dickie, that's Allen, and that's Jerry…

Back to the future of 1996…before school started for Susan, we planned another adventure; this one with my pretty little sister, (Casey was away at gym camp), to the awesomeness of the Canadian Rockies. We arrived in Calgary, rented our car and took off for the mountains—none of us had been here before, and were anxious to see what Canada had to offer. We stopped along the way at a restaurant that served steamed, or boiled (I'm not sure which), corn on the cob; all three of us concluded this was absolutely the best corn we'd ever had. It came to us right off the stalk—you had to shuck the corn at the table yourself; somehow, this trapped in the flavor and juices and aroma of the corn that made it unlike anything we'd experienced before…the trip had started off well.

We drove to the little mountain town of Banff, high in the Rockies, set amidst the grandeur and panoramic views of the glaciated Rocky Mountains. We awoke the next morning, from the little cabin we'd rented, to find several elk asleep in our little front yard. That was different. We shopped in Banff and all bought identical, matching red and white sweatshirts that read CANADA across the front, which we all still have by the way. We rode the mountain lanes, were awed by the unbroken beauty of the still snowcapped mountains, we hiked many trails and viewed unnamed vistas, ridges, peaks and valleys. On one hike, it started raining on us, then it sleeted, and finally snowed on us…as they say in the mountains, "if you don't like the weather, just wait 15 minutes." On the top of one peak, we sat down to rest and a Canadian jay alighted on my foot and stared at me. Why? It either wanted to ask me something, or tell me something…I didn't know which; at that point in time, I sure wish I'd known how to speak bird to know what was on its mind.

We visited Lake Louise, famous for the indescribable color of the water (which means, I can't describe it…you'll have to go there and see for yourself); listened to a Scottish bagpipe band play at the Lake Louise Hotel, bought a large bag of cherries from a roadside stand and ate every one of them—turning our fingers, lips and teeth cherry red. We traveled up national park roads, clogged with mountain goats, elk, deer and big horn sheep…all of which came up to our stopped car and ate cookies from our hands. One elk forced its massive head inside the window of our car, slobbered all over the seat, and Anne, ate a couple of cookies, then left us screaming with laughter, awe and wonder. We drove from Banff to Jasper National Park, absorbing more beauty than we imagined was possible in this remote wilderness; we saw a mama bear and three little cubs off to the side of the road scrounging for berries in the thickets—we did not let them eat from our hands. But we ate up the atmosphere of this vast region, longed for more time to explore and were extremely happy we'd decided to visit this wonderland that is the Canadian Rockies.

1996 was a magical year for me, but in a sense it was a sad year as well; I'd lost my passion for tennis. Most of the guys I'd been playing with, moved on, or aged out of competitive tennis; and as I mentioned earlier, tennis was a dying sport—people just didn't play any longer. It was so hard to find matches, that I'd become discouraged and disenchanted with the process. One fall Saturday, a guy who Anne went to college with, called me to see if I'd like to play; honestly, I didn't want to, I can't describe the feeling now (or then), but I just didn't want to. But, I agreed, because he'd been on my tennis team for a few years and had the best fake laugh I'd ever seen. For descriptive purposes, I'll call this fellow Johnny...well, I'd played Johnny many, many times over the years; he'd never won a set from me. In fact, most of the sets weren't close. But, this day—I didn't care—ME, master of competitiveness—did not care. Johnny beat me 6-0 / 6-0. All I could think of from the first point to the last was "I want to go home." When the last point was over, I shook his hand, packed my tennis bag, went home and didn't play again for over 10 years.

Allen, Jerry, Dickie, Larry, and Susan

25

Susan and I visited Las Vegas in January, 1997...it's similar to a cruise ship in that the only way to have a bad time, is to try to have a bad time; and trust me, there are people who do. We didn't. We liked to visit all the spectacular new casinos on the Strip and see how they all tried to outdo each other: the MGM Grand, The Luxor, Caesar's Palace, The Bellagio, New York, New York, Paris, etc., etc., etc. We were especially looking forward to this trip because we had tickets to see the magic show of Siegfried and Roy playing at the Mirage. Incredible show! You know in your pragmatic mind that these tigers are not actually disappearing, but when you sit in that audience and "see" them disappear...well, it's truly amazing. I'm glad we were able to experience that before the accident to Roy stopped their shows.

We had another vacation planned during the summer with Jerry and Wandre, this one at their urging—a visit to Jamaica and the resort villas of Sandals. An excellent choice. Sandal's had three locations in Montego Bay; of course, we stayed at the best one. All food and meals and all drinks were included in the price, as well as all beach activities and excursions; we took advantage of all these. We went out to a reef and I snorkeled for the first time in my life—the others did not, they were satisfied to watch me and soak up the sun's golden rays on board. All I can say is "wow," I had no idea snorkeling was that much fun, or that you could see so well under water. Truly, with my mask on, I could see as well under water as I could above water—it was that clear! Fish of all sizes and colors, reefs and underwater plants that were indescribable...it was a virtual wonderland that had eluded me for nearly 47 years.

Jerry and I also went parasailing, harnessed together, floating over the sea like two convicts freed from prison, looking for adventure. Great fun until the Jamaicans in the boat pulling us decided to suddenly slow down, losing our air and dunking us in the ocean with no notice. It happened so fast, we didn't know what was happening...one moment we're soaring like eagles, the next, we're under water struggling to breathe. I don't know why, or how, we held onto our cameras as we were dunked—but we did. When the Jamaicans sped up the boat and the sail pulled us back into the sky, we looked around, figured out we weren't dead, and saw the crazy Jamaicans laughing at us in the boat. At that moment, I wished our friend Allen was with us to punch those wacked out rasta boys smack in the nose...that would have been sweet. We made it back to the shore, however, had a Jamaican beach drink, a hamburger and some fries, and sat next to the two prettiest girls on the beach while we dried out. The rest of the afternoon, old Jer kept rubbing his eyes and complaining of foggy vision—we figured the dunking in the ocean and the salt water had upset his sensitive little eyes...but no, we later learned that Jer had lost a contact during our dunking and that was the reason everything was looking foggy to him—now, we really needed Allen to punch those guys in the nose!

When we arrived in Montego Bay, we were waiting in line to pass through customs and saw O.J.'s lawyer, Johnnie Cochran standing in line next to us, with his full entourage of hangers-on...he was world famous at this point in time. We wondered if there would be any other celebrities on the island with us...we didn't have to wait long to find out. Jerry and I were in a little boat with 6 other people, taking us out to do some water activity, and sitting directly across from us—our feet actually touching hers, was the singer Cheryl Crow. She noticed our wedding bands and pretended not to be interested...but Jerry and I could see that look in her eyes...right Jer? We snubbed Cheryl, and continued with our activities: drinking, slumbering, eating, drinking, napping and trying to solve all of Dickie's problems. We weren't up to the task. But we did do some ocean kayaking, some paddle boating and visited the other Sandal resorts on the island (not as nice as ours); we gorged on a poolside buffet that included every type of food mankind has ever invented—then, being totally stuffed, we went to an exclusive Italian restaurant and did nothing but move the food around on our plate. We were gluttons, tempted by the aromas of succulent Caribbean cuisines, unable to control our desires and our cravings—oh, how sweet it was!

***

Back home again, I started doing some running, not much, 3-5 miles around the neighborhood; I had to find something since tennis was gone—I just didn't know what. Martha and Clarence had their combined 50th birthday parties in August and it was a big celebration; too big really, when all 50 candles were lit and blown out, the smoke almost set off the fire alarm. We had a big Halloween party at our house for Shelley and her friends, she enjoyed it and we enjoyed doing it, especially Susan in her witch's costume. However, the month before, in October, I made another trip out to Utah, this time to do a mountain biking excursion into the wastelands of southeastern Utah.

Our base for the week long trip was in the old mining town of Moab, dead in the center of the most beautiful place in the world—Arches and Canyonlands National Parks. The biking company, Escape the City Streets, picked all the bikers up and transported us in a van to the different sites; there were a total of 8 guests as well as the two tour guides. Again, I didn't know anyone else on the tour, I was there to experience the scenery and land. The first day, as the guides fitted us to our bikes, one of the other guests hit something in the trail and flipped him over the handlebars, flat on his back before he had gone twenty yards from the van. Two minutes into the week, he was out of commission; the next day he and his friend left the group and went back home. The rest of us rode on wilderness trails, up switchbacks, across deserts, up peaks, down valleys and over the slickrock wilderness that is southeastern Utah. I only had one major accident, which didn't hurt me too bad, just skinned me up a little. Our ride that morning started off on a canyon rim and we were to descend to the bottom and eventually ride a trail along the creek at the bottom. The trail down was alternately steep and hilly...I was coming down a particularly steep part of the trail, with a lot of speed and ran into a big muddy section I couldn't ride around. I thought the bike would just go right through it, so I lifted my feet off the pedals so they wouldn't get wet, but instead of going through the mud, the bike stuck, but I kept on going—over the handlebars, head first, landing face down at the end of the mud puddle. Fortunately, I did land in the mud and not the hard packed trail we were on; the mud softened the fall, and all I really hurt was my pride, being covered in mud for all the others to laugh and giggle at.

I found that mountain biking out there was not the fun I thought it would be. I was thinking that being on the bike would allow me to see more of this beautiful country than I could see trying to hike it. I was wrong. Biking, for me, meant constantly looking down at the rough trails, making sure I didn't hit any boulders, rocks and stumps that would wreck me. Instead of looking up and around at the incredible slickrock scenery, I spent most of my time looking down at the well-worn bike tracks. It was still fun being there, soaking up the Utah desert, but just not what I had expected—I'll stick to hiking in the future.

Back home, I continued to run until the pain in my left knee got so bad I couldn't run. The doctor's told me my meniscus was torn and shredded and that I would need surgery to repair it. So, I had my first ever operation that December—it was no fun. However, we had some fun scheduled soon, another cruise over the New Year's holiday, this time to the Caribbean with Anne, her new husband Nick, Casey, Susan, me and Shelley. Again, on Royal Caribbean aboard the ship "Sovereign of the Seas"; we left from Miami, with stops in Cocoa Cay, Nassau and Key West. Really, it didn't matter where we went, the fun was with being together with our family, especially having Shelley spend time with Anne and Casey...it was very nice. We let the girls do any activities they wanted to and Anne seemed to enjoy everything as well...Nick was not the kind of guy to let his emotions show, I assumed he was having a good time, it was really hard for me to tell...those one-syllable guys are hard to understand at times.

Susan and I had experienced this all before on previous cruises, but it was still great fun; the new place for us was Key West; I hadn't been there before and was looking forward to our day there. We loved walking down the little streets and shopping, buying stuff we didn't need, and finding gifts for our friends and family. We visited the Hemingway House, one of my favorite all-time authors, saw his writing room, and desks and typewriter, as well as the famous six-toed cats of the house. The cruise was capped off with a marvelous New Year's Eve party on board, with whistles, ribbons, balloons, confetti, drinks, a band and plenty of good times...cruise ships certainly know how to entertain. What a way to end another wonderful year in the fairy tale life of Gary Raymond Hope.

1998 would be a big year for Shelley Hope. She turned 16 and got her first car, and from that point forward in her life, I'm pretty sure she never listened to anything I said, or paid any attention to any advice, either her mom or I ever gave her again...up to, and including, today,

July 29, 2014. Oh, we tried, we all tried; but her little friends had much better advice than we all did...and that's who she listened to. Susan had another one of her school trips scheduled that spring to London, we decided we'd arrange for Shelley and Susan's niece, Wendy, to go along as well; open Shelley's eyes to another culture and foreign country. They saw all the sights of London that make it so special, including places I didn't get to see, like Stonehenge. We look at the pictures of that trip today and in nearly every one of them, Shelley looks unhappy, certainly as though she did not want to be there. When I asked her about that trip several years later, all she could say was that it was cold.

While they were traveling to London, I had another trip planned to my beloved Utah, this time a hiking trip all by my lonesome. There were several places I wanted to visit that I'd read about in my favorite book of all time, "Desert Solitaire," and going alone meant I could spend as much time as I wanted to, or needed to, at each of the magical spots I'd planned. I won't bore you with the details of that trip, because what's important to me, certainly won't be to you—that's understandable. Hiking all day in some remote, desert, wilderness region does not appeal to many people—certainly not when I was there; most days, I never saw another living human being all day long. Getting a little lost and just a bit frightened was part of the deal. Surely, being miles from nowhere and near no one had dangers...a broken ankle, or a fall, or any number of minor incidents could lead to disaster when you're out all alone. But, you don't think of things like that (till later), I just thought "my gosh, how beautiful is this?"

One day trip I'll mention is the one to the "confluence" of the Green River and the Colorado River, in the remote area of Canyonlands National Park. I made that hike, which lasted almost all day, all alone (as was my plan) and didn't see anyone either on the way out, or on the way back—which was just fortunate. Even though I have vivid memories of that hike and the things I saw that early spring day, seemingly, my memory wasn't what I thought it was, or, I dreamed a lot of it through the years. I made that same exact hike about 12 years later with Susan, Anne and Marky and I would have sworn it was not the same trail I did in 1998. Nothing looked familiar, things I'd remembered then, I did not see later; I built a rock cairn, a good solid rock cairn, about 2' tall, at a conspicuous point in the trail—one that couldn't be missed and was inconspicuous to all but me—the builder. Under the cairn, I placed a 1998 quarter, so that years later I could return and find that quarter and bring back those memories. 12 years later, I never saw my rock cairn, could barely find the trail, did not recognize, nor remember, hardly anything I saw that day. Had I changed? Had my memory become that bad? Was I on the right trail? I could not figure out what was so amiss...and I never did; only that the Park service confirmed that the trail was

Susan and the coast of Ireland

the ONLY trail there, the only one that had ever been there. My quarter was lost, my memory let me down, I was a little disappointed and confused.

That early spring day in 1998, I hiked to the confluence in a mixture of rain, then sleet, then a few snow flurries, then sunshine, then a little more rain. When I reached the end of the trail and the overlook where these two mighty rivers meet, the sun broke through again to clearly show how the two rivers converged, yet did not actually merge initially. The darker Green River and the muddier Colorado River actually met and flowed side by side as far as I could see downstream...a distinct line in the middle of the newly formed river clearly delineating the old Green river from the newly formed Colorado River. Soon, the torment and rapids and falls of the upcoming canyons would mix them both together into one foamy, muddy torrent, so all the good people of Phoenix and Los Angeles could wash their cars and fill their pools. Oh, Colorado, what a mighty, untamed river you are..."too thick to drink, too thin to plow."

In early spring we met Jerry and Wandre at Hillsborough, at an old, quaint B&B for the weekend; it just happened to be the weekend of the local "Hog Festival" as well...lucky us. It's always nice meeting our two dear friends, but we were a little distracted by the fact that we were planning our first ever trip to Ireland in a couple months. We'd thought of Ireland before and the fact that my grandparent's grandparents came from Ireland, and that Susan's mom had been there and kissed the Blarney Stone, made it an ideal destination for us.

We flew into Dublin, we would never make this mistake again, rented our car and experienced the maze and mire that is Dublin's traffic. We first parked and walked around a bit, inhaling the Irish culture—which is unique. Dublin is indeed nice, but, in reality, it's just another big city—Irish no doubt—but a big city. We enjoyed the sights and pubs and Trinity College and the old castle, a tour of the Guinness brewery, but other places were calling us, so after a few hours we decided we'd begin our journey. The only problem was we couldn't find our way out of Dublin...the streets didn't run at right angles, in fact, we could never figure the streets out. After a couple of hours of being lost and frustrated, we finally hired a taxi driver to lead us out of town.

We finally made our way north out of the city to the little town of Howth, where we would spend our first night. Having flown from the US overnight, toured Dublin most of the day, gotten lost and frustrated, we were very happy to find our little hotel on the bay about 7:00 that night. We secured the room and went downstairs to the little pub/restaurant there for dinner, before going to bed and getting some needed rest. It was the prime occasion for me to try my first Guinness. It was memorable. I'm assuming, the combination of being tired, with no sleep, hungry and not a seasoned drinker all combined to affect me rather quickly. A little over halfway through my first pint, I could feel the effects of that black potion in my little head. By the end of dinner, I was quite sure I could not stand, nor walk, and had to elicit Susan's great help just to make it to our room. I have no other memories until I woke up the next morning—a nice introduction from Mr. Guinness.

The first part of our journey would take us up to Northern Ireland, where we were going to meet two guys I had worked with at B/E Aerospace, Peter and James. We were mesmerized by the Irish countryside...green and lush—and cloudy and rainy—but gorgeously beautiful. We passed the checkpoint into Northern Ireland, which was manned by the British army with sub-machine guns, with no issues—I'm assuming we did not fit the terrorist profile. A little ways into the country, we came to an overview of a lush valley, prototypical stone walls, sheep grazing—your ideal picture of what Ireland looks like. I pulled over to take the first of many pictures that day and noticed a sign posted on a pole about 12' up that said, "Caution: Sniper Alert." I took a quick picture of the valley, then of the sign, got quickly back into the car and sped off...you don't see signs like that very often in Robeson County.

Obviously, the religious differences that affect these countries run deep and are not easily solved. We met our two Irish friends, Peter and James, (James is pronounced "Jims") in Kilkeel and had a nice visit...they showed us the local castle and the cliffs above the ocean—the wind was blowing so hard that day, we could barely open the car door to get out. We met James' wife and baby, he had to go to work later, but Peter was going to be our guide the rest of the day. Peter took us to his hometown, where an IRA bomb had killed 17 people a few years earlier; guided us through this beautiful country and treated us to dinner that evening—he was a great and fun guy, who's goal was to ultimately find a job in the US and move there—he truly enjoyed his work experience here earlier in the year.

We left this beautiful, but confused country, many unsure if they should be called British or Irish; seemingly the British don't want them, with all their problems, and the Republic of Ireland doesn't want them with all their problems—hard to understand if it will ever be settled. Back into the Republic's 26 counties (6 in the North), and pass through the idyllic little village of Adair, with its main street packed with iconic thatched roof houses and businesses—certainly a nice stop on the tourist trail, which was evident by all the tour buses there. Down to the east coast through Glendalough and the excellent Gaelic churches and graveyards; onto to Waterford, Youghal and other nameless, yet memorable little villages on the east and south coasts of Ireland. There was no GPS available in Ireland on this trip, so we spent a lot of time getting lost, trying to find our way out and then, getting lost again. One morning, we stopped at one of the many overlooks to see a little stream that was tumbling over the edge into a fantastic waterfall. I wanted to get a nice picture of this, but it was wet and slippery on the rocks around the stream, and of course, there was no fence or railing on the edge of the road where the stream was tumbling down the cliff. I got my camera out and told Susan to be very careful on these rocks—as soon as I said the word "rocks," I slipped and fell, the camera flew from my hands, bounced on a big rock and bounded for the edge of the cliff, luckily sticking in some black muck, preventing it from tumbling over the edge. I was not so lucky.

I didn't go over the edge, but instead, bounced on my butt, landing in the blackest, nastiest bog you'd find in all of Ireland. I looked up, Susan was laughing hysterically, 3 or 4 other tourists were gawking at me; my camera was on the edge of disaster and my butt was killing me. I retrieved the camera (since the case hadn't been opened yet, it was okay, just a little dirty), and carefully made my way back to the top—my shorts and shoes and socks and shirt, and even my underwear, were completely and thoroughly soaked and BLACK with bog. I had to get into the back seat of the car, take off all my clothes and put on dry ones, while trying to maintain my dignity—not easy to do with Susan still laughing at me.

After several wrong turns, we finally made our way to Blarney Castle, truly, a nice place to visit, even with all the tour buses—it's nice. Susan wanted to follow in her mother's footsteps and "kiss the Blarney Stone," which she did—I did not want to kiss that nasty rock myself—I just watched and took her picture while she kissed it. We drove on to the west coast and out to the end of the Dingle peninsula to the little town of Dingle...we would return here many times. I'm not going to try and describe the wild, scenic west coast of Ireland, because I know I can't. Up the coast we continued, finally arriving in Clifden, one of my favorite little towns in northwest Ireland. Lakes and mountains, sheep in the road, islands off the coast...too much to describe, too much to ever forget. The entire trip seems like a fairy tale now; I wonder now if some of the things we saw were real, or if I only dreamed them—or thought I saw what I saw—Ireland will do that to you—or, it did it to me, but I'm special that way—sometimes it's nice living in a dream world, especially one as beautiful as this.

Back home, Ireland in our minds, but N.C. in our hearts. Susan and Shelley back in school, me...well; I could talk about work, but why? Work is a long ways down the priority list...don't get me wrong, it's important that I work—it's important that everyone works, everyone. But, in my own priority list, it's not close. God is first, always and forever, without my faith I simply could not live...period. Second is Susan, third is Shelley and now Kali, fourth is Anne and Casey and Marky; fifth is the rest of my family, including Susan's family—her dad, Barbara, Martha, Clarence, Wendy, Robyn, Eliza, Luke and Seth. My friends, Jerry and Wandre, Dickie, Larry, Allen and Bill—God bless him. And...finally me. All priorities are very close together, except the most important one, the first one. Now, back to 1998.

I have decided I will try golf; I don't have any golf clubs and haven't played golf in many, many years...and never seriously; but I need something, something I can do on my own, without finding a partner to play with. I go to a golf store, tell the guy I want the best clubs available, he asks me what kind I want, I say "the best you've got." I don't care what the brand is, as long as they're the best. He sells me Bubble shafted, Taylor Made irons and woods (not really wood any longer). They look cool, slate colored shafts, not iron colored, really distinctive looking. Then I drove over to Pine Brook Country Club and joined the club. So, here I am with brand new clubs and now a member of a country club and I haven't hit a golf ball in about two decades. I hope I like it.

The pro at Pine Brook asked me what my handicap was...aside from not playing in 20 years, I didn't have a clue—he got a good laugh over that. The reason I chose Pine Brook was because they had a driving range where you could hit all the balls you wanted, for no additional charge; they also had two putting greens and a practice chipping area with a sand trap. I had determined to follow Ben Hogan's advice, when asked what the secret to golf was—he correctly said, "The secret is in the dirt." You just have to pound that dirt, over and over and over and over, until you unlock the secret that is you. It's not easy and there are no shortcuts. So I started pounding, every day, every day and every day...I sliced, I hooked, I hit them fat, I hit them thin; I threw clubs, I threw golf balls, I threw my bag and I threw tantrums—yes, golf brought out my bad side at times. But I LOVED it! Let me re-phrase that...I LOVED IT!!!!

As with all beginners, I did not score well, sometimes pretty bad, sometimes not so bad—but never good; and I was very inconsistent. One day I could hit the driver well, and my irons stunk; the next day I hit irons good and couldn't putt or chip; then I'd putt well but couldn't a driver in the fairway—golf is not a fair game, it doesn't show you any pity, it doesn't give you anything...it is what it is. What I liked so much was that I played against me...no matter if I was playing with 2 or 3 other guys, I was still only playing against ME. Later, when I began to improve, I was still playing against me, but I then started playing against par—an even tougher opponent than I ever was.

Golf took a short break that fall when Susan and I met Jerry and Wandre, and Anne and Nick in Las Vegas for a four day weekend at the MGM Grand—and it was grand! We took everyone to the Siegfried and Roy show at the Mirage and they loved it like we did; we played some blackjack, ate at nice restaurants, visited all the big casinos and won a few slot jackpots—at least Jerry and Wandre did. We had a wonderful time, but...there was something about Anne's husband Nick; I could never define what that something was, but there was something.

***

1999, the last year of the century would bring all sorts of wackos out in public, saying all the computers would malfunction when year 2000 arrived; the so-called Y2K phenomenon would crash the computers, stop all the clocks and disrupt life as we knew it. Skip to Dec. 31 and Jan 1...nothing happened. However the year was full of promise for us all...our family reunion was held once again and all were still in good health, even Aunt Mary, who was beginning to have serious diabetes issues. Golfing had become a passion for me, and I spent at least part of most days at the golf course, I'd usually play all day (36 holes on Saturdays and Sundays—walking of course).

Susan and I planned a trip to Italy during the summer and welcomed our niece Wendy to join us...she's a good old girl. We flew into Milan, rented a car, and tried to figure out how in the world to get out of the traffic maze in that Italian metropolis. We finally found some pedestrians who spoke a little English and gave enough directions to lead us out of the congestion. Our first destination was north, across the Alps, into Switzerland. How beautiful that was...I don't remember the names of the towns and lakes we visited, but it was all that you imagined Switzerland would look like—I wasn't disappointed. We drove east and south into France to indulge my yearning to visit the site of the 1968 Olympic games in Grenoble, where Jean-Claude Killy captured the imagination of the world in the winter games. Really, not much to the town of Grenoble, we had lunch at a restaurant there where no one spoke English, and the menu was in

French and we didn't have a clue what we were ordering—but we survived and left that little town headed for the magical place that was Venice.

We had to park our car in a parking lot outside of Venice and ride a bus into the city, for obvious reasons. There, we were dropped off where we boarded one of the local ferries that took us down the Grand Canal and deposited us at St. Mark's Square, in the middle of this fascinating place. We were in Venice for three glorious days, I wished it could have been more...it was truly a wonderful place to visit. We took several gondola rides in and around the canals, passed under the Bridge of Sighs (look it up), took a boat out to some islands, walked the streets, ate at local restaurants and generally soaked up the atmosphere of this flooded little city. We had a wonderful time there and really didn't want to leave for Florence, but we did.

Florence was, for me, both incredible and irritating. The art alone makes it one of the most desired places to visit in the world...just seeing Michelangelo's "The David" was probably worth the entire trip. Shopping on the Ponte Vecchio, visiting the many art galleries and churches—truly, a once-in-a-lifetime experience. But, in Florence, you had to endure some unpleasantness along with the good stuff. The city was overrun with little motor scooters, everybody there drove one, and seemingly, no one obeyed any traffic laws whatsoever. The pesky little things would buzz by you and around you, making that infernal racket that sounded like you were being chased by a nest of bumble bees.

We were walking one afternoon when a young girl approached us with a newspaper hanging off her arm, speaking Italian and coming closer and closer to us as she did. I kept saying "no," "no"...whatever she was selling or asking, I didn't want. Suddenly, her accomplice (a young boy about 14-15) came up behind us and tried to steal either my camera or wallet from my pocket. I wheeled around quickly and grabbed him by the front of the shirt, lifting him off the ground, saying a few choice American words to him. I don't know if he understood these phrases...but I guarantee you he knew what they meant. I sort of pushed him away as I let him down and he and the girl took off running. It scared Wendy, I'm truly sorry about that, but I did what I had to do. I kind of liked it—brought out the Robeson County hidden in me.

All in all, we thoroughly enjoyed Italy, especially Venice; even with the distractions in Florence, it was very nice and I'd love to visit there again. But, for now, back to our home and family and golf and w...not, I won't say that word.

26

Well, it's 12:01 AM, in the year 2000 and no Y2K disaster... I'm standing outside in the street to make sure. All the lights are working and all services are operational, including the phones, because I got a call from Uncle Donald, in Texas, at 12:30 AM. We talk for over 30 minutes and I helped him bring in the New Year with good conversation and a glass of wine or two, or three, or four, on his end...or five. My little girl turned 18 years old in February; I remember holding her in the hospital as a newborn baby; funny, but when I close my eyes and think of her, it's as a 6 or 7 year old—I wonder why that is?

Tough year for Aunt Mary...her husband, Kelly, died and she's all alone in Florida. She also had one leg amputated because of diabetes (that dreaded disease that would keep visiting us throughout the years). Susan flew down there in February to help with the arrangements to move Aunt Mary up here, initially to Sara's house, but we'll see where it ends up. Susan has a heart of gold, always doing for others without regard to her own feelings or wants...I'm lucky.

I made a note in my journal on March 14 that gas had risen to $1.59 per gallon—and I was disgusted. I remember feeling the same way back in the early 1970's when it rose to $0.55 a gallon. And I remember working at Eddie's Esso one day in my youth, when I thought a man requested $5.00 worth of gas, which I pumped in his car, when he said he only ordered 5 GALLONS worth of regular at $0.24 a gallon…good old Eddie smoothed it over with this irate customer and didn't say a word to me. Had this guy done this sort of word game before to get free gas? Or was Eddie just protecting me because he liked mama so much? During the so-called oil embargo of the early and mid-seventies, when people were lining up around the blocks to buy gas, Eddie always let mama come in early in the morning before he opened, to fill her tank for the commute to Fort Bragg. He was a good guy and treated me better than I deserved.

On April 1 of this year I shot a 77 at Pinebrook, my lowest score yet...then I followed that up with an 86 the next day—that's the nature of golf, why it's so beautiful and so cruel all at the same time. I made the following observations in my journal on April 8, of things I needed to do more of:

- ∴ Exercise
- ∴ Play guitar
- ∴ Read
- ∴ Spend time with Susan

∴ Call Shelley

∴ Call Anne

∴ Read the Bible

∴ Have patience

Then, made a list of things I needed to less of:

∴ Watch TV

∴ Worry about money

∴ Snack

∴ Waste time

Fourteen years later and not much has changed in those two lists.

More golf news...one Saturday in May, I played 36 holes (as I usually did) and shot 86 on the first 18, then, being tired and worn out, I shot 74 on the second 18. I'm pretty sure I'll never figure out this crazy game. In June, we had the family reunion in Red Springs at Uncle Earl's house, all the brothers and sisters, except for Aunt Mary, were still vibrant and healthy. I took some time and went around the corner to stand in what used to be the front yard of Granny and Granddaddy's house at 215 S. Cross St.—it's a parking lot now for the Piggly Wiggly. But, it still contains a lifetime worth of memories that no parking lot can ever cover up.

From now on, as I write this, I'm going to try to limit my golf stories and scores, as I'm sure it's just tedious, frivolous information, important to no one really; but, I did shoot my first score under par, a 71, on June 29. Somehow, I was able to tear myself away from golf to start planning another trip for us...Ireland was beckoning again, and I couldn't resist the urge to return to the Emerald Isle once again. This trip would be different however, we had booked a hiking trip with "Joyce's Hiking Trips of Ireland." Joyce would take us on day long hikes in remote areas of Ireland, places people don't normally see or visit—truly off the beaten path. There were only 6 of us hikers, plus Joyce, and we got along pretty well—Joyce made sure of that.

Our first hikes were up north near Ballintoy in Northern Ireland; on this July 9 day, it was 50 degrees and the wind was blowing about 30 mph, with intermittent rain and sunshine—a typical summer day in Ireland. After each day's hike, Joyce always arranged dinner at a local pub that had live music—which includes almost all Irish pubs—amazing musicians, they sort of look at each other, then start playing; what a joy it is to experience that. We visited the Giant's Causeway and hiked along a cliff about 300 feet or so above the ocean, with the wind blowing so hard, you had to walk bent over at a 45 degree angle to make any progress. Poor Susan couldn't even do that, she ended up crawling on hands and knees into that headwind, until the trail turned away from the wind a little. I lost my hat to the wind that day and I'm pretty sure lost some more hair from the top of my head as well. At that point in northeast Ireland, we were only 14 miles across the ocean from Scotland and could even see the Scottish coast off in the distance.

On to Ballycastle for more hikes, and over the border, back into County Donegal, in the Gaelic speaking region of Ireland. One rainy, misty day on the Horn Head Peninsula, we came out of some woods along the coast and entered a large area filled with stones and boulders—which can describe most places in Ireland. We stop for lunch and all of us find a nice big rock to either sit on or lean against to eat our sandwiches and try to stay warm. I had recently had an eye exam and been fitted for glasses to overcome my near-sightedness (I couldn't see distances clearly any longer). The glasses were great, except I didn't need them to read with or any up close vision...so, I took them off while we ate lunch—placing them on a rock next to me, within easy reach. We finished eating, packed up our backpacks and started off; almost immediately I realized everything was a little fuzzy looking—I'd forgotten to put my glasses back on. We'd only walked about 25 feet or so, I turned around to get my glasses and looked at about 10,000 rocks strewn about that field, all looking exactly alike. Susan and I walked through those rocks for at least 15 minutes and we never found my glasses...$300 donated to the first near-sighted sheep that comes along.

Down the northwest coast we travel, stopping at one of Ireland's most sacred spots...Croagh Patrick, County Mayo. The place where St. Patrick retreated to after driving all the snakes out of Ireland; it was nearly mandatory for all Irishmen to climb this little mountain at least once in their lifetimes to pay homage to Ireland's greatest hero—many would climb it barefoot in honor of Patrick to relive the pain he went through for all Irishmen. It was a typical Irish day: wind, cold, rain, fog and low clouds. We all started for the summit, but the weather and the steepness and rockiness of the trail drove them all back, except for me—Patrick, I'm coming! Alone I continued up the mountain, I met, nor saw, anyone else on the journey; it was very steep in places and extremely rocky and treacherous...how anyone could ever climb this barefoot was beyond my comprehension.

The last third of the hike to the summit was engulfed in low clouds, I can only see 15-20 feet ahead of me at any time; as I neared the top, the so-called trail levels off and I look up and see a "cross" in the distance, seemingly floating in mid-air. As I approach, I find the wooden cross is attached to a small chapel, which was painted white, and all but invisible wrapped in the clouds. I tried to take some pictures, but none came out well, just too foggy and cloudy. My shirt was wet from the climb, and soon I was freezing; I didn't bring another shirt with me on the hike, so I had to take off the wet shirt and just wear my vest and raincoat on the way down the mountain. The rest of the group waited patiently for me in the little shop at the trail head—I thank them for that; all ended well, except the little shop did not serve Guinness...the only negative to a wonderful experience.

The next day, July 14, was Susan's birthday; how many people get to spend their birthdays hiking across Ben Levy in County Galway, with large lakes in the distance, on both sides of the mountain...one of them being the largest lake in Ireland, Lough Corrib. We stopped for a celebratory birthday lunch and snack in the middle of a large field, rainy, windy, cold and very happy to be where we were. I would make sure that evening that we had a proper birthday celebration for my lovely, little wife, who so bravely endured this day with no complaints at all.

On we traveled through Westport, a charming little town, through the village of Cong, stopping for a pint or two and finishing at our stay for the night at Cregg Castle, about 10 miles from Galway. We would have Susan's birthday party at a thousand year old castle set it the highlands and bogs of western Ireland. The next day we would travel back to Dublin for our flight home...it was a memorable week hiking the wilds of Ireland...in my journal I noted these perceptions of our week there:

∴ Friendliness of the people

∴ Guinness, Harp, Smithwicks, Irish coffee, Bailey's

∴ Potatoes: chipped, baked, broiled, stewed, souffled, hashed and fried—all good

∴ Clouds and rain

∴ Beautiful coastlines and countryside

∴ Stone walls

∴ Sheep, sheep and more sheep

∴ Full Irish breakfasts

∴ Crough Patrick

∴ 80 mph winds

∴ Bogs

∴ Traditional Irish music in the pubs

∴ And Joyce...a great guide and friend.

I notice that in Dublin my right arm is sore, for some unknown reason, when I woke up the next day to go to the airport, I can't lift anything with that arm...poor Susan has to carry most of the luggage. On the flight back I'm having severe pains from my elbow down to my wrist; and my fingers are numb! Something BAD is wrong. Advil is not working and I'm getting very concerned. First day home I go to the doctor and he concludes something bit my elbow...there are now vivid red streaks running from my elbow to my fingers and swelling has started. He prescribes some medicines and sends me home, but nothing is working; that night, the pain is now shooting up into my shoulder as well and I'm in great pain...nauseous, headaches, lightheaded. I get two more shots the next day and still no relief and the red streaks are redder and longer. The doctor sends me to a specialist and they take blood samples and send them to the Center for Disease Control in Atlanta, and after doing research, they tell me there are no poisonous spiders or animals in Ireland that could have bitten me...that's no help.

They take me to the hospital and do x-rays and more blood samples and give me more shots for the pain—it's not working. Three days after arriving home and there is no relief and the doctor is worried to the point of saving my arm. Tiny blisters are now forming from my elbow down to my fingers and everything is swollen...I'm truly scared now, not only for my arm, but for my life—this is way too serious. More prescriptions, more blood tests, more shots...finally, five days after arriving home, the little blisters, the swelling and the red streaks start to fade...and some of the pain. The reports back from the CDC say they have no idea what happened to me, the doctors had no idea what caused it and all were completely baffled. By the weekend, feeling had come back to my fingers, and my arm was getting back to normal...neither me, nor the doctors, had any explanation for this ordeal...but it's over now.

***

In August I had laser eye surgery so I could see distances better...it had gotten to the point that when playing golf I couldn't see the ball after I hit it off the tee. I had no idea where to go look for my ball—down the middle, left or right...it was very frustrating. So, I had it done, about $3800 at the time; the surgeon who did it ran an ad the following week for a special price of $1895; talk about bad timing on my part. What I failed to realize was that fixing my eyes to see distances clearly, meant that now I would need reading glasses to see up close—a tradeoff of sorts. At least now, when I sliced one in the woods, I knew exactly where to go look for it.

Little Casey traveled with her gymnastics team to Russia this summer, where they trained with the Russian national team, which included the eventual Olympic gymnastics champion—some skinny, blonde-headed 8-syllable named girl. Anne's worthless husband, Nick (that sorry one-syllable dude of a husband), filed for divorce from Anne, effective August 10. I know it was hard on her, but in my opinion—good riddance! Susan and I had our 10th wedding anniversary coming up Aug. 18 and I wanted to do something special...something she'd remember. I had the perfect idea.

I surprised her with a three day trip to New York City, staying at the Waldorf-Astoria Hotel; dinner at the Bull's and Bear Restaurant and drinks at the Waldorf pub—Bailey's of course. What a day. We took the train the next afternoon out to the Bronx to Yankee Stadium, good old Susan indulging me again. Yankee Stadium—I could hardly believe I was there—it was like a dream come true. I looked down on the outfield grass that Babe Ruth and Joe DiMaggio and Mickey Mantle and Roger Maris had played on; over at first base where Lou Gehrig played, second base for Bobby Richardson, Tony Kubek at shotstop, Clete Boyer at third, Yogi Berra and Elston Howard and Thurman Munson catching; Whitey Ford, Don Larson, Goose Gossage, Ron Guidry pitching; Casey Stengal and Ralph Houk managing— it was almost too much to comprehend. And the Yankees did me proud that day beating the Angels 8-0; I'm sure they did that just for me...I'm special that way.

We went to Broadway that night and saw the musical "Chicago" at the Shubert Theatre...yup, New York is a very special place. The next day was equally spectacular, 74 degrees, sunny and magnificent in the greatest city in the world. After a $50 breakfast, we walked down Madison Avenue, which was closed to traffic so that a pedestrian shopping area could be set up...block after block after block; vendors selling everything from jewelry, to cotton candy to paintings to nesting dolls and everything in between—we bought stuff until we couldn't carry anymore. We visited Central Park West, (specifically 8th and 73rd Streets) where the Dakota apartment building stood...across the street from Strawberry Fields park. We stood in the entrance way where John was shot...

Back to Rockefeller Center for lunch in the plaza and easy strolls through the city; the Chrysler Building, the Empire State Building and the World Trade Center, where scarcely 13 months later, the unimaginable would happen. I loved New York, very nice and very expensive...two drinks at a bar on Broadway was $47.50, including the tip. Dinner was $125, before the tip. Our room at the Waldorf was $360 a night, but it did include free usage of a bath robe and a complimentary pen—I kept the pen. Sunday evening, flying back home, all I can think about is that entrance way at the Dakota. My, oh my.

***

Oct 10, 2000 was significant to me, not to any others...it was the last day in my 40's. When you're in your forties, you don't really SOUND that old, heck, baseball players, basketball players, a lot of golfers still play at a top level in their 40's. Fifties is altogether different—it sounds old. I still feel great, am still able to do anything I want to do, but it sounds old.

Election day this year is Nov. 7...Al Gore and George W. Bush, it will be a memorable one. Gore won the popular vote (which really doesn't mean anything); the electoral votes (which do) are deadlocked and waiting on the recounts from Florida; which is controlled by Republicans who are trying to figure out how they can steal the election from Gore without the American public actually knowing they're stealing it.

∴ Nov. 10: still recounting Florida's votes
∴ Nov. 17: still counting
∴ Nov. 22: still counting (a sad day to count actually)
∴ Nov. 27: still counting...yawn
∴ Nov. 30: still counting
∴ Dec 2: still no President
∴ Dec 5: still counting
∴ Dec 7: still counting on Pearl Harbor Day
∴ Dec 8: still counting on John's birthday
∴ Dec 12: still counting
∴ Dec 14...the Supreme Court finally found a way to let Bush win without causing riots, by a 5-4 margin

On the last day of the year I wrote a list of 100 things I hoped to do before I died...now 14 years later, I'm going to list some of the things on that list that I still have not done, yet hope to do before I do pass on...here they are:

∴ Hike parts of the Pacific Coast Trail
∴ Go to Cooperstown
∴ Hike in the Maze
∴ Learn to dance

∴ Go to the French Open

∴ Play Pebble Beach and Pinehurst #2 and St. Andrews

∴ See the Northern Lights

∴ Visit Australia

∴ Take a Beatles tour in London and Liverpool

∴ Be the father of a bride

∴ Go to the Masters

∴ Take a hot air balloon trip over the desert

∴ Ride a bike either across America, or on the west coast from Mexico to Canada

∴ See 30' waves

∴ Make a hole-in-one (with witnesses)

∴ Watch Shelley be successful at something meaningful

∴ Own a motorcycle and ride it out west—all over

∴ Live a summer in Carmel

∴ Catch a foul ball at Yankee Stadium

∴ Lead someone to Christ

∴ Spend a stormy season at Big Sur

∴ Take a two week Mediterranean Cruise

∴ Visit Normandy

∴ Discover Grace

∴ Be able to fill a void in Shelley's life

∴ Be the most important person in Susan's life.

27

"Be kind whenever possible. It is always possible."

In Feb of 2001, I flew out to Reno to see one of Casey's gymnastic meets; unfortunately, she had sustained an injury and could not perform. We just spent some good time together, well, as much as we could, Anne was in training for a marathon and was running 14 miles that day. On March 2 Susan left on another school trip, this one to the Netherlands; she was excited...rightfully so. I was not excited...NASDAQ had cost me most of my life's savings; I was now resigned to being broke forever.

Golfing is improving, my nose is not...I had to have a somnoplasty done May 7—don't ask, it's terrible, and I'm a terrible patient and will not follow the doctor's orders. Susan has another school trip lined up with Dianne Tutt, this time going to Italy, leaving June 2. Anne ran in the San Diego marathon, 3 hr, 35 minutes—excellent time. Susan is off on another trip with Dianne Tutt, leaving June 28 for London...in four months, she's gone to the Netherlands, then Italy, and now London. However, the London trip is a mess, Dianne leaves her alone, Susan is unhappy, I tell her to just come home; it's a disaster.

July 4, 2001, on a Wednesday, I break 70 for the first time when I shoot a 69, witnessed by my friend Jack Braswell...what a day! I came to the 18th hole, which is a par 5, needing to eagle it to actually break 70—I'd eagled this hole once in my entire golfing life...so, my chances were not very good. I hit a good drive, but it ended up just in the left rough, with a good lie, about 200 yards from the green. The problem was that there was one small limb sort of overhanging the fairway in my line of sight; I stared at that limb for several minutes, ultimately thinking there's no way I could hit that limb, even if I tried to. So, I hit my three iron as sweet as I could hit it, and yep, you guessed it—I hit that tiny, stupid, inconsequential limb. My ball popped up in the air and landed about 60 yards short of the green. Chances of eagle...gone! Chances of birdie...mostly gone; now I was just hoping to make a 5 and still be under par for the round.

After fuming and fussing about my bad luck, Jack told me to calm down and make a good shot. Jack was smart, I listened to him. I took out my sand wedge and hit a shot directly at the pin...it took one hop and rolled right into the cup for an EAGLE 3! Jack ran across the fairway, we high-fived, yelled and screamed—what a good guy to share that moment with. I bought him a drink in the clubhouse and shared my story with anyone who would listen, including the club pro, Ross. He burst my bubble pretty fast, telling me to savor this day, because it would probably be many months, or even years, before I broke 70 again. Huh??? Why did he say that? Why ruin my moment? I would show him...I'd prove him wrong! The only thing was...he was right. I kept shooting good scores, 73, 75, 72, etc., etc...but nothing close to 69; maybe Ross was right.

Susan's Dad, a great man, and his wife Barbara invited us, and Martha and Clarence to go to Hawaii with them in August—and pay for the trip—what a deal! We'd fly out there and board a cruise ship, which would tour several islands, making various stops along the way...we were very excited. It took us 24 hours of actual travel time, from leaving W-S for the airport, to eventually Los Angeles, to Honolulu to board the cruise ship. The first day we sailed toward Hilo, on the big island and visited Volcanoes National Park there. That night, the ship sailed past an active volcano, which had lava flowing from the top of the mountain all the way down into the sea— and, it's been flowing like this non-stop for 20 years! This island averages about 130" of rainfall a year, on the windward side, and only 20" a year on the other side (leeward).

In Kona, I went parasailing again, this time harnessed up as a tandem with Barbara. It was a little windy and we were swaying pretty good up there; I got a little queasy, but Barbara got really sick. As we were being pulled back into the boat, she started throwing up over my shoulder, into the boat; Susan's Dad was video-taping the whole affair and got the whole scene recorded for posterity—it was not pretty. Fortunately for me, they needed to get Barbara back on shore quickly, I was glad because I had a snorkeling trip lined up with Clarence and I thought I was going to be late for it. Back on shore, my legs were a little wobbly, but, I thought I'd be okay; I got off our boat and ran over to the other sailboat to meet Clarence and off we sailed—out about an hour to a reef in the Pacific. Boats and me are not friends even in the best of times— this was not the best of times. The seas were choppy and the little sail boat was rocking and rolling; combine this with my parasailing a few minutes earlier and I was fearing the worst. Finally, we stopped and got our gear on for the snorkeling...as soon as I got in the water, I felt fine; as in the Caribbean, the water was as clear as looking out a window—I could not tell I was under water, except for the multi-colored fish and reefs we saw.

I don't know how long we swam around, but time went far too quickly for me...I loved it; the whistle sounded, telling us to come back to the boat. I looked up and was still pretty far away, but started swimming back; I was the last to arrive and as poor old Clarence was giving me a helping hand into the boat, I suddenly, without warning, started throwing up. I had no control over this bodily function and could not stop throwing up...all over Clarence, all over the boat and anyone, or anything else within my spewing distance. I was not the most popular passenger on the boat. The captain was yelling at me to "puke overboard."..but I was halfway in the boat and halfway out...I had no control where my vomit was going. I just knew it was coming up and out. Once again Clarence...I apologize!

Parasailing and snorkeling in choppy waters, back-to-back, were not a good combination for me. We learned later that day that Susan and Martha had gone on a glass-bottom boat tour, also in choppy waters, and had gotten sick and thrown up as well. Therefore, of the six of us that day, four of us donated our lunches back to the vast depths of the Pacific Ocean.

August 15, the next day, I was recovered and rented some golf clubs to play at Makaha Country Club, about an hour north of Honolulu. The golf clubs I rented were really no good, but the scenery was spectacular! Not only the scenery, but I saw several birds around the course I'd never seen before. The most fetching was a Hawaiian robin, which had a red head, with a blue body and a white neck ring...truly beautiful. We did all the tourist stuff, including a Polynesian feast, with dancing and singing, the Hawaiians really know how to entertain you. The next day we went to the Arizona Memorial there in Pearl Harbor, where 1177 men were still entombed in its hull. If this doesn't affect you, then probably not much will.

We shopped, drank piña coladas, lounged around the ship, all the while watching Honolulu, Waikiki, and Diamond Head pass by us...a nice rainbow forming from Diamond Head into the ocean as we rounded the bend. Today, Aug. 16, was Martha and Clarence's 32cd wedding anniversary...what a memorable way to enjoy it. Our last day aboard the S.S. Independence was spent on the magnificent island of Kauai. Susan and I signed up for a "bike" ride to Wiamai Canyon. Actually, a van drives you to the top of the mountain, then you get on the bike and coast down to the shore...never pedaling once during the 12 mile ride. On one side of this mountain, they receive about 450-650" of rain a year...while on the other side of the same mountain, 12 miles away, they receive only 6" per year. Nights on board were spent listening to and watching Barbara and Conrad sing and dance at the talent shows—they were a great hit; and watching the stars and islands pass by from up on deck. All amazing sights.

The next day, Aug. 18, we spent our 11th anniversary about 35,000 feet over the Pacific, between Hawaii and Los Angeles. I listed the memories of Hawaii in my journal then...I won't rehash them now...needless to say, indescribable. Conrad and Barbara...thank you, thank you, thank you.

***

Sept 11, 2001...A day that will live in infamy. In my journal for that day, it was not immediately known how many people had died...reports were ranging up to 20,000. College football was called off for Saturday, Sept. 15, rightfully so, as our nation still grieved for those killed four days earlier. Susan and I went to Asheville again over Thanksgiving and stayed at the Grove Park Inn...always a nice place to visit.

George Harrison died November 30, after struggling for a few years with cancer...such a sweet, sweet man. This will take a while to accept. We didn't really do anything the rest of the year to talk about...met Susan's Dad and Barbara at Myrtle Beach in mid-December for some shows and dinners...it's always nice spending time with them. Other than that, I only played golf and we stayed at home—pretty unusual for us. On Dec. 30 an owl somehow got in our house, we saw it perched on the mantel piece in the living room. It was so still, I wasn't sure it real when I first saw it. Then, it flew upstairs and we knew we had a situation. We didn't really know what to do, so we called Clarence for advice; he told us to get a blanket and try to catch it in that way. As I went near it with the blanket, it flew across the room, directly into the window and knocked itself out. I picked it up with the blanket, not really knowing if it was alive or dead, and its talons instinctively latched onto my fingers, even though it was completely unconscious.

I took it outside and it took both hands for me to get free of those steel-trap like talons…I laid it down on the driveway and walked back under the carport to keep an eye on it; I didn't want a cat, or some other animal to come along while it was knocked out. After maybe 6-8 minutes, it started moving, then raised up on its legs, shook it's head two or three times and just looked around. After 2-3 more minutes regaining its senses, it gracefully lifted off, into the trees and out of our lives…but not out of our memory.

This was not a good year for me…I lost a bundle in the stock market, never to regain; Shelley seems completely lost with no clear direction in her life, except "having a good time." The nose operation, some skin cancers burnt off my face, 9/11…one of those years that you have to endure in your life's journey. Two things that got me through this mess, two things that never change, two things I had (and have), that I probably don't deserve: the Lord's love and forgiveness and Susan's love and understanding…two constants I can always count on.

Shelley turned 20 years old on this day, Feb. 6, 2002; I wish I could say she was in school and doing well. I wish I could say she was working and doing well…there's a lot of things I wish I could say.

***

I had a nose operation on Feb 13 of this year…one of the worst experiences of my life. They packed my nose with a plastic tube, surrounded by gauze, so that I couldn't breathe. It was supposed to stay in my nose for three days while it healed…I pulled it out that night. Susan was extremely upset at me, but when you can't breathe, you can't breathe—and extreme steps must be taken…that's my story and I'm sticking with it.

I flew out to Las Vegas in April, staying at the Excalibur Hotel, to meet Anne and Casey and see Casey's regional gymnastics meet held nearby in Henderson. She won a medal in the vault, I was very proud of her, as was her mom. Paul McCartney was in concert at the MGM Grand while we were there, tickets ranged from $250-350…I thought really hard about it; but ended up not going, instead, I donated that money to the blackjack tables in Vegas. Stupid me.

On May 7, I shot my lowest score ever, a sweet, sweet 68! (witnessed by Mike Dees and Clay Setzer) It was last July 4 that I shot 69, and the pro told me it would be many months, or even years before I would be in the 60's again…he was close, it took me 10 months. I made this note in my journal that day on the golf course…Hole No.6, which has a lake down the left hand side; on this hole alone, I saw: 2 swans, 3 ducks, 14 geese, a blue heron and a couple of red-winged blackbirds. I guess it was just my lucky day.

At the family reunion this year, Uncle Paul and Aunt Mary verified what I thought I already knew—that Granny's grandfather and his two brothers immigrated from Ireland to the U.S.— they were Newtons. They think the Townsends, (granddaddy's grandparents, came from Scotland). Granny was born in 1903, her dad about 1875 and her grandfather around the year 1840…exactly the time of the great potato famines in Ireland.

I was very fortunate this year to play golf with two of heroes…Alfred Paul Townsend and Charles Donald Townsend. It made no difference to me how we all played, only that I was there with them…what a special day with two special guys.

Susan and I left for Ireland (again) on June 7 and arrived in Shannon early in the morning of June 8…tired, sleepy and very excited. Secured the rental car and started out for Kerry and the pretty little town of Killarney—got lost briefly, found our way and continued on. We had to take a short (4 hour) nap at the hotel, then we hiked about 4-5 miles up the Gap of Dunloe. Had some delicious vegetable soup at Kate Kearney's Cottage and a glass or two of Guinness to cap off the day.

My notes from that day say the temperature was 58 degrees, raining and windy; as an old woman once told me over there, "you don't come to Ireland for the sunshine!" She was right. Most days started off a little rainy, but usually ended up with periods of sunshine that absolutely take your breath away as you look out over the Dingle Bay into the rough highlands of the Ring of Kerry. Oh, the quaint little towns we passed through…all magical to me, each with its own special appeal: Eyeries, colorful; Glengariff, shops; Kenmare, homey; Castletownbere, working class; Sneem, the waterfalls; on and on it went. Each little town unique to itself and to us…we would visit these places many times hence.

We didn't really want to leave Killarney, but we had to…The Aran Islands were calling me. Down through the Burren (look it up), into the little village of Doolin, where we'll catch the ferry tomorrow out to the islands—the weather's a little ominous, but, it's Ireland, not Myrtle Beach. The next morning we catch the little ferry, which holds about a dozen people I'm guessing; it has about 4 rows of bench seats—no individual seating.

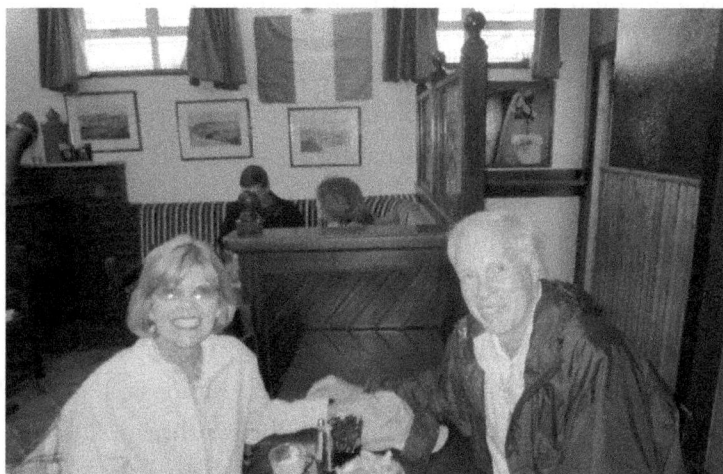

Irish pub

The captain tells us it's a little over an hour's journey out to Inishmore, the largest of the islands, set out in the Galway Bay. It's 51 degrees, raining and very windy as we leave the shore.

Immediately, the little boat is whipped by the waves; one second you're looking directly up into the sky, then the boat comes off the wave and you're looking directly down into the sea. Up and down, Up and down, Up and down…we literally had to hold onto the seats with both hands to keep from being thrown onto the deck of the boat. Within the first five minutes of the trip, I knew I was in deep trouble; with over an hour left to travel, I did not think I'd live through it. It only got worse, the further out into the ocean we went. Finally, nature took over, Susan got me a seasickness bag and I started heaving…my full Irish breakfast came up first, then last night's Shepherd's Pie followed, then last week's vegetable soup, followed by a corn dog I had eaten at Fall Festival in the sixth grade. Somehow, I made it to shore alive…I don't know how; I threw up some things that were attached down there, but came up anyway—I guess they weren't important. When we stumbled off that boat, I was soaking wet from the perspiration I endured from all the vomiting. We went into the first store we saw and Susan bought me all new, dry clothes to put on. After a while, I felt as though I could actually walk around, after enduring all that, I had to see what was out here…and what was out here was fantastic!

At the end of the island was an old circular fort, Dun Aengus, 2500 years old, perched about 500' above the raging Atlantic Ocean. The fort, the stone houses, the Gaelic churches and graveyards all made Inishmore a special place. I loved it. I did not love the thought of having to ride that boat back to the shore, another hour amongst those churning seas. But, with Susan's help, I made it safely back to shore, I had nothing left to throw up—the corn dog was the last of it. I had to lay down in the car seat and let Susan drive, the simple task of trying to focus on anything was more than I could handle at that time.

With Susan driving most of the way, we made our way to Galway for the night. In the hotel, we saw a pamphlet for a company that takes visitors out to the Aran Islands on a jet boat that rides on a cushion of air…REALLY? A cushion of air? No seasickness, no throwing up…oh, Gary, tell me it ain't so.

After Galway, we drive up the coast to a favorite place of mine, the little town of Clifden, where we spend a couple of days exploring some old castles, visiting some hidden lakes, driving down some narrow, twisting roads, trying to avoid the sheep grazing on the shoulders; sampling the local fares, buying junk we don't need—but want…living the dream that is hidden in the Irish countryside. Where, you might ask? It's in your heart…you'll know it when you get there.

We fly home June 15, sad to leave, but with a treasure trove of new memories to store in our minds and hearts forever…thoughts of Guinness, Bailey's, Harp, rock walls, vegetable soups, rain & mist, twisty, narrow roads, Gaelic, brown bread, and the aromatic smells of peat burning in the fireplaces of hidden pubs where old men sit and play guitars and fiddles well into the Irish night.

***

Back home, back to golf, back to life…I shot another 69, playing with Susan's dad, they had come up to help us celebrate Susan's birthday. It's always nice to spend time with Conrad and Barbara, they're so much fun, and Susan's dad is so very interesting to talk to—extremely intelligent.

On October 7, Shelley, Susan and I go to see Paul McCartney in concert once again, this time in Raleigh. In my journal, I wrote: Wow! Fantastic! Amazing! That about sums it up; even Shelley was impressed, which is really saying something. Paul played a total of 36 songs for us that night, and we loved them all.

My lifetime friends, Dickie, Jerry and Allen came up for a weekend of telling stories, eating at nice restaurants and reliving old days and times—doesn't get any better than that. Susan left on another school trip, this one to Korea...that should be interesting. I decided to go up to Stone Mountain and hike while she was gone...being late November, I was quite alone at the summit, just me and the wind and the buzzards. I don't know why, but there were about 40-50 of them riding the thermals up the bald, stone side of the mountain. I sat as near the edge as I felt comfortable doing, watching them soar and float, sometimes above me, sometimes below me; sometimes gliding so close to me I could hear their feathers ruffling in the wind. I wondered what they thought of me...unable to soar as they did, grounded for eternity, bound by the confines of gravity...if possible, would they change places with me? I sincerely doubt it. Would I change places with them, if possible?

28

"When wealth is lost, nothing is lost; when health is lost, something is lost; but when character is lost, all is lost."

On Jan 2, 2003 Anne called to tell me they had found a melanoma on her back…not the kind of news you like to hear starting off a new year. They operated and took it out, with good results…seems as though they got all the cancerous cells…let's hope so.

I joined a local "hiking" club and went on several winter hikes with them…one day in particular was memorable for me; on Feb 1, we had hiked 11 miles, up and around Pilot Mountain; I was cold, hungry and tired as I got in my car to drive home after the hike. Normally, I don't turn on the radio, but I did that day and heard the tragic news that the space shuttle, Columbia, had broken apart and crashed as it entered earth's atmosphere, killing the 7 astronauts aboard. It was traveling about 12,000 mph and about 207,000 feet above the earth's surface when it disintegrated.

I made a note in my journal that the war with Iraq started March 20…that's all I said about it, which seems strange now. And for some reason, which I don't understand now, I quit playing golf in 2003. I don't remember now why I stopped; I made no comments in my journal about quitting, didn't refer to it at all and have no recollections whatsoever of what happened (if anything), to make me stop. I just know that I stopping golfing and started running 3-6 miles a day…I'm flabbergasted now, looking back on this…why did I do that?

In June, I took my buds, Jerry and Dickie, into the mountains for a hiking/ rafting trip. First, I hauled them up Stone Mountain to see the wonderful views up there, then down the trail to view the waterfall. From there, we went deeper into the Appalachians to the Nantahala River, where we took a raft trip down that remote mountain river. It wasn't a wild ride, like you would experience out west, but it was a good trip down the river with two great guys.

Susan is leaving for London again with Dianne Tutt on July 13…I hope Dianne treats Susan better this year than she did before. While Susan's gone, all my journal says is that I'm running every day…the golf thing still has me perplexed.

In August, I flew out to Las Vegas, then drove up to Reno to surprise Anne and Casey on Anne's 50th birthday. I flew to Vegas because I wanted to drive up through the desert to Reno and see the nothingness that was out there. I'd made Anne a video tape of her life (so far) and I wanted to surprise her with it…she needed some good news after the Nick fiasco. They were happy to see me and we had a great time, especially the night of her birthday when we drove up to Lake Tahoe for dinner at Anne's favorite restaurant, Jake's on the Lake, directly on the lake front…it was gorgeous. Anne and I shared a bottle of California's finest and let Casey drive us home later that night; I could've driven, if I'd been awake.

We played tennis together, went running with Elvis, played some slots and blackjack together; went to a BBQ festival, and finally went bowling, where I beat Casey rather handily (sorry Casey, I have to tell the truth). Great girls, great times, I'm lucky to have so many wonderful girls in my life…but, as you know…I'm special.

The rest of the year was spent running, reading and meeting Jerry and Dickie for various college and high school basketball games. But not golfing. The only other noteworthy news was that, apparently, my thyroid had stopped working. On my yearly physical, the doctor asked me if I was rundown? No. Was I tired? No. Was I this? No. That? No. "Well," he said, "you should be." He was very disappointed I had no symptoms, obviously, I was not a good patient; he gave me a prescription and told me to take one of these pills every day. Okay, I will. They must be working, because I still don't have any symptoms…He's a good, old doctor.

***

Before I progress in this chronicle, I want to explain a few things that I've either omitted, or emphasized in the previous chapters of my story and life—as I see it. First, being that I am a Christian—always have been and always will be. The Lord Jesus is the most important thing in the world to me; just because I don't write about it in every chapter or emphasize it more often should not be an indication of how important my faith is to me. It's what keeps me alive and functioning in a somewhat and sometimes dysfunctional world…I am truly blessed in every facet imaginable, there have been heaps and gobs of blessings bestowed on me that I don't deserve; it is by Grace that I exist and continue to breathe the fragrant aromas of this life.

Next, I haven't said a lot about my daughter, Shelley Christine Hope; not because I don't love her with all my heart, because I do. I will love her forever and ever; there are some things she does (and doesn't do) that I don't approve of…it doesn't mean I don't love her. I've found that not commenting on certain aspects of her life, and our relationship, is better than trying to explain it…when the only thing that matters is that I love her. Do I wish things were different? Yes! Do I wish she would make better decisions? Yes! I wish a lot of things…but who among us doesn't? Who among us doesn't wish for better things for their children? As I was looking at my journal for 2004, I made references to Shelley every few days, but yet, I'll probably not pen any of those thoughts in this history. So, reader, as you look through these pages, don't determine by Shelley's absence, that she wasn't in my thoughts and prayers and concerns DAILY, because she was.

And…I am quite certain I have the best friends a man could ever have. I've written about these unique and wonderful men before, so I won't elaborate here in these pages. Just know that because you don't see their names in each and every chapter, it doesn't mean they haven't been a part of my life in each and every chapter…because they have. Also, I have many regrets; many, many things I wish I'd done differently, many decisions I'd like to make over again, many actions and words I'd like to change. The apostle Paul once said that he was the "chief among sinners"…I'm right there with you buddy; however, I know that the Lord has forgiven me, so I don't dwell on these transgressions. I only hope that the men and women in my life will also forgive me for any hurt I have inflicted upon them through my selfish actions and words. That's asking a lot I know; I hope they will all have forgiveness and passion in their hearts for me…I know I don't deserve it, but hopefully, they're all better people than I am.

***

Inexplicably, I started playing golf again in 2004…I don't know why I stopped a year earlier, nor do I know why I started back again. I made no reference to it either time in my journals. I just see now that I started playing again and scoring very well, mostly in the low to mid 70's. I've found that golf was similar to tennis and to playing guitar, in that once your muscles learn what to do, then that muscle memory will kick in whenever you ask it to in the future. I had quit playing golf for over a year, then started back and almost immediately was able to shoot scores near par…it's a funny game.

In February of this year, we had to put Aunt Mary in an assisted living place in King…she would never leave there. It was very difficult, but Sara simply could not care for her any longer, Aunt Mary needed full-time care and attention. The woman who loved me, spanked me, took me to my first Beatles movie, took me to Gatorland (and yes, the Tupperwear plant), the woman who I lived with for two years, who gave me an enema and gave me baseball cards, was lying in a nursing home, with both her legs amputated, her heart damaged, but her mind as sharp as a tack. It's hard to make those decisions for someone who's taken care of you nearly your whole life— very hard. Later in February, Susan's Aunt Doris died. She was a tremendous woman, great Christian wife, mother, sister and aunt…we'll miss her.

***

Early spring, I drove down to Lumberton to meet my "bloods"; Jerry and I were going to run in the "Rumba on the Lumber," Dickie was going to walk it with Wandre. We started out running with the pack and after a couple of minutes Jerry looked over at me and said, "Is this the pace you're going to run at?" "Well," I thought…since I don't have those huge lungs of yours, yes, this is as fast as I'm going to run. So, I said, "take off buddy, show these Lumbees what you're made of." And he did. Within 30 seconds, I had lost sight of him. When I finally arrived at the finish line, Jerry had cooled off, changed clothes, had a Pepsi to drink and finished a BBQ sandwich with fries and hushpuppies. Dang, that boy can run!

I flew out to Las Vegas once again in March to see Casey in another gymnastics meet. I truly don't know how Anne can stand to watch these things every month…they are extremely nerve-wracking to me—and dangerous! The way those girls jump and twist and turn and balance is astounding, and that balance beam—turning flips on a 4" wide piece of wood??? I had to close my eyes when Casey flipped on that thing. At any rate, it was great spending time with them; I think my sister has mostly forgiven me for the things I did to her in her youth, and I know Casey loves her Uncle Gary…don't you? Poor little girl, she tries as hard as she can, but she just can't beat me at anything…putt-putt = Uncle Gary; bowling = Uncle Gary; running = Uncle Gary; ping-pong = Uncle Gary…I know if I could only take a few weeks off and practice some gymnastics tricks I'd probably beat her at that as well…but I won't, I've got to let the little girl win at something…I'm special that way.

On March 17, St. Patrick's Day, Casey turned 17, amazing to think that little red-headed, bug-eyed squirt is now 17 years old. Susan and I celebrated the "wearing of the green" at a Mexican restaurant, but we did have green limes in our Sangria. As I ate my chimichanga and nachos, I was remembering one cold, rainy, misty day when I climbed to the top of Crough Patrick and paid homage to the man himself…"Come fairies, take me out of this dull world, for I would ride with you upon the wind and dance upon the mountains like a flame!" Yes, Billy, we would indeed.

***

Death continued its never-ending journey in our lives, when Susan's Uncle Ralph died on May 11. He was 92 or 93 years old, I'm not sure; it didn't really matter, what did matter was the type of man he was. A good one. He started working at RJR when he was 12 or 14, there were no age restrictions back then, he lived at home and took many of his paychecks in the form of RJR stock, which he kept until he had more money than the Reynolds' family had (that might be an exaggeration, but not by much). Long after Uncle Ralph retired from Reynolds, they still called him when something broke down and they couldn't fix it. He'd go over to the plant, repair the machinery and teach all the engineers and mechanics a few good lessons. Uncle Ralph outlived two wives and soon found himself a third one as he was approaching 90; with a new Viagra prescription in hand, he and his bride started a new and exciting life together—everything with Ralph was exciting.

Before his third marriage, when he was in his mid-to-late 80's, Susan and I arranged to pick him up one night and all go over to Martha's house for a Christmas party. We told him we'd be by about 6:30 that evening, he lived in a big, old house on South Main Street, with about 5-6 steps from the sidewalk up to the porch. As we pulled in the driveway to his house, we saw him come out the front door, take about three steps and leap off the porch, over the steps and onto the sidewalk…bow tied up and ready to go!

There are lots of stories about Uncle Ralph and his money, I don't know if they're all true or not, but they're good stories. Here's a few of my favorites: first, I know this one is true because Susan's Dad and Barbara were participants and witnesses. They had taken Ralph on a trip somewhere and had stopped at a restaurant for dinner that evening. Now, Ralph was rich, but he was also "careful" with his money. They were seated at the table for dinner and the waitress asked them what they wanted to drink, Ralph said "nothing, I'm fine." When she left, he got up and went to the counter where they had these little milk containers—the kind you put in your coffee—maybe an ounce each. He grabbed a handful of these little things and an empty glass and that's what he drank at dinner. He actually wouldn't order anything to eat either, Susan's Dad had to buy something for him and give it to him!

Second, Uncle Ralph had an old car he drove, (why buy a new one, when the old one ran just fine), and he liked to pack the trunk of that old car with old and rare coins and go to "coin shows" around the area. He had so many coins in the trunk of that car that at night the headlights were shining up in the air instead of on the road. He left the coins in the trunk of his car, parked out in the driveway in a section of town that had changed dramatically since Ralph's youth…it was an area you probably wanted to stay away from after dark. However, no one ever messed with his car or his coins…if those desperados had only known what he had back there…

Finally, I don't actually know if this story is true or not, but it sheds light on the nature of Uncle Ralph. Clarence was his lawyer and went to pick him up one day to do some legal work for him (Clarence was good that way), they had to go downtown for some reason and Uncle Ralph said he'd drive. Clarence hopped in the passenger seat and as they were going down the road, he noticed an envelope stuck down between the backrest and the seat cushion. He pulled it out and asked Uncle Ralph what it was, Ralph didn't know and asked Clarence to open it for him. Clarence opened it and found a $100,000 CD inside the envelope. He looked real close at it to make sure it was real, then asked Uncle Ralph about it, and Ralph said, "Oh, I wondered where that was." Skimming milk and losing $100,000 CD's…that was Uncle Ralph in a nutshell.

29

"We are the products of our past, but we don't have to be prisoners of it."

As the year progressed, I continued to play golf, I was good now and the "big boys" were calling me to play with them. However, in my journal, where I had been noting my scores, I was now noting other things in place of my score for the day. A good example of this is my journal entry for May 12, which said I walked 15 holes after work and saw the following: geese, a groundhog, buzzards, swans, bluebirds, turtles, a snake, American Goldfinches, squirrels, a worm, grackles, and a bunch of little grey birds. Nothing about my score or how I played, or who I played with…a telling sign I think.

I still could not get Ireland out of my mind, I thought about it all the time; someone told me," Gar, you can't keep going back to the same place year after year." "Why not?" I thought, if you love it, why the heck not? But, I let others unduly influence me and started thinking of someplace else we could go this summer. Maybe it'll be a good idea to ask Susan—YA THINK?

We left July 16 for another Alaskan cruise. 2 ½ hour flight to Minneapolis, then 5 more hours to Anchorage, then a 3 hour bus ride to Seward where the ship was—my friends, that's a long day. The bus ride was really pretty nice, through the Alaskan back country—mountains, glaciers, rivers, lakes…what a wonderland. Finally, we arrived at Royal Caribbean's "Vision of the Seas," a truly magnificent ship. Alaska's climate then was similar to Ireland's, around 60 degrees, sort of misty and rainy…nice day to visit a pub, or the ship's bar—which we did.

This cruise, we would leave Seward and sail down the Alaskan coast to Vancouver; on our first day we stopped at Hubbard Glacier…a true glacier by any definition. It was roughly 300' tall, and about 5 miles wide—that, friends, is a glacier. As we slowly slipped into the bay we started hearing thunder, rolling thunder, which seemed a little strange since it was only about 48 degrees outside. But, we soon found out it wasn't thunder at all that we were hearing, it was the "calving" (or, breaking away) of ice from the main glacier. As these 200-300' sheets of ice would break from the main glacier and fall into the sea, the noise it made sounded like thunder to us on the ship. Our ship stayed in the bay about 4-5 hours while we were mesmerized by the hundreds of icebergs floating around the ship and the thunderous calving sounds and sights of the glacier itself. I wish I could describe this incredible scene better, but I don't know how—you need to go there.

Our next stop was Juneau, as we docked there, we were looking out over the bay and we saw an eagle glide down to the ocean, grab a fish from the water and fly back into the trees. You seldom see that in Robeson County…this trip was starting out pretty darn good. We'd made reservations in Juneau for a "whale watching" excursion; I was pretty skeptical about this, I didn't really understand, or much believe, they could leave the docks at 1:00 and actually go out and see whales. Did they have the whales in cages or chained up? How could they guarantee you'd see a whale? But, that's exactly what they did, if we did not see whales (plural), they would refund our $100 tickets—that's a pretty big gamble on their part.

The little boat probably held about 15 people, including me, (who was doped to the max on Dramamine). We left the harbor and hadn't gone 5-10 minutes out into the bay when we saw our first whale breaching the surface. Then another one, and another one; the boat stopped and we watched spellbound as these magnificent creatures kept showing off for us. Alaskan law prohibited us from getting closer than 100 yards from them, but that was okay…that was just okay. Occasionally, they would surface about 50 yards from us as they frolicked in the ocean. Frolicked? I don't actually know what they were doing…watching us watching them…I have no idea; but I do know that was probably the best $100 I've ever spent. Just before we turned around to head back to the shore, four whales surfaced together, rolled on their sides, flipped up their tails and went back under…quite an encore.

We left rainy Juneau (they get precipitation there 300 days a year) for Skagway, where we took another helicopter ride up to the Denver Glacier—insanely beautiful! From there, down the coast to Ketchikan to the Misty Fjords, snow covered mountains, blah, blah, blah—the beauty is so monotonous…Alaska, can't you simply be plain and dull? Obviously, not!

Coming home from Alaska, or Ireland, or England, or Italy, or Utah, etc., etc…took a while for me to adjust to the normalcy of life. I started golfing again and the old muscle memory kicked in high gear; less than a month later I won our golf club championship at Pinebrook, shooting even par on the last day. Scoring in tournament play is much tougher than usual, because you have to make every 1 and 2 footer, nothing is conceded—this plays on your nerves. I was playing in the last group on Sunday with the guy who was in second place, I'll always remember him—Turk Turgliafaro. He may have lapsed into history unknown, if he hadn't pulled a stunt on the last hole of the tournament that upset me and consequently, inspired me.

Old Turk was one shot behind me coming to the last hole, which was a par 5; he smashed a drive way down the fairway, easily within reach of the green in two. I hit a good drive, not nearly as far as Turk's, and knew I could not reach the green in two shots. I hit first and laid up about 40 yards short of the green, whereas Turk hit a beautiful shot onto the green about 20' from the hole. I hit my little chip shot to the green okay—not great, just okay, about 15' from the pin. If Turk made his 20 footer, he would at least tie me, if not win the tournament—he barely missed and tapped in for a birdie; which meant, my 15 footer was also for birdie and if I made it—I had won the tournament by one shot over Turk.

My putt was on a little sidehill lie, with maybe 6-8" of break in it; as I was lining it up deciding exactly how to putt it, Turk walked behind me, stopped ever so briefly and said, "wow, that's got a lot of break in it." Something happened in me when he said that…I knew he was trying to disturb me, that he was sinking to the lowest form of gamesmanship he knew; but instead of being more nervous, that comment somehow made me focus so much on the line of the putt, that I could actually see the ball rolling in the hole before I ever hit it! All I had to do now was put the club on the ball and I KNEW it was going in—I KNEW IT! And, it did. Turk said, "nice putt," and walked off the green…I wanted to scream, or cry, or yell "take that you #$&#@?&%$#!!!" I didn't…but I sure wanted to. Several people watching came over to congratulate me, the pro gave me the trophy and shook my hand, which was unnecessary because my whole body was shaking. That was as proud as I've ever been of myself in a sporting event. I carefully carried my beautiful, glass vase trophy home and showed it to Susan and she said, "where did you get that?" I said, "I won it." She looked me right dead in the eye and said, "Really?"

***

On November 26, I played my last round of golf at Pinebrook…fittingly, I shot a 1 under par round. The club was having financial problems, the economy had caused a lot of members to leave and they had to keep "assessing" the remaining members some fees to cover the costs of running the club. After the second assessment, I decided to quit and not pay any more…in retrospect, a rash decision; I loved Pinebrook and loved golfing there. But, I did it and almost immediately started asking myself "what now?" Before I end my golfing saga I want to write about the funniest thing I've ever seen on a golf course (except for all my temper tantrums of course). I played a lot of golf with two close friends in those days, Mike Dees and Jack Braswell; Jack was a good golfer, about a 10-12 handicapper. Mike wanted to be a good golfer, Lord knows he tried, but he just didn't have it in him. Mike would try different swings, different clubs, different thoughts—nothing worked; he had the worst slice you've ever seen and could never correct it.

To have the ball land safely in the fairway, he would have to aim it 50 yards left to allow for the slice—it was that bad. On hole number 6 at Pinebrook, there is a cinder block restroom facility just in the front left of the tee box, with a water cooler outside the door. Well, old Mike has to aim left, because of his slice, but on this particular day, he aimed a little too far left, and he probably hit the ball a little on the heel of the club; at any rate, when he hit the ball, it went straight at the restroom, bounced off the cinder blocks, ricochet off the water cooler and rolled right back up the tee box, stopping directly between Mike's legs, next to his tee. Jack and I were howling, fortunately, we'd already hit our shots…if not, there's no way we could've recovered enough to swing. Poor old Mike took it good enough and even today, will sometimes smile himself when we recall that episode.

30

"I've learned that I still have a lot to learn."

My little sister had been running marathons, she even ran in the Boston Marathon; this inspired me to see if this was something I could do as well—not Boston, but just complete a marathon, to see if it was possible with this 55 year old body. Since golf was now over, I could devote my full attention to running…the problem was, I hated it. I'm sorry, but running is no fun; it hurts your feet, your ankles, your knees, your back, and most importantly it wears on your mind. The simple fact of knowing you have to come home from work and run 6-8 miles is gruesomely sadistic…it ruins your whole day. I found that MAYBE one day out of ten was pain free, the rest of the time was torture. Well, why did you do it Gar?

Shelley had become pregnant early in 2005. After all the mental and emotional adjustments we all made with that news, we started preparing for a new life in our family. We had lost so many aunts and uncles on both sides of our families recently, we were excited about a baby. Judy, Susan and I all went for the sonogram, which showed Shelley was going to have a little girl…I was glad. On September 18, precious little Kali Christine Hope was born, with all of us in the room witnessing her arrival. All ten toes and fingers, pointy little head and just the prettiest thing you'd ever seen in your life. I was a very proud Grandpa.

Life pretty much revolved around Kali, rightly so, she looked like Shelley then, and she still does—it's amazing the similarity. I was around a lot because I had changed jobs in mid-2005 to work at Goodwill Industries of NWNC…hopefully, the last job I'll ever have—a very good company. So, having no vacation time accrued, we didn't travel this year…I just ran and ran and ran…trying to accustom my body and mind to the torture that is long distance running. What I soon figured out was that my mind actually controlled how I felt and how I performed—not my body. If I knew, in my mind, that I had to run 9 miles that day, then I could run 9 miles fairly easily. But, if my mind knew the next day that I was only going to run 3 miles, then that's ALL I could run…not one step over 3 miles—I physically couldn't do it. I found that I could only run what my mind told me I had to run. If the schedule was 12 miles, then I'd run twelve, it was only 4 miles, then all I could do was 4…no more—my mind controlled what my body was able to do.

In December, I ran my first half marathon here in W-S, the Mistletoe Run; lots of people running on a very cold, windy morning. First thing I noticed was some guy running barefoot.

Then I looked around and saw older people than me (much older), fat people, skinny people, sick-looking people, ugly people and a few whom I couldn't tell if they were male or female people. But, they were all runners. For some reason which I have never understood to this day, I ran that 13.1 miles (the most I'd ever run up to that point), and I never got tired, I never got out of breath and at the finish line I felt as if I could've kept on going for another two hours. The only time in my life I'd ever felt that way, before or since. Then, I knew, the full marathon was next…I knew I could do it.

Anne and Casey came to our house at Christmas and we all had a great time playing with Kali and with each other…a baby sure makes the holidays special. Now, reader, I am going to skim through time, omitting some fascinating, humorous and touching stories—not wanting to bog you down with what you may consider the trivialities of mundane everyday life—I'm special that way.

So, we skip ahead to my training for the marathon, I was up to 20 mile runs by February, and hating every bit of it. Finally, marathon day, March 25 arrives. It's the Ellerbe Springs Marathon, basically run through the farming and rural areas in and around Ellerbe. I'm going to skip all my crying and complaining and whining about how hard it was and how much I hated it, and skip to the end…4 hours and 48 minutes later. I was disappointed with my time, I had wanted to be under 4 hours, but the course whipped me into submission. There was not a flat spot anywhere in the 26.2 miles; up one hill, down another, up, down, a succession of heart-breaking hills that drained my energy and will power. One particularly brutal stretch in the middle had a 2 ½ mile long uphill grade, not steep, but all uphill. It was beyond my capabilities and what my training had prepared me for. Fat women were passing me, old guys were passing me, I was trying to maintain my dignity and not start crying. Honestly, I was lucky to finish the course without medical attention. I had run a marathon, but the marathon had won.

In May I went to Atlantic Beach to meet my homeys: Dickie, Jerry, Larry, Bill, Furman and Nickie. What a joy to spend time with these guys…it would be the first of many trips and times we'd start spending with each other. Then in early June we had our family reunion again at the nursing home where Aunt Mary was living. Aunt Annie Lou had died the previous winter and Uncle Earl was alone, but looked good, as did all the others…time was taking its toll however. The brevity of time is one of the most amazing aspects of life, especially as we get older and start putting things in perspective.

Life, life, life, life…it just rolls on, days into days, memories made and memories forgotten; if not for my journal notes, I couldn't distinguish one year from the next—life just happens. I had a colonoscopy on my birthday—not the kind of present I was hoping for. We met Jerry and Wandre again in Blowing Rock one cold, windy weekend in late October. Dickie, Larry, Bill and Jerry visited in November, we went to a basketball game and a football game, however, we could've done nothing but sit around and re-tell stories for three days and had just as much fun. We don't need any entertainment, other than ourselves.

Anne and Casey came for Thanksgiving; we ate a lot, went to movies, shopped, laughed, played with Kali—all the things that make life special. Susan spoiled everyone, took them shopping, took them for pedicures, let Anne shop in Wal-Mart all she wanted, let Casey pick out the movies, and let them sleep as long as they wanted.

My friend, my blood, my homey Dickie had a heart by-pass operation in December and I went to Chapel Hill and sat with him in the hospital…it was scary. We're pretty much just alike…open heart surgery???

Shelley and Kali

Time marches on, our bodies slowly deteriorate, youth fades, middle age passes, old age beckons…we lose aunts and uncles and moms and dads. But, our friends, our contemporaries, ourselves—how do we cope with that? How will we manage that? Will our faith carry us through these hard times?

***

I read 84 books in 2006 and our country has now been at "war" in Iraq for 46 months; I like the book statistic better, especially considering that during this so-called war, more than 3000 young Americans have been killed. What a huge waste of precious lives. I was out running on January 13, a wonderful 70 degree day, and my right heel felt like it imploded. It felt as though I had stepped on a piece of glass, or metal, that cut through the bottom of my shoe. What really happened was that the cortisone shot I'd taken in my heel for the plantar fasciitis had ceased working suddenly. I was about 5 miles out at the time and had to limp back home…beaten and dejected. I had planned to train on the hills and improve my time in the Ellerbe Springs marathon this year…so much for that.

Anne moved from San Francisco to Kansas City for a better job opportunity; she's afraid she won't like it there, she's been a west coast girl for quite a while now. (She'll like it). Met all the boys again at Emerald Isle, told stories (the same ones, but with different names), laughed, told some more lies, talked sports and laughed some more…sounds awful doesn't it? For the third year in a row, Susan and I did not take a big vacation; plenty of quick, short trips, but nothing big. Anne and Casey came for Thanksgiving and Christmas this year; again, always such a joy to have a houseful of people…Shelley and Kali came and a wonderful time was had by all. Anne and Susan went together and gave me a gym membership for Christmas…hmmm, wonder if I'll ever use that?

31

"If you find yourself in a hole, stop digging."

I flew up to Michigan to visit Casey on her 21st birthday at Western Michigan University. As I was flying in to the Grand Rapids airport, I noticed all the little lakes and ponds were frozen over...it was March 15, and they were still frozen over; and as we landed I saw snow piled up around the streets. I left home in shirt sleeves and arrived up here freezing. Anne and Casey met me and we toured the university, Casey's apartment and Kalamazoo, while I was still marveling at all the snow piled up on the streets. She had a good gymnastics meet and tasted her first Guinness on March 17—she didn't like it. Anne and I had the opportunity to ride around town some alone and she mentioned to me a guy she'd been seeing recently; his name was Mark (already a bad one-syllable omen). We'll see.

We're now at the 5 year anniversary of the so-called Gulf War and our country is spending over $12 BILLION a month to finance this fiasco, which is nothing compared to the cost of young lives lost and devastated by injuries. This spring I competed in the Senior Games here in Winston Salem, competitors from all over northwest N.C. came here to complete in track and field events. I entered four events: 100 yard dash, 200 yard dash, long-jump and standing long-jump. I finished second in all four events...to the same guy, losing the 100 yard dash by only one step...pretty frustrating.

Met all the boys again at Ocean Isle in May and started to really enjoy my gym membership Anne and Susan had gotten me for Christmas. In July, Dickie, Larry and I went to Baltimore to attend a couple of Baltimore Oriole baseball games, Bill had gotten us tickets, through Baseball USA which were eight rows behind home plate—thank you Bill. We walked around Baltimore and the Inner Harbor, and generally enjoyed our weekend there; mostly we enjoyed each other's company.

Again, no vacation for us, time spent visiting Kali and Shelley and Aunt Mary and other family members...I'm worried about Shelley, wish there was something I could do. She had a terrible car accident in October and was lucky to survive...I'll let it go at that; not much else positive to report. And on November 4, we elected a Black President. All the boys came back up in November for a football game, we've sort of gotten addicted to each by now and we keep looking for excuses or reasons to all get together as often as we can.

Anne, Casey and Anne's boyfriend Mark came for Thanksgiving...Mark loved sports, loved to watch sports, loved to talk sports and enjoyed a good, cold Guinness; I've got to figure out a way to add a syllable to his name. He's a good, old boy and we broke him in right with a lengthy visit at the nursing home with Aunt Mary—he endured it well. Anne and Casey came back for Christmas, leaving poor, old Mark in the hinterlands...we'd see him again soon enough.

The year passes quietly, life moves on; some good things, some not so good things. As I near the end of this history of Gary Hope, I'm going to speed write through the remaining years; hitting a few memorable trips and occurrences...to be honest, I getting a bit tired of all this writing, as I'm sure you are tired of reading it.

So, forgive me for compacting the remaining years into a few pages; but let's move on—okay?

***

Anne's job in Kansas City was as a Vice President at Grantham University, an on-line school; soon, she got me on board teaching Geography to these college students. This was in late 2008, by early 2009 I was also teaching classes in World History, American Government and a couple of other introductory subjects. It was fun and I enjoyed it and it paid pretty well. By July I would have 26 different courses I was teaching at Grantham...it was indeed a full time job—but would it last?

My friend Bill, who was the town manager in Cary, NC had recently had the Olympic baseball stadium named after him, because of his hard work in having it located and built in Cary...The William B. Coleman Field...we are all so proud of him. Since Bill is the namesake of the stadium, he arranged for all the boys to meet there one weekend in July and take infield and batting practice on this immaculate field—and we did. We fielded ground balls, tried to throw them to first base, we hit, we ran bases, we laughed and had the best time a bunch of 60 year old men can have. Dickie on first, Bill on second, Larry at short and me at third...just like old times, 40-50 years ago! Time fades a lot of things, it cannot fade our friendship or love for each other.

We met Jerry and Wandre and Anne and Mark in Nags Head in September; I hadn't been there since 1977 and had forgotten how beautiful and wonderful the Outer Banks can be. We climbed the sand dunes, visited the Wright Brother's Memorial, walked the beaches, watched surfers, ate generously and had a glorious five days on the ocean. I think I'd better come up with a second syllable for Mark pretty quickly. All the boys came up for another football game in October and we celebrated Larry's birthday on the 5th as well...he's Bill's hero, so we had to give him a hero's birthday party—Susan did just that.

In November, Grantham cut me off for the year, they said I had too many students...1133 so far. Just as I suspected, I need to come up with a new syllable for Mark, he and Anne married on November 19, 2009—my sister is indeed lucky to have old Marky—yes, from now on, he's Marky...he knows it, he accepts it, we will not tempt fate. Congratulations Anne and Marky! I saw the boys for some more games, and spent time with Kali and tried to with Shelley...pretty frustrating there. Anne, Casey and Marky came for Christmas and we celebrated it with a White Christmas! First time in my life I'd experienced that, mama would have loved it. Gary, are you slowing down? Has the wanderlust left your heart? Are you getting old? Be patient reader, I'm just getting started.

32

"One word is worth a thousand pictures…if it's the right word."

2010 was another year of meeting the boys for baseball games, basketball games and football games…taking them to Foothills, Finnegan's, Vincenzo's, Village Tavern, the Deacon Tower Grille, Chelsea's, Hutch & Harris, and other favorites of ours around downtown and beyond. But, as Dickie would say, we could eat out on a Pepsi crate and a cinder block and have just as good a time. Little Kali was getting more beautiful by the day and I was getting more worried every day about her mom.

Over the years I had been secretly and psychologically planting the idea of Ireland in Casey's mind…she doesn't realize it, but I can easily manipulate her thoughts and actions without her knowing it—I'm special that way. I had convinced her, unconsciously of course, that her mom should give her a trip to Ireland for her college graduation this year. Anne asked me what I thought of the idea and would we go with them…well, "I don't know," I said, "Let me think about it." I then let the idea stew for a few days (with Casey calling me, urging me to go every day or two); finally, I said, yes, we'd go—only because of little Casey's graduation. They are so easily manipulated.

Off to Ireland we go, Anne and Marky, Susan and me, Casey and Marky's son Scott (who proved to be just as good as his dad)—all 6 of us on a great adventure, hopefully with no seasickness, or poisonous bites from anything…a nice safe holiday. It didn't start out well. We had all boarded the plane for Shannon when they announced the plane had a mechanical malfunction and we had to exit the aircraft and board a different plane. That's not a comfortable feeling when you're getting ready to fly 6 hours across the ocean.

No problems however, and we landed safely in Shannon, got our two rental cars and headed for Killarney, jewel of Kerry, emerald gem of our hearts. We arrived in Killarney in typical Irish fashion, rainy, windy and cold. We couldn't check in to our hotel yet, the beautiful Loch Lein House, so we all piled into one car and drove up to the Gap of Dunloe—breathtaking mountain scenery, dotted with lakes and stones and sheep and waterfalls. The other four of them got out of the car, overwhelmed with the Irish scenery, and started walking and running in the rain, Susan and I, having been here before, opted to stay dry in the car and follow them along the muddy one-lane, unpaved road. They romped in the rain, chased sheep, climbed to some waterfalls and were having a blast. I would pull off the road as much as I could to watch them, but there wasn't any room to do much moving on the narrow little muddy road, boarded closely by rock walls. They finally decided they had enough and wanted to turn around and go back...well, how do I do that? There are no turn-offs, no places to do anything...I finally found a little place where I thought I might be able to turn, as I turned the wheel as far as I could, the car started sliding sideways off the road. No matter how hard I applied the brakes or turned the wheel, we were sliding sideways, right into a big boulder...well, not actually that big, it only left about a 24" gash in the side of the car. Could've been worse.

***

Sharing Ireland with our family was fantastic, it was like new to us again, seeing it through their eyes. The Dingle Peninsula, all the way to the little town of Dingle and out to Slea Head, the scenery is beyond description. The Ring of Kerry, the lakes of Killarney, Torc Falls, we showed them all we could in our three short days in Killarney. We drove next up the coast to the Cliffs of Moher and across the Shannon towards Galway; this time we would board a larger boat for the trip out to the Aran Islands. We loved Galway...the city was alive! Bands playing, pedestrian malls, pubs, restaurants, it was as vibrant a city as I've been in. We sat out and watched one little street band play and even bought their CD's...do you remember their name? (Mutefish). We also celebrated Marky's and Susan's birthdays in Galway, hard to find a better place for those celebrations. We took the boat out to Inishmore and I didn't even get sick—but it was close. We visited the old fort Dun Aengus, walked the rocky roads, gazed into the misty Atlantic and dreamed of Irish days and nights, long ago.

On a previous trip here I had noticed a sign that said "Newton Castle," but Susan and I didn't stop then, I told myself I would stop this time if I could only see that sign again...after all, my grandmother's grandparents were Newton's and immigrated from Ireland sometime in the 1840's...the potato famine era. We spotted it finally and cruised into the grounds; there it was, my birthright, my heritage, my claim to Irish princehood. And it was closed. We had to settle for taking pictures, walking around the castle and posing with Anne in front of the doorway...prince and princess, finally at home with our ancestors. You can call me Sir Gary from now on.

Our next stay was in Clifden, where we spent the night before traveling up to Donegal, a place I had longed to visit. On the way to Donegal, we spotted on old rock, watch tower, so we pulled off the road to inspect it; what a find, it was from the year 1100, and across the street from a little church that had a small graveyard containing the grave of William B. Yeats. After several pictures of the church and the dead poet's grave, we started off again in our two-car caravan for the remote outpost of Donegal which seemed by the map to be about two hours away. We drove the twisty, narrow little roads of northwest Ireland and enjoyed the pristine scenery that you'll only find in Ireland. We passed one field with several horses grazing in the lush green pasture, I looked at Casey, pointed at the horses and said, "Do you know what they call those in Ireland?" "No," she said, "What?" "Horses, Casey, they call them horses." She failed to see the humor in that.

After about an hour and a half of driving we spotted another stone tower, similar to the one we'd seen earlier; we pulled off the road to check it out, looked across the street, and there is the church with William B. Yeats grave! What the #&*$@%!!! What had we done? Somehow, we got twisted around and rode in a big circle for an hour and a half and ended up back where we started. Marky, why didn't you bring a GPS? Oh well, actually, the scenery looked better the second time around.

After a few minutes back on the "correct" route, we decided to stop in a little village just short of Donegal to have an afternoon cup of soup and a liquid refreshment. As we were ready to leave I asked the waiter about how far it was from here to Donegal...he said, "Where?," "Donegal," I said...he had never heard of it. Lived here his whole life, Donegal was the largest city in the region, the county seat and no more than 15-20 minutes away...and he'd never heard of it. Very odd, so we went outside to the car and I asked an older gentleman the same question, how far to Donegal? "Where?" You cannot be serious! This guy also had never heard of Donegal...I was flabbergasted, but in retrospect, I should not have been; this was Ireland, not America. People here were born and raised and seldom left the little towns and villages they were from; they truly had no concept of travel, and only dreamed of "going to the States," actually venturing up the road for 20 minutes to a different city was as alien to them as it would be for us to travel to Timbuctu, or Katmandu, or even Kalamazoo. The Gaelic region of northwest Ireland was indeed a land in and of itself.

Donegal was great, a wonderful castle in the middle of town, dating from the 1300's, beautifully restored; marvelous coastline, exquisite scenery. And to top it off, the hotel we stayed at was hosting an Irish wedding, complete with bridesmaids, tuxedoed men and drunken priests...you gotta love Ireland. We visited the local pubs there, Marky and Scott rooted for the county Hurling team and the Donegal Gaelic football squad as they played Galway (Donegal won). We didn't clearly understand the rules of Gaelic football, and certainly not hurling...but it was great fun rooting for the local teams.

Understandably sad, our journey was nearing the end, the long drive back to Shannon, the long flight home, the memories of this trip forever etched in our minds and hearts. Chasing a group of sheep in our car, down a tiny, wall lined road; Guinness in the pubs, walking in the rain, marveling at the waterfalls...on and on, memory upon memory spent with those we love.

Our family also grew by two this year, Susan's niece Robyn, had twins! Eliza and Luke came into the world healthy and wise—wise, because both their parents graduated from Duke. Robyn loves me, even though she tries to hide it at times (Wendy just loves me out right); I know she and Seth will be wonderful, loving parents—they can't help but be—they have great role models. One Seth story and I'll move on...I played golf at Pinebrook several times with Seth – who is a great golfer by the way, even though he won't play anymore. We were on hole # 16 which was a long par 4, we stood on the tee and Seth looked down the fairway and said, "Is that overhanging limb in play?" "What limb?" I asked, I didn't know what he was referring to. "That one...down the left hand side." I looked where he was pointing and saw the limb in question, and said, "That one? Heck no! I can't even hit a drive that rolls under that limb." Yep. Seth hit the limb on the fly. I sort of ducked my head and started walking away, waiting for Seth's response to my terrible advice. He never uttered a word, just continued on to his ball, went about his business and parred the hole. That's Seth.

I turned 60 years old in October, a great month, and in November I competed in the North Carolina Bodybuilding Championships in Greensboro. Senior division of course, all eight competitors were at least 60 years old. I came in fourth, which stunk, because the top three places received trophies. All that work and pumping iron and dieting and all I get is a pat on the back and a "good job, keep up the good work." I had bulked up to 210 pounds during the summer, and had dieted down to 188 pounds for the competition…I should have stayed big. All the other guys in the competition were in the 220-240 range, most of them pumped up on steroids as well; they were all huge compared to me, I just had less body fat than a few of them and a little better defined musculature, that's why I finished 4th, instead of last. I don't think I'll do any more shows or competitions, simply because shaving my body is too traumatic—I'm a very hairy dude, in case you haven't noticed. I liked the training part, the lifting and even the dieting wasn't too bad…but that shaving, Susan hated it, and without all my hair, I sort of looked like…Jerry.

***

My beautiful wife finally retired from the school system after 38 years. Jan 31, 2011 was her last day, it's about time, the stress and all the junk associated with the job were taking its toll on her…I'm glad it's over. We visited Wilmington in April with Jerry and Wandre and, of course, had a great time; Wilmington has done a great job of revitalizing its downtown and river areas—it's a very nice place to visit, or even live. At the end of April, the 30th, Susan and a group of her school associates decided to celebrate their retirements by renting a limousine and taking a tour of several local wineries. They were just leaving the first winery of the day, Childress Winery in Davidson County, when another car slammed into them broadsiding their limo, turning it over several times. Miraculously, no one was killed, several went to the hospital, but Susan only received bruises and cuts from all the broken glass. That accident has affected Susan to this day, she flinches a lot in traffic now when she sees cars come a little too close, especially as a passenger when she looks up and is surprised by traffic…I can understand how she feels—it was a bad, scary accident.

We decided to paint our house this spring and started getting bids from several companies to paint the outside and a couple of rooms inside maybe. It was expensive, so we decided we'd definitely paint the outside and maybe one or two rooms on the inside depending on the cost. The best deal we had was around $1800 for the outside and a couple of inside rooms; as I was mulling this over one day at work, I asked a couple of my Mexican employees if they knew any people from their church who did painting. Of course they did, so I asked them to come over and give me an estimate as well. Two very nice professional looking guys came and surveyed the house, took measurements, talked in Spanish, pointed, gestured, walked around and around and finally said, yes, they'd love to do it and would be back tomorrow with their price. Great, I thought, maybe I could save a little if they did it.

The next afternoon they came over, one speaking English, the owner could only speak Spanish; I asked them how much and the younger guy said $600. I said, "What? $600??" The younger guy looked at the older guy, said something in Spanish, they talked, then looked back at me and said, "okay, $500." No, no, no...are you sure of this price, to paint all of the outside and the rooms inside? Yes, they said. We settled on $1200, saved me a bunch of money and made them double what they were initially asking...they did a very nice job and we were all happy.

Susan and I left May 7 for a hiking trip in Utah where we'd meet Anne and Marky for a week's adventure in the most beautiful place in the country. Arches National Park and Canyonlands National Park are beyond description, so I'll spare you the time of reading my inadequate accounts of the scenery. We go to different trails each day, including the one to the Confluence Overlook I described earlier, where I could never find my missing quarter, hike all day, become mesmerized by the beauty of it all, then return to the little

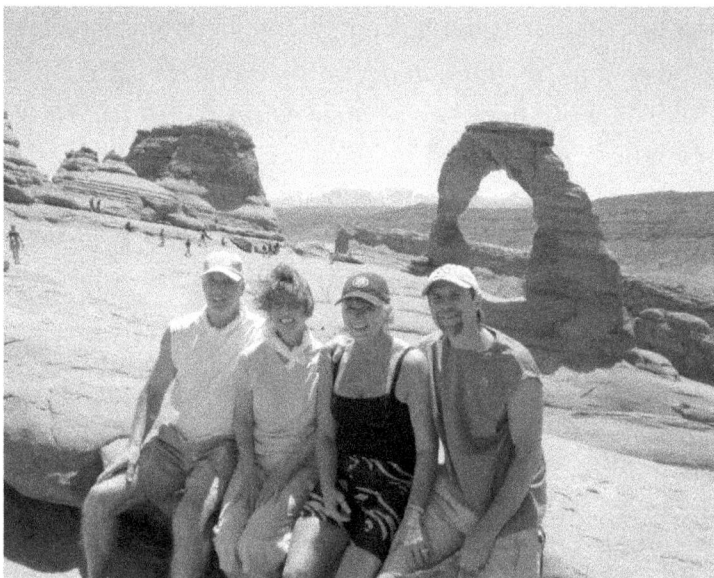

Anne, Mark, Susan and Me in Utah

town of Moab each evening for dinner and drinks at the Moab Brewery—home of Black Raven Stout, my favorite. The Needles, Dead Horse Point, the Island in the Sky, Grandview Point, Delicate Arch, Mesa Arch...too many to list, too beautiful to describe. The view of Balanced Rock with the La Sal Mountains in the background was enough to overwhelm me and bring a sane man to tears; but of course, there is no sanity in this heartlessly beautiful land. Do not travel here, it's too dangerous for you, too many things that will stick you, prick you and bite you; too many places you'll get lost, twist an ankle, fall down, skin your arms; and too many places that will make you sit down and dream the undreamable, and think the unthinkable. No...stay home, go the beach and watch the waves crash upon the shore, sip a pina colada and thank your lucky stars you are where you are.

***

In early August I took Kali up to Stone Mountain and let her walk through the woods, play under the waterfall, collect little shells, while we made a list of all the animals we saw that day, which included: deer, wild turkeys, a rabbit, a hawk, some geese and a few goats—it was a fun day. How lucky we are to have such a beautiful little girl in our family. Later in August, I flew up to Milwaukee for a Goodwill meeting, but in all honesty, we didn't meet very much, mostly in was going to dinners with people, drinks with people and for me—going to see the Brewers play the Dodgers three nights in a row—fantastic. I liked Milwaukee (of course, I haven't been there in the winter time), great, enthusiastic crowds and a beautiful new ballpark, wonderful friendly people...in the summer, it was a great place to visit.

***

Aunt Mary died this morning, Sept. 17, 2011...she'd known me and cared for me and loved me for 61 years. No other person on earth could claim that. She was special...she had her ways and could exasperate you to no end, but there was something about Mary, something we'll never forget and something we'll always remember. I'm sure my mama met her in heaven, along with Joe; she left here without both legs, but arrived up there in full heavenly body, the woman we'd grown up with and loved, healthy and vibrant again.

We buried her in Red Springs, next to her first husband, Herbert Grady Fowler, on one side; and my mom on the other side—so she could take care of them and they could take care of her. Sisters together again...they had always looked out for each other. Back home the next day, I saw a peacock standing on the side of the road, with its tail fanned out in all its fantastic colors. I hadn't seen a peacock in years and years, and have never seen one since...but I surely saw one the day after we buried my Aunt Mary.

***

Life kept on rolling, time kept on passing…I had a cancerous lesion cut off my ear (no fun at all), all the boys came up for football games, baseball games, heck—any reason we could come up with to visit that all the wives would believe. Truth was, we NEEDED each other, we needed to hear Dickie's stories, we needed to kid Jerry and listen to all the people Allen beat up, I needed to talk to Larry—I wanted to find out what he was thinking—I still do. He can't remember much, but sometimes he can say things that make you think. I need to confide in Jerry, I need to be with Dickie—we're so much alike; I love being around Bill, soaking up his confidence and humor...we need each other like the crops need the rain to grow and prosper.

My Uncle G.C. died on Oct 14; I've written about him in another book, a true American hero; winner of the Silver Star in WWII, father of 6, grandfather to many more. Of course, all my uncles and grandfather were heroes...I'm special that way. Another special man is Susan's Dad, who's also in my second book, we went to his 90th birthday party in late October, and it was a grand affair, fittingly, for a great man.

I drove down to Red Springs in early November to meet all the guys and go to a UNC-Pembroke football game. I had not been back on campus since I graduated there in 1974. I was amazed at what I saw, first, I didn't recognize anything; I was totally lost and if not for Jerry and Dickie, I couldn't have found my way around. Second, I was very impressed and proud at what my old school had done...I'm proud to be a Brave. The next morning, Dickie and Larry and I drove all over Red Springs, riding by all the houses where we and our friends used to live, where we used to play ball, where we used to go parking with Vardell Hall girls, places we loved and times we'd never forget.

Anne and Casey and Marky couldn't come for Thanksgiving this year, so Susan and I decided to make our own Thanksgiving tradition...we'd go on a cruise! We drove to Charleston and boarded Carnival's "Fantasy"; we had always cruised on Royal Caribbean in the past, but were pleasantly surprised by Carnival and the ship. Thanksgiving on the ocean sailing down to Nassau, 78 degrees, sitting out by the pool, Pina Coladas and Kiss on the Lips, reading, dozing and people watching...I love Thanksgiving. Our ship had a 24 hour ice cream bar and a 24 grill that served hamburgers, cheeseburgers, fries and chicken wings—if your cholesterol didn't rise appropriately, it was your own darned fault.

We docked in Freeport and saw nothing that impressed us and went back on board as quickly as we could; however, we did like Nassau and walked up and down the streets there, and the straw market; ending up on a restaurant balcony, overlooking the main street, while we drank a couple of Kaliks and kept trying to solve Dickie's problems...again, we failed. Nights were spent going to shows on board (a great Beatles tribute one night), visiting the casino and generally doing whatever we wanted to do...which was mostly having fun and doing nothing.

A grand and wonderful year...but, aren't they all?

33

"Of course I want to hear about your problems…just let me Irish up this coffee first."

Mr. Mattox, please forgive me, but I joined the Methodist church today, Jan. 8, 2012. I'm not that happy about it, but you do what you have to do and try to ignore the rest. A Methodist…doesn't sound right does it? All the boys came up again in February; Deacon Tower Grille, Finnegan's Wake, Hutch & Harris, basketball game and a baseball game. It's probably not fair for us to be having this much fun, but we're special like that; so, it's okay.

Susan and I went back to Ireland in June, arriving in Shannon again and driving down to our favorite little town of Killarney. Outside the airport, it's 48 degrees, raining and the wind is blowing about 35 mph; we plug in our GPS, no getting lost this trip, and start searching for fairies and leprechauns as we make our way down the sheep infested streets of Limerick and Kerry. Our weeklong destination is the Castlerosse Hotel and Golf Resort in Killarney, with magnificent views of Loch Lein and the Dunloe Mountains from the dining room, bar and our bedroom (room no. 131, this will be important later in my story).

I won't bore you with details, but suffice it to say, we were overwhelmed with beauty and history at the Muckross House and gardens. We drove the Ring of Kerry again and stopped at every overlook available to stretch our gazes and imaginations out over the Dingle Bay to the far side of the wild Kerry Peninsula. We stopped at the Dingle Brewery and tasted the Tom Crean Lager, named after one of Ireland's most famous men. Tom Crean, who walked 18 miles in 24 hours in -44 temperature to get help for his friends, who were starving and freezing to death at the South Pole on Shackleton's last voyage. Truly, a brew worthy of Kerry's heroic native son.

We drive to Cork and visit the wonderful Blarney Castle again, Susan re-kissing the Blarney Stone, touring the grounds, wishing time would stop…or, at least slow down—please slow down and let us enjoy this. Our second day there, I felt a little guilty about the food and Guinness intake, so I visited the little exercise room at the hotel; not much in there, but they had one set of dumbbells I could use with a couple of 10 pound weights on each end…not much, but maybe I could burn a few calories. As I started my first set, one of the ten pound weights came off and fell directly on my big toe, breaking it. Extreme pain cannot describe how my toe felt…it immediately turned dark blue, then black in a matter of minutes. I hopped back to the room, where Susan was getting dressed for our hike today (which wouldn't happen now), she wasn't real proud of me. Seasickness, poisonous bites, car wrecks and now a broken toe…what is about my homeland that is causing one of its native princes so much pain and agony?

We have to alter our plans now that I can barely walk; gone are the hikes and day trips we'd planned, now we're looking for shorter, car driven sites to visit. Our bartender at the hotel told us about the "Meeting of the Waters" and said it was nice and an easy walk. Well, an easy walk turned out to be 20 minutes of excruciating pain for me. The only good thing on that walk was a tree stump that had a large patch of shamrocks growing around it—the only shamrocks I'd seen growing in the wild in all of Ireland. The "meeting of the waters" was simply where two lakes converged…nice, but not 20 minutes of pain worthy. So, we started back for the car and noticed a 6" sign off the trail that pointed to the "Old Weir Bridge." What the heck, let's check it out. 6-8 more minutes of limping through the woods and we come upon an old stone bridge, over a rushing Irish stream that absolutely stunned us. Certainly one of the best scenes we'd encountered in all our trips here—and we were the only ones there. We took dozens of pictures, walked up and around the bridge, soaked it all in and could not believe our good fortune at finding this unknown gem in the middle of an Irish forest.

Around the Ring of Kerry, collecting a bottle of Kerry dirt and rocks to take back home with me, driving around in a dream of greens and blues and water and sky. Through the idyllic little town of Glengariff and around the Beara Peninsula, we cannot get enough of this surrealistic landscape, which is laden with lakes and valleys and mountains and fields and overlooks into Bantry Bay and Dingle Bay and all points westward into the vast and wild North Atlantic Ocean.

One late afternoon, on our way back to the hotel, we stop in a scenic little town on the Beara Peninsula called Castletownbere. It might take you 3-4 minutes to drive through this little town, located right on the bay, but we were thirsty and spotted a tiny little pub off the road on the right…so we pulled in. Inside was a grandmother type lady behind the bar and one other gentleman at the far end—no one else. We ordered a Harp and a Guinness and said hello to the lady, who recognized Susan's accent as not being from around Castletownbere. She didn't get many foreigners in her little pub and started talking to us and asking questions and being just as

Laurels, the cross

friendly as she could be, (which most Irish are). We told her where we'd been, what we'd seen and where we were still going…she loved hearing of our travels; she knew we were Americans, but didn't ask any further questions about it.

In a few minutes, a young lady and a little girl came into the pub and the little girl ran behind the bar and hugged the woman, who was obviously her grandmother. They talked a little and then the grandmother pointed at us and said, "these two visitors are from the U.S." The little girl stopped, looked at us and said, "Are you from North Carolina? I love North Carolina!" What??? We couldn't believe the little girl said that, we hadn't told anyone there where we were from. Susan said, "Yes, we are…how do you know North Carolina?" Anyway, we made instant friends, the little girl Muirann, the mother, Dierdre and the grandmother. They were such a joy to talk to and seemed very excited with anything Susan said—maybe they just liked her accent.

Soon, Dierdre and Muirann had to leave and we were left alone with the grandmother…a sad look came upon her face and she said she wanted to tell us about her daughter and what had happened to their family. Dierdre's husband was a fisherman, on one of the ships that go out to sea for 3-6 months at a time, he was on deck and a steel cable somehow malfunctioned, whipping around where Dierdre's husband was, cutting him in half—it sliced him in half. Poor Dierdre, now a widow, with three young kids, the youngest being pre-school; hard to understand how she coped with that then—or how she copes with it now. The story broke our hearts, Susan asked the grandmother if it would be okay if we sent them some gifts from America, she gave us their address and ever since then Susan has made sure they get presents from us on all holidays and special occasions. What a special family they are.

Our last day there we spent around Killarney and the beauty that is Kerry. We took one last drive out to an overlook called "The Ladies View," named for the ladies in the court of Queen Victoria, who loved the views from the cliff side. It had been raining much of the day and everything was soggy and slippery; but it didn't affect me too much, because we did little walking with my toe still broken. We got out of the car to enjoy the view down into the valley full of lakes and streams. Wait a minute, I thought, if I just move down the hill a little bit, I can get a better picture of the lakes; "No, don't do it Gary," "Susan," I said, "don't worry, it's just a few feet, I'll be okay." Famous last words! The hill was steeper than I thought it was and much wetter and slipperier. I lost my balance and started falling down the hill, the only way to keep from falling face first was to start running to avoid disaster. Toe killing me, I was hurtling down the slope, trying to keep my balance and not face dive into the muck and mire of that hillside. As the hill started to flatten out a bit I ran directly into a thick, black bog of a mess. My feet immediately sunk into the bog, sucking off my shoes and one sock, however, gravity kept pulling me down the hill. I finally stopped, without ever falling down—I'm special that way—but I was shoeless, sockless and covered in black, mucous bog.

I searched the bog for my shoes and sock—but, they were sucked into oblivion, donated to the local leprechaun colony; never to be seen again. I trudged, shoeless, back to the top, where Susan was, you guessed it—laughing at me. Covered in bog from my waist down; I stood there, among several other tourists, who were gawking at me; wondering, what the devil just happened? Just then, a young man walked around a car towards me with a box of baby wipes, he handed them to me and said, "Here, take these, I think you'll need them more than we will." He was right…I did.

Back to the hotel, get in the shower and try to rinse the bog off me; luckily, I brought two pairs of shoes. No more picture taking today, let's go downtown on our last night, find a nice restaurant and have a going away meal and drink. Killarney is a vibrant place, as are all city centers in Ireland, full of pubs, restaurants and meeting places. We saw a pub/restaurant in the middle of town, called The Laurels, walked in, saw an open table in the corner to the right, and sat right down…very good fortune. We were in the mood for some American junk food, so we ordered an Irish pizza as our last dinner of the week…and it was a good one. Our waitress/bartender was a very friendly young lady named Eileen; we asked her if she would take our picture there in the corner and she happily did. We could immediately see it with the digital camera, and the picture shocked us. The corner we were sitting in had white walls, with a brown beam going horizontally around the restaurant; and the corner had a brown beam going from the floor to the ceiling. The picture had me and Susan centered at the table, with our pizza and Guinness; and the two beams made a perfect cross in the background. It looked like we were sitting in front of a cross. We showed the picture to Eileen, we were all laughing and she started showing it to all the other waiters and staff…it was a great hit. I told Eileen, I'd show this picture to people back home and tell them that even the churches in Ireland served Guinness! She made us promise to make an extra picture for her and send her one, which we did when we got back home. That was a great night and great fun to end our week in Ireland. We wouldn't soon forget our times and adventures here and our new friends, Dierdre, Muirann and Eileen…a special week for us to always remember.

***

On returning home from Ireland, to 100 degree temps, I learned that my friend Allen's wife, was dying of cancer. Janice had been struggling for years with treatments and now the grim news was the cancer had won the battle. I felt bad for my friend; it's so hard to watch those you love waste away and struggle painfully with this dreadful disease. Janice died on July 5, my heart is breaking for my friend Allen…I feel so helpless, helpless, helpless. Dickie, Larry and I decided we'd go down to Allen's home near Hilton Head and spend a weekend with him after he got settled a little. We went down on Susan's birthday, July 14, and had a wonderful time together…telling old stories, remembering old times, letting Allen reminisce of olden times and golden times; filling us in on stories and travels he and Janice had done over the years—it was a good time for us all.

The boys came up for baseball games, tennis matches, football games, tall tales, fables, and once in a while, even the truth—the truth was not nearly as fun, but we endured it. We even endured a Wake Forest soccer match, in honor of our friend Larry, who obviously has forgotten what real fun is and sometimes loses his grasp of reality thinking that soccer is actually enjoyable.

On Sept. 5, (the day my mother died 24 years ago) I usually get a little melancholy—at least, that's the excuse I'm going to use. In my journal that day, I made a list of things I was thinking about, here it is:

∴ Thought about God

∴ Thought about Susan

∴ Thought about Shelley and Kali

∴ Thought about Anne and Casey

∴ Thought about Marky, Dickie, Larry, Jerry, Allen and Bill

∴ Thought about Ireland

∴ Thought about God some more

∴ Thought about Conrad and Barbara

∴ Thought about Martha, Clarence and Wendy

∴ Thought about Robyn, Seth, Luke and Eliza

∴ Thought about Aunt Elizabeth

∴ Thought about exercising and weight lifting

∴ Thought about writing another book

∴ Thought about work

∴ Thought about my relationship with Jesus

∴ Thought a little about me and things I have to do to be the man I want to be.

Anne and Mark came to visit in October for a few days, nothing special, she just loves her brother and wanted to see him…I'm special that way. Later in October, I was riding bikes with my friend David Lusk on Country Club Rd. when I hit a pothole, blew out both tires, flew up in the air and landed in the middle of the road on my shoulder. Fortunately, the cars behind me didn't run over my bruised and skinned body. David was in front and didn't see the wreck and kept on biking; he finally realized I wasn't with him and came back to help. We called Susan, she came and picked me up, we loaded up my wrecked bike and went home bruised, skinned…but still alive.

More bad health news in late October when our friend Bill told us he had been diagnosed with pancreatic cancer, maybe the worst of all the cancers. That was not the news we wanted to hear…it made me think of my own mortality—on my birthday, I was now 5 years older than my mother when she died, and 20 years older than my father when he died…my gene pool truly sucks! Then, we get the news that Anne has a melanoma again, that requires surgery—her second episode of this type cancer. The surgery goes well, thank the Lord, but this cancer thing is getting way to frequent here lately.

Susan and I leave Nov 23 for our annual Thanksgiving cruise to the Bahamas…blah, blah, blah. Fun, eats, drinks, shows, napping, sleeping, relaxing…you know the rest of the story. Don't make me repeat it. We leave Dec 26 for Kansas City to spend some time with Anne, Marky and Casey, we're looking forward to it.

Susan and I love K.C., seems like a great place…lively and varied downtown, good roads and easy to get around. We visited the wonderful Truman Presidential Library—it's great, go there someday if you can. We ate some Kansas City BBQ—not what we would call BBQ here in N.C., but it was good; we went to an Irish pub/restaurant, had dinner with Markey's family—all great and fun people and generally just enjoyed hanging out with each other, even though it was way too cold out there for my tastes. Casey cooked us all banana bread and other desserts, we played with the best dog in the world, Elvis; and savored the holidays, the companionship and the love we all had for each other…I'm a lucky guy.

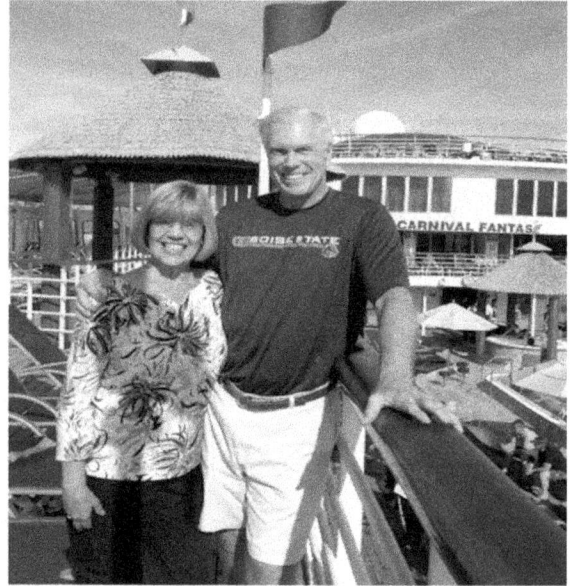

On a cruise

34

"So, give it your best
And don't worry about what some may say
Follow your dreams
It's really all that you can do

Give it your best
And remember that life is what you choose
Follow your dreams
And do what you love to do"

Shelley and Kali

35

"My home is in heaven. I'm just traveling through this world."

My employment as a professor with Grantham University was terminated at the end of the year. No reason given, only a short, one sentence email from them that stated I wouldn't get any more classes. No explanation, no thanks for 5 years of work…no nothing—such is the way of business now.

The boys, minus Bill (who is taking heavy chemotherapy treatments), all came up again in early spring. We rode up to Pilot Mt., then onto Mt. Airy to visit Andy's hometown. We walked around the streets, ate some BBQ, saw an Otis impersonator and took our picture next to Andy's patrol car. Seemingly, Mt. Airy has a thriving business based on the memories of Mayberry and Andy and Barney—and, they were good memories.

Susan and I met Anne and Marky out in Colorado in June to do some hiking in the mountains around the ski village of Breckenridge. At about 10,000 feet, the hiking proved to be all we wanted. As opposed to other hiking trips in my life, this was different; first, you hiked straight up mountain—no level ground, all uphill; then, you come back down. Going up, your lungs and legs are burning; and coming down wore out your knees…it wasn't the most fun I've ever had. The views were great, especially some of the snow covered tops and lakes we visited, but I prefer the rolling terrain of the Utah desert for hiking, as opposed to the straight up and straight down of Colorado. We all went to a Colorado Rockies baseball game one weekend and walked the streets of Denver one afternoon…it's a big city.

Bill invited us all to come to Cary for a game between the USA National

Kali and Susan

team and the Cuban National baseball team, held at William Coleman Field. We went and were shown the royal treatment by Baseball USA and the stadium's namesake—and the USA won the game. Later that month, they all came back to our house for the Winston Salem Open Tennis tournament, which John Isner won for the second consecutive year. Then, we got two bad pieces of news: Bill's cancer had spread again, and the doctors were telling him there is only a 30% survival rate. And, secondly, my precious little granddaughter, Kali, was diagnosed with type 1 diabetes, which meant she would immediately have to start pricking her finger and then giving herself four shots of insulin a day…she's 7 years old…7! Within a year, she will have given herself nearly 1500 shots of insulin…think of that the next time you start feeling sorry for yourself.

***

We celebrated Larry's birthday on October 5 in grand style…Susan got him balloons and a horn and made him cupcakes. Then we all went to a Wake Forest football game, with drinks at Finnegan's later—a grand birthday celebration. October is such a wonderful month…college football, World Series, my birthday…oh yes, it's the best month by far. It was especially great for my friend Jerry who told us he was RETIRING! Best news I've heard in a long while; he had been working mostly six day work weeks and was not enjoying his life like he should…like he deserves. I am so happy for my friend, maybe one day, he can return the happiness for me.

Also, in October, I completed writing my second book, "Gary's Hope," which I'm very proud of. Even today, after reading it over and over through editing and the final version, I still cry at some of the stories I chronicled of my heroes and friends. If that weren't enough for the great month of October, Dickie, Marky and I topped off the month with a trip to the World Series in St. Louis. That's right friends—The World Series! Good old Bill had been asking us for years if we wanted to go and we finally pulled the trigger and committed; Bill got us tickets through Baseball USA and we were set.

Dickie and I flew out there to meet Marky, and sat across from Curt Schilling in the airport as we were waiting on the flight. We attended two games in St. Louis, both with bizarre endings. The first game ended with an interference call on the third base line…how weird was that; no one really knew what was happening…the players just sort of walked off the field. We couldn't tell what was going on. Sitting in the stands, without television replay, we didn't know what had happened. However, we didn't really mind, since we were freezing! We sat on the very top row and the wind ripped through us all night, if it hadn't been the World Series, we would have left in the third or fourth inning—it was that cold.

The second game ended just a strangely…with a runner on first and the Cardinal's best hitter at the plate, Carlos Beltran, the guy on first base gets picked off to end the game. Totally incredible! Our seats to this game were much better, half way down the first base line, very comfortable—except for all the St. Louis fans around us…we were sort of pulling for the Red Sox.

During the days, we rode by the Arch, went to the Mississippi River and stuck our hands in the water, and spent all afternoon at Forest Park, an immense park and fun area outside the city.

Tennis courts, golf courses, music, museums, walking trails, fountains, a river running through it, an aluminum tree and a Korean War Memorial, which our friend Dickie got a kick from, since he spent 13 months of his youth in Korea, protecting our way of life and entertaining the local female population over there. I let Dickie spend all the time he wanted at the Memorial, just as I let Marky spend all the time he wanted at an Irish pub near the ballpark… I'm special that way.

***

My book was published in November and sold quite a few copies, I was happy with that. I received a few phone calls, several emails and Facebook postings about it—they all made me feel very good; I'll keep those memories to myself, I'm just glad my friends and family enjoyed it. We had another cruise set up in late November, this time with Anne, Marky, Casey and her friend Danelle coming with us. I hadn't met Danelle before but Anne sent a picture that showed how long Danelle's toes were, compared to Anne's fingers—the toes were longer. We picked them all up at their hotel to transfer everyone to the ship, Danelle hopped into the front seat with me and I asked her what she was going to call me…she said, "I'm going to call you 'Uncle Gary,'" I say "Great," then she asked me what I was going to call her. "LT" I said. Everyone looked at me and said "What? LT, what does that mean?" "Long Toes" I said, "from now on she's LT." And, so she was for the rest of the trip.

Even though this particular cruise was old hat for me and Susan, it was also new, in that we could share it with our family and LT. We had a wonderful time sharing the fun and adventures of the ship and the Bahamas with each other. Anne, Casey, LT and I went snorkeling while Susan and Marky kept the bar open (somebody had to do it); we went to the shows on board the ship, where they "volunteered" me to go on stage one night. We took pictures, we laughed, we ate too much, we visited our favorite restaurant balcony overlooking main street in Nassau—introducing them to Kalik, and we shopped in the straw market. The girls all dressed up for dinner a couple of nights and they were gorgeous, Marky tried to pour us all a glass of wine at the dinner table one night, but neglected to take the top off the bottle—it works better when you take the cork out. Susan and I chaperoned Casey and Danelle one afternoon on

Anne and me

board ship—we actually fell asleep and don't have a clue what they did; but when we woke up, they were still alive, so I'm assuming we did our job okay.

There are times I've felt that it wasn't totally fair for me to be so blessed with a such great friends and family; that it was unfair to others that I've been able to see and do so much, that I've had the love of so many people surround me for all my life; that I've been blessed with good health and a few abilities…but, I guess I'm special that way. That's all I can figure, I certainly have not deserved all the good things the Lord had sent my way.

Susan and I spent a few days in Asheville after Christmas, one glorious afternoon sitting out on the balcony of the Grove Park Inn in our shirt sleeves, basking in a warming afternoon sun, watching the sun slowly descend over the distant peaks of the Blue Ridge Mountains. A very nice late Christmas present, and a fitting way to cap off yet another incredible year.

Well reader…here we are nearing the end of this saga, one more year to go. I'm getting a little nostalgic now, I should've written a lot more about some things, and probably a lot less about others. But, since it's my book and my life (sort of), I get to choose what is in these pages, or not. I hope I've not hurt any feelings and I also hope I've brought back some memories that have been forgotten. I purposely left out most of the mistakes I made over the years and certainly did not include my many, many regrets and things I wish I'd done differently—what would have been the point in that. So, let's move on to the year 2014 and complete this select history of the world, as I see it.

36

The year starts off great with the boys coming up in January…why? I don't remember, and it doesn't matter, does it. As long as we tell stories, eat, drink and revel in each other's company…who cares what we do? I'm sure we went to some sort of game, but the main attraction this winter has been the abundance of buzzards in our region, especially our neighborhood. I had told the guys about them, but I think they were surprised by how many there were…at least 25-30 in the trees and sunning themselves on one roof in our neighborhood. What a life they must live…floating around on the thermals all day, never expending any energy, enjoying the view, knowing that lunch or dinner will always be there…always. You do realize I'm referring to the buzzards, right?

The next week we saw a dead deer that had been hit by a car, just up the street from us…this gave us a close up look at these magnificent birds. All they're doing is what God put them here for, not gruesome, or nasty, just doing their jobs in the natural chain of events. Oh, by the way, Wake Forest beat Notre Dame in a "who cares" basketball game.

My friend Allen is retired, Jerry's retired, Larry's retired, Bill should retire, but Dickie and I keep on trucking…however, I sometimes wish the truck would stop and let me off. Please let me off! We had a "friend" of ours from Red Springs die in early February, he and I had the shared the same birthday. I'm not going to mention his name, for personal reasons, but his parents were outstanding people. His mom died several years ago, but his Dad is still living and I called him on the day of the funeral. Amazingly, he recognized my voice and we had a wonderful, nostalgic conversation. We talked about old times, his wife, his sons and all the ballgames he used to watch us play as we were growing up…according to him, those were the best days of his life. He was, and is, a good man who deserved more out of life.

My little sister has, once again, been frequented by the most unwelcome guest of all…cancer. This time it's endometrial cancer, and it's not good. Fortunately, they've caught it early, but we are all still wrecks over this news…Casey, Marky and me all worrying about the unthinkable. Waiting on the operation was torture, the days drug by so slowly; finally, they operated and had fantastic results which showed they had gotten it all and she should make a full recovery. Anne Hope—you've got to stop this! Now!!

***

We had all planned to visit Ireland again this summer, Anne, Mark, Casey and us; but with Anne's surgery and Casey's new job in Seattle, it will only be me and my cute, little wife trying to stay out of harm's way on the Emerald Isle. We will sacrifice a pint of Guinness at the first pub we see, hoping this small token of our gratitude will appease the fairies and leprechauns that somehow influence seasickness, poisonous bites, broken toes, shoe-sucking bogs and wrecked cars. Maybe we'll donate two pints.

We arrive in Shannon on June 14 and head directly for our home away from home—Killarney. Our favorite hotel, Castlerosse Hotel and Golf Resort, was booked up, so we made arrangements at the Riverside Hotel for our stay. Unfortunately, our room was directly over the bar and we didn't get any sleep all night long. About midnight, I found a phone book and called Castlerosse, hoping for a miracle—we could not stay at the Riverside any longer—the leprechauns were smiling on us that night, they had recently had a cancellation and YES, we could book the room for the entire week.

At daylight, we packed up our things, checked out of the Riverside and drove immediately to our wayward home—we were so happy. The Castlerosse is a pretty big hotel, with a great restaurant and pub...we didn't care where they put us, we were simply happy to be "home." I did the paperwork, paid the bill, got the room key and grabbed our luggage...let's get in the room before they change their mind. As we're walking down one of the long hallways, it all comes back to us...yes, I remember this hallway, and yes, I remember this turn, and yes I remember this couch and chair and light—holy cow Susan—we're in the exact same room that we had two years ago...No. 131! That second pint of Guinness had worked its black magic.

Same old incredible scenery, same cliffs, same lakes, same mountains, same stone fields, same castles and forts and bays and rivers and streams...yep, all the same; and yet, we could gaze upon this majesty for days and nights untold—at least by human standards. The only difference this trip was the sunshine...you'd have thought we were in Phoenix! No rain, no clouds, no mists...just day after day of boring, monotonous sunshine.

We drove way out to west Cork one sunny day, where a young lady from Dingle had told us the "true Irish" people lived. I said, "Well, aren't YOU true Irish?" She said, "Yes...but they're TRUE Irish!" I didn't know what that meant, I still don't know what it means—but we drove out there to see. Unfortunately, all I found way out there on the wild coastline of west Cork, was an anchor on the side of the road, covered with weeds, that some fisherman had abandoned, that my front fender now uncovered. I discovered that when an anchor and a flimsy front fender meet—the anchor always wins. I should've donated 3 pints.

We toured the old Ross Castle once again, walked out to the old Weir Bridge (found our long lost patch of shamrocks), visited Blarney once more—that never gets old; wandered about Muckross House and the 900 year old Abbey and dreamed away our thoughts and concerns in that magic kingdom. We made a great, new friend at one of our favorite pubs, Molly Darcy's, she was a young lady working her way through medical school there. I cannot spell her name correctly and can barely pronounce it correctly, but it sounds like "nee-um." That's close enough…she befriended us, took care of us and saved me a bowl of Banoffee every night—she liked me—I'm special that way.

Susan had arranged, through emails, for us to drive down to Castletownbere and meet the Irish family we'd met two years ago, Dierdre, Muirann, Keeland and Albva (I'm not quite sure how to spell any of the names). We arrived in front of their house and they all ran out to meet us, smiling and thrilled we were there. Susan had brought them all presents from North Carolina and we had a great time watching them open all the gifts. We hugged, took pictures, told stories and listened to events in their lives…we had a grand and wonderful evening. Deirdre then insisted on taking all of us out to Castletownbere's finest restaurant and paying for everything (much to Susan's chagrin). The kids competed for minutes to tell us their stories, especially to Susan, whom they just loved. Muirann, who was 13 years old I think, was sitting across from me at the dinner table, watching my every move and telling me all her thoughts—it was great. I figured that by the time dessert came, she was my fast friend, and thus subject to my Jerry Elkins shenanigans. She absolutely loved dessert and was thoroughly enjoying the plate of ice cream in front of her; when she finally looked up from the ice cream, I looked over her shoulder and pointed, saying, "Who's that over there?" As she quickly turned to look, I took a big spoonful of her ice cream and ate it. Everyone at the table started laughing when she turned back around to notice something was missing from her plate. I don't think she fully understood what had happened, and as much as she loved ice cream—I wasn't going to tell her. Back at their house after dinner, both grandmothers came by to see us, the grandfather came, aunts and cousins—everyone they knew came to see the Americans…what a special night.

When we finally left, for the drive back to Killarney, we were both very happy and very sad. We wished we could see them more often…Dierdre had asked Susan if it would be possible for them to be "life-long friends." Of course it would…what a wonderful family.

***

After spending time with that amazing family, the next day's visit to the 800 year old Cahir Castle seemed almost anti-climactic, as well as our journey up to the Rock of Cashel. On our last day, we took one last drive out to Dingle and visited the Dingle Brewery again and shopped in the little picturesque village on the bay. Our hearts were still in Castletownbere, but the scenery and ambiance could not be ignored. We decided that our last night in Killarney would be dining at The Laurels restaurant, downtown, where we'd had our picture made "beneath the cross" two years earlier. We arrived at rush hour and the place was packed, however, as we walked in the door, a couple got up from the corner table, over to our right, and exited the restaurant—the exact same table where we'd sat two years earlier.

We sat down quickly, stunned at our good luck to be at our favorite table. While we were deciding what to order, I told Susan I'd go up the bar and order us a couple of drinks, which I did. As I was looking at the selections, a waitress came up to me from behind the bar and said,

"Gary?" I recognized her from two years ago as our same waitress. I then pointed over to our table and she said, "Susan?" She then came around the bar, over to our table and hugged us both. Of all the thousands of customers she'd had, we were amazed she remembered our names from that one night, two years ago. I said to her, "Now Eileen, I'm really going to be impressed if you can also remember what we ordered that night two years ago." Without skipping a beat, she said "Pizza!" Which was exactly right...oh my gosh!

Susan had sent her the picture of us sitting at the corner table, beneath the cross, and she had put it on her refrigerator, she told us. Then she said, she just looked at it a couple of weeks ago wondering how we were and what we were doing. We hugged some more and listened to part of Eileen's story; she actually lived in Kenmare and drove over an hour, each way, to work every day. She also told us her husband worked in Saudi Arabia and was over there for 6-8 months at a time—only coming home for 3 weeks, before going back again. The intricacies of people's lives are so fascinating. We had our pizza and Guinness, we talked to Eileen some more, and we became saddened by our impending departure the next morning. We might leave Eire, but parts of our hearts would stay with Eileen, Dierdre, Keeland, Muirann, Albva, Nee-um and the magic that is Ireland.

37

37 chapters and I'm finally done, my fingers are indeed tired from all this typing, I hope I haven't bored you too much with my stories. But, I have to admit, I haven't written this for anyone but myself (for selfish reasons) and for Kali, in case, many years from now, she would ever wonder about her Grandpa.

I met with all the boys again in Cary, to visit Bill in late June; he is not looking good—in fact, he looks bad, and I'm sure he knows, as we know, the end is approaching. It's very sad witnessing what cancer is doing to our friend…very sad. And then, July 23, I wake up having a heart attack! Me…two hours a day in the gym, strong, healthy, don't smoke, eat pretty good, but yet my heart attacks me. Bad genes is the culprit, my doctor says—that, plus stress. Three days in the hospital, and $56,000 later, they release me. "Do what we say," they tell me. "Don't worry," I say, I most certainly will. As I headlined a few chapters earlier, "Heaven is my home. I'm just passing through here." But, I'd like to pass through a little longer, if it's possible.

Bill and Larry came to visit me, Jerry came, Dickie came; my sister calls me every day, Casey checks on me, Kali calls me and says, "Don't worry Papa, it's going to be alright." Friends and relatives call and send cards, Susan pampers me, Martha and Clarence take us out to dinner, Aunt Elizabeth checks up on me and the Lord continues to bless me…I truly don't know why, but it's nice being loved.

I only stay out of work one week, but my perspective on work and retirement changed during that week. I need to think.

Uncle Earl died August 10, he was 93 years old, parachuted behind German lines on D-Day, fathered 5 wonderful children, was an excellent husband, son, uncle and role model, as well as being a committed Christian his entire life. I'm certain the Lord is getting an earful of advice from Uncle Earl, he was never bashful offering it. We'll miss him.

Believe or not, I'm done. I'm not going to get all sentimental in this last paragraph. Hopefully, this is only Volume 1. I'm really looking forward to experiencing Volume 2. I know we're going to lose our great friend Bill very soon. Shelley has a multitude of problems to overcome, but I'll always love her, no matter what. My heart causes some concerns, but overall, things are great. I've lived a fairy tale life (still on-going), blessed with a wonderful wife, excellent relatives and the best friends that could ever be imagined. And, there are still some hidden places in Ireland I want to see. I finish this story on my sister's birthday, August 29, 2014…wishing that everyone could be as happy and blessed as I have been.

Love, Dad
Love, Grandpa
Love, Gary

www.ingramcontent.com/pod-product-compliance
Lightning Source LLC
Chambersburg PA
CBHW081229090426
42738CB00016B/3239